The Soul of Ministry

The Soul of Ministry

Forming Leaders for God's People

RAY S. ANDERSON

Westminster John Knox Press
Louisville, Kentucky

© 1997 Ray S. Anderson

Scripture quotations from the New Revised Standard Version
of the Bible are copyright © 1989 by the Division of Christian Education
of the National Council of the Churches of Christ in the U.S.A.
and are used by permission.

Book design by Jennifer K. Cox
Cover design by Pam Poll

First edition
Published by Westminster John Knox Press
Louisville, Kentucky

This book is printed on acid-free paper that meets the
American National Standards Institute Z39.48 standard. ∞

PRINTED IN THE UNITED STATES OF AMERICA
97 98 99 00 01 02 03 04 05 06 — 10 9 8 7 6 5 4 3 2 1

Library of Congress Cataloging-in-Publication Data
Anderson, Ray Sherman.
  The soul of ministry: forming leader's for God's people / Ray S.
Anderson. — 1st ed.
    p.   cm.
  Includes bibliographical references and index.
  ISBN 0-664-25744-5 (alk. paper)
  1. Theology, Practical.   2. Clergy—Office.   3. Church work.
I. Title.
BV660.2.A53   1997
253—dc21   97-11496

Contents

Preface

We were riding in his van on the way to dinner with his family. Greg was a young man in his late twenties. His wife and young son, along with his parents, were in the back. I was sitting up front. "Tell me," he suddenly asked, "what is ministry?"

I thought a moment. Here was a young adult whom I had held in my hands as an infant in dedicating him to God. Only recently had he and his wife shown much interest in the church and, in fact, had only recently begun attending a large church that I knew quite well where the emphasis is on every member as a minister.

"What I really want to know," he said again, not waiting for me to respond, "is what does the noun *ministry* really mean? They talk about having this ministry and that ministry. But what does *ministry* really mean?"

I thought about explaining the word in the original Greek as it used in the New Testament and just as quickly discarded the notion. As I recall, I said something like, "It means doing something that God wants done to help other people." He never answered, and I realized that he had thrown me a slow pitch when I was looking for a fastball, and I struck out.

In all of my years of teaching both seminary students and pastors, I have never had the question put to me in exactly that fashion. At the same time, if there is one theme that has preoccupied me during these years it is that of a theology of ministry.

I doubt that this book is one that Greg will read and find an answer to his question, at least not yet. Maybe someday. But I have a notion that his question, What is ministry? is the right question, and I have attempted to answer it with each chapter.

Another question that I have heard repeatedly from pastors with whom I have shared my own theology of ministry is, "Where is this written down so we can read it? Where is there a book that we can take home with us that has in it what you are telling us?"

Here it is then. Immodest as it may appear, I have made no attempt at writing a definitive and scholarly book that depends on the insights and thoughts of others. While I have read and reflected on scores of books in this area, I have freely drawn from them to stimulate my own insights and convictions. Instead of distracting footnotes, I have placed all references for each chapter at the end of the book, with an extensive bibliography of sources.

This book is not the final word on the subject, though I have distilled and refined these thoughts through many years of ministry and teaching. The interaction and challenge provided by a host of students and pastors have shaped what I now say, though the words and thoughts are my own and I take full responsibility for them.

The thrust of this book points toward God's mission and ministry as succinctly captured in this verse: "For God so loved the world that he gave his only Son, so that everyone who believes in him may not perish but have eternal life" (John 3:16). The ministry of God is to the world, for the sake of the world, and it is in the world that the continuing ministry of Christ is carried out by the people of God.

I have anticipated questions and reactions in each chapter, though I have not attempted to answer and respond at each point. I only ask that the reader have the patience to read through the entire book before deciding that a statement or position I have taken is untenable. In the end, I suspect that there will remain many questions and challenges. That is as it should be. For theology is meant to be an open and continuing inquiry into the truth of God revealed through God's ministry as Creator, Redeemer, and Sanctifier.

I am writing this book for thoughtful laypersons, busy pastors, and anxious students. My hope is that it will stimulate further questions among those who like to think about these things, and provide direction for those who are actually doing these things.

I

Ministry as
Theological Task

1

Ministry as
Theological Discovery

"Where is the theological beginning point in the Old Testament?" I asked a group of pastors in our Doctor of Ministry program. I received a variety of answers, with Genesis the most often cited. "No," I replied, "I want the theological beginning point, not the chronological."

"Exodus," someone shouted out, and we were off and running.

Exodus precedes Genesis in the same way that knowledge of God as Redeemer precedes knowledge of God as Creator. Exodus precedes Genesis in the same way that the seventh day precedes the sixth day and that ministry precedes and creates theology. Let me explain.

The concept of the seventh day (the sabbath) cannot be logically found in the sequence of days beginning with the first day. To know that the seventh day is the "last day" one must have a special word of revelation from God. The meaning of the first six days is thus revealed through the seventh day. In this way, one can say, theologically, that the seventh day precedes the sixth day. In the same way, God's ministry precedes our concepts of God. It is through God's ministry of redemption that we understand the meaning of God's work as Creator.

All of God's actions in history are what we mean by God's ministry. Ministry is first of all what God does by speaking and acting within the framework of human history. God's actions reveal God's existence and make possible true knowledge of God. It is God's ministry that expounds God's nature and purpose. In obedience and response to God's ministry, we gain knowledge of God and of ourselves. This obedient response to God's ministry becomes our ministry which, in turn, serves as a theological exposition of God's nature and purpose.

"Who was the first theologian in the Bible?" I ask the same group of pastors. Again, I get a variety of answers until someone shouts out, "Moses!" They are now on to my game! And they press me for more. "Why Moses, and not Abraham?"

Abraham, Isaac, and Jacob are storytellers and actors in the redemptive drama and they, too, in living and telling the story of God's acts, expound a theology of God's ministry. But it is Moses who ultimately tells *their* stories as part of his account of God's purpose from the beginning of human history. Moses is the first theologian in the Bible, because everything told of the Genesis account of creation is written from the perspective of the exodus event.

Moses is not simply a storyteller, a recorder of events. Rather, he received directly from God a commission that carried a new content of revelation as well as produced a new event in salvation history. Moses became, as it were, a "god," with Aaron as his prophet. When Moses protested that he could not perform the task assigned to him because of a speech impediment, God chided him, "Who gives speech to mortals? Who makes them mute or deaf, seeing or blind? Is it not I, the Lord?" (Ex. 4:11). When Moses continued to beg off from the assignment and asked that someone else be sent, the Lord responded by saying that his brother, Aaron, would accompany him to speak for him. "He indeed shall speak for you to the people; he shall serve as a mouth for you, and you shall serve as God for him" (Ex. 4:16).

What Moses did not clearly recognize at the time was that his speech impediment was no barrier to God's Word, for the Word of God itself creates "out of nothing," so to speak. In the meantime, Moses would expound the revelation of God as it came to him with his brother Aaron as his spokesman.

As we shall see later in this book, the ministry of Moses as God's servant-leader in bringing the people out of Egypt to the very threshold of the Promised Land was also the revelation of a core theological paradigm that is foundational for all of the Old Testament. Without the theological paradigm revealed through the exodus, one cannot read and understand the Genesis account of creation nor can one follow the subsequent unfolding of God's redemptive history.

When someone asks where they should begin reading in the Old Testament, I never tell them to begin with Genesis, but rather with Exodus. Exodus is the theological beginning point that serves as the exposition and explanation of all that precedes.

It is actually the third chapter of the book of Exodus that is our theological beginning point. Here we find Moses confronted by the strange phenomenon of the bush that burns without being consumed. As he draws near he hears the voice of God calling out to him from the bush, and from that encounter he learns the new name of God—Yahweh—which was not known to his ancestors, Abraham, Isaac, and Jacob (Ex. 3:15; 6:2–3).

With this new name for God came the revelation of God's purpose to redeem the children of Israel from bondage in Egypt. Through this mighty act of Yahweh, the innermost being of God will be revealed. Every step that Moses takes, even reluctantly and not always perfectly (!), will expound the glory and grace of this *name*. Moses will become God's minister in achieving the liberation of his people. Each stage of this ministry produces revelation concerning the nature and purpose of God.

Abraham, Isaac, and Jacob were actors in the drama that preceded the revelation of God as Yahweh—the God of covenant love. They could not expound on what had not yet been revealed. It is Moses who learns the content of the divine *name* through Yahweh's encounter with the powers that hold his people in bondage. And it is Moses who expounds the inner mystery and meaning of that *name* through the formation of a people who are no longer merely the children of Israel (Jacob) but "children of God."

Through the prism of Yahweh's mighty act of liberation, Moses expounds the inner logic of God's purpose in calling Abraham, of God's judgment and grace revealed through Noah, and of the creation of the first humans in the divine image and likeness. Yahweh is the theological beginning point for all concepts of the deity, for Yahweh is the God who breaks the "silence of the gods" and reveals a divine pathos in which both mercy and wrath are expressions of a love that is creative and redemptive.

Yahweh is known as the God who sees, hears, and speaks. This distinguishes Israel's God from all other gods. As the psalmist reminds us, "The idols of the nations are silver and gold, the work of human hands. They have mouths, but they do not speak; they have eyes, but they do not see; they have ears, but they do not hear, and there is no breath in their mouths" (Ps. 135:15–18).

All ministry is first of all God's ministry. Every act of God, even that of creation, is the ministry of God. God's ministry of Word and deed breaks the silence and ends all speculation about whether or not there is a God and of how the deity might be disposed toward us. In responding to the cry of the people of Israel suffering under bondage in Egypt, God's ministry of hearing reveals the nature of God as one who cares and acts.

In answering the plea of Abraham for a son and heir, God's ministry of creative grace reveals that barrenness is no obstacle to God's promise, and that God is faithful to keep his Word (Genesis 12, 15, 17). In searching out and clothing Adam and Eve, who have fled from the presence of God in confusion and shame, God's ministry of healing and hope reveals the nature of God as forgiving and life-giving (Genesis 3). It is only through God's ministry that God's nature and purpose are revealed.

Ministry Precedes and Creates Theology

Theology has the task of expounding the revelation of God. The initiative thus lies with God as revealer. If the heavens and the earth are the handiwork of God, as the psalmist sings (Psalm 8, 19), and if humans are created in the image and likeness of God, one might assume that creation itself is a revelation of God and therefore expounds the nature and purpose of God.

The created world, however, has no "theological voice," as the psalmist reminds us (Ps. 19:3). The human perception of God became hopelessly skewed at the very beginning, as Paul reminds us (Romans 1). As a result, God's ministry of revelation through *personal* word and act stands at the beginning of all theological reflection.

Was it not so even at the very beginning? The author of Genesis, who stands at the center of the exodus event, tells us that it was. In that original garden of God's good creation, there is a personal ministry of God through his Word and act. The "not good" situation of the solitary "earth creature" is addressed by God and resolved through the simultaneous emergence of the first humans, male and female, in the divine image (Genesis 2).

This is God's ministry of grace, preceding the occasion of the first sin (Genesis 3). It is a ministry of God's personal Word and act standing over and against the silence of God's good creation. When the first humans turned away in disobedience from this divine word and grace they heard "the sound of the Lord God walking in the garden at the time of the evening breeze," and they fled into the foliage of the garden as though to hide from God's presence (Gen. 3:8). We are given reason to believe that this nocturnal visit of God was not unusual. Only this time it caused them to feel shame and they sought concealment amid the impersonal world of nature.

If, however, it was a daily occurrence for God to meet them in the cool of the evening, does this not suggest that from the very beginning God's ministry was one of communion and communication with humans? This means that there never was a time when humans were solely dependent on the impersonal, created world to expound the nature and purpose of God. This means that God's revelation to humans was originally one of personal word and gracious presence. This means that God's ministry is the primal word of creative love and grace for humanity.

There is no other way to say it. God's ministry is the revelation of God to humans and the basis for all human knowledge of God's nature and purpose. There is no theological task that has any basis in God's truth other than the task of expounding the ministry of God.

When the Ten Commandments were given, they were prefaced by the announcement, "I am Yahweh your God who brought you out of the Land of Egypt, out of the house of slavery: you shall have no other gods before me" (Ex. 20:2). The very first commandment is thus grounded in the knowledge of God as restricted to that of Yahweh, whose name is forever bound to the ministry of liberation from bondage and the promise of a new future. This command not only forbids idolatry, it also stands as a warning against any theology that is not expounded as the ministry of God.

All ministry is grounded in God's ministry, and all theology is dependent on God's continued ministry as the source of revealed truth. To claim a revelation of God apart from the ministry of God is to violate the first commandment and to clothe ourselves with fig leaves. Any theology that has not been called forth out of the network of its own devising is shame-based and ends up concealing more than it reveals.

Like busy spiders, theologians spin their webs of sticky strands in the open spaces of a conceptual cosmos hoping to snag a wing of an invisible deity. Meanwhile, Yahweh stuns a lonely fugitive named Moses with a bush that explodes with transcendence and arms him with enough magic to bring a powerful Pharaoh to his knees. God's ministry is God's transcendence made visible and accessible to anyone who lives within a stone's throw of a burning bush. And it doesn't take much of a bush to burn when Yahweh drops a little glory on it!

Ministry is God's way of reaffirming and expounding the truth of who God is and what God wishes to reveal through what he has said and done.

Every Act of Ministry
Reveals Something of God

Whether we realize it or not, every act of ministry reveals something of God. By act of ministry I mean a sermon preached, a lesson taught, a marriage performed, counsel offered, and any other word or act that people might construe as carrying God's blessing, warning, or judgment.

What we may intend as a very practical application of a biblical principle or church rule says something about who God is. Not everything we say or do is ministry, of course. But when we speak and act as a Christian we give others reason to conclude that we are speaking on behalf of Christ. When we speak and act out of the authority of the church, we give others reason to think that God's nature and character, as well as his will for persons, is embodied in our words and actions.

If I say, "I'm sorry, but our church does not permit children to partake of the communion service," I may think that I am explaining church polity but, in reality, I am saying something about God. The parent of the child will conclude that God does not want children to taste and touch of his own grace even though they can freely feed on the same food from which their parents eat at home. While the motive might be to protect the "holy sacrament," the effect might be to portray God as accessible only to those who are qualified by an enlightened mind.

Jesus expounded a theology of supreme importance when he took the children in his arms and blessed them, despite the protestations of his disciples, and thereby proclaimed, "Whoever does not receive the kingdom of God as a little child will never enter it" (Mark 10:15–16).

Suppose that I should even say, "I cannot perform this marriage because you have been divorced and it would be contrary to the Bible's teaching." Surely one might think that having a biblical text as support for one's ministry would be sufficient! But even here we must ask the question: What does this act of ministry (refusal to marry a divorced person) teach about God? If it should be construed as teaching that God can forgive all sin but the sin of divorce, and that God's grace is not available to one who has committed that particular sin, would this be in accord with God's Word itself?

Every act of ministry teaches something about God. When Jesus forgave the sin of the woman caught in adultery and refused to sentence her to death—which the law of Moses demanded—his act of ministry taught something about God that even the law did not teach. In this case it was not enough for the religious authorities to say, "the Bible teaches," but rather, they were responsible to recognize that the Word of God was even then incarnate in their midst and acting so as to reveal God's ultimate purpose, which is to liberate persons from the law of sin and death and to free them to recover their humanity as God intended.

Jesus was often condemned by the religious authorities for his actions and his ministry of healing on the sabbath. Jesus responded by saying, "The sabbath was made for humankind, and not humankind for the sabbath" (Mark 2:27). When Jesus experienced the work of God in healing, even on the sabbath, he expounded that healing as the ministry of God that gave a new meaning to the sabbath.

When Paul experienced the coming of the Holy Spirit upon uncircumcised Gentiles, he expounded the ministry of the Spirit of God as theological truth and said that circumcision no longer was a binding requirement following the resurrection of Christ (Gal. 6:15).

Every act of ministry reveals something of God.

A Methodist minister is asked to go to the hospital and baptize a baby who will be stillborn. With no guidance from his ministerial manual, and

with conflicting thoughts about the implications of his actions (he had refused to baptize a baby only a few weeks ago because the parents were not
churchgoers!), he heads for the hospital. Once there, he realizes that he is
confronted with ultimate questions as to where God is in this human
tragedy. Summoning up his courage, he responds by taking the infant in
his arms and performs the baptism. His own theological reflection on that
event revealed new depths of God's grace and comfort, both to himself
and the parents.

Ministry is much more than the teaching of biblical concepts and the
application of pastoral skills in accordance with approved rules and
guidelines. Within the framework of biblical truths and in accordance
with sound pastoral care, there yet remains an understanding of ministry
as theological exposition.

In this chapter I have set forth a basic thesis that will be explored and
developed at many levels and in many ways throughout the rest of this
book. *All ministry is God's ministry from the very beginning.* There is no revelation of God's truth that is not rooted in God's ministry and expounded
through God's continuing ministry by those who are empowered by the
Spirit of God.

Let no one claim to be a theologian who has not stood "unshod" at the
burning bush, and let no one claim to be a minister of God who is not prepared to say something about the nature and purpose of God through that
ministry.

2

Ministry as
Theological Discernment

"How can you decide what is the right thing to do in a ministry situation if you cannot always follow the clear biblical teaching?" The question was generated by my suggestion that the refusal to marry a person who has been divorced may convey the impression that there are some sins, like that of a failed marriage, that God cannot and will not forgive.

Every act of ministry teaches something about God. And if a teaching about God results from a ministry decision that violates what we already know about God through his own acts of mercy and ministry, then we should pause and consider. *The Word of God is also the ministry of God.* God's truth cannot be detached from God's character.

"Does not your view of ministry reduce the command and Word of God to pure subjective content so that each person can decide for himself or herself what the Bible teaches? Does not the text of Scripture provide us with an objective truth that we can discover by reading and interpreting it in an attempt to determine the single intent of the author?"

My answer to both questions is, not necessarily. And here are the reasons why.

The Inner Logic
of Theological Discernment

There are two directions that the human mind can go in responding to what comes through sense experience. The brain does not function without sensory perception. This reminds us of Aristotle's famous dictum: There is nothing in the mind that is not first of all in the senses. The five senses, smell, touch, taste, sight, and hearing, flood the brain with sensory data. The mind seeks to organize and clarify this data.

One direction the mind can take is to abstract away from sense experience and form concepts that are devoid of time and space. These concepts form a network of interlocking relations and lead to formal knowledge based on logic. This knowledge yields principles, such as: It is always wrong to tell a lie, because it is a violation of the universal principle of truthfulness. One thus enters into every situation guided by a principle of what constitutes truthful words and actions as against untruthful ones. If one holds to this rule, God's truth will be judged by formal principles and divine revelation will be understood as knowledge based on the capacity of the human mind to be in conformity to the divine mind. René Descartes, often considered to be the founder of the modern period in philosophical thought, abstracted thought from experience in an absolute sense when he said, "I think, therefore I am." The human mind thus becomes the criterion of that which is real and true.

Another direction the mind can take is to seek to penetrate into the structure of things and events as they are experienced in order to discern the nature of things as revealed through our encounter with them. In this case, the mind seeks to understand the intrinsic structure of reality as it presents itself to us through experience. When we do this, we are attempting to discern the "inner logic" of reality as we encounter it as contrasted with the "formal logic" of a mind that abstracts away from sensory experience and retreats into a timeless and contentless world of ideas and concepts.

For example, we have all attended weddings where we know one of the persons about to be married in a more negative way than the other. As they stand before the minister, we may whisper to a friend, "For the life of me, I can't see what she sees in him!" Translated, this means, I would never want to live with this person based on how I have seen him behave in our fellowship group! In this case, observation of his actions led to conclusions concerning his personality and character that resulted in a strong opinion concerning who he was. This is what I mean by *formal logic*. Concepts are derived from experience that forms an objective knowledge of another.

Suppose that the person who expressed the negative opinion based on certain knowledge of the man is invited to the home of the newly married couple. In this encounter, the formal logic of what one knows about the one person is set aside in order to enter into the experience of the newly married couple without prejudice. During the evening, the couple reveal dimensions of their relationship that could only be known through experiencing them in their own setting and in their mutual love. Leaving the couple's home, the same person could well now say, "I now see what she sees in him! They have something going for them that I never would have believed!" This is what I mean by *inner logic*. Suspending, for the moment, judgment based only on formal logic, one is now open to the revelation of the inner reality of this new relation.

Discernment requires submission to the clear and continuing observance of reality encountered through experience. Refusal to open one's mind to this actuality for the sake of clinging to concepts one has abstracted from experience closes the door to new revelation. Truth, as the original Greek word denotes (*aletheia*), comes through disclosure or openness. Formal logic is a "closed" concept of truth. While this form of truth is necessary and valid in our day-to-day living, without discernment we can "miss the many-splendoured thing," as English poet Francis Thompson once put it. What formal logic may fail to see, discernment can perceive as an inner coherence connecting visible to invisible reality.

Nicodemus failed to discern the inner meaning of Jesus' words, and so stumbled over his own certainty. "We know that you are a teacher who has come from God," he announced. But when Jesus probed for a deeper discernment on his part, Nicodemus retreated to his own formal logic. "How can anyone be born after having grown old?" he protested (John 3:2, 4).

Using the Absurdity Test

The formal logic of Nicodemus illustrates the difference between revelation of truth that comes through discernment and revelation, and that which is held as formal, or propositional, truth. What is important to understand is that, while both are important, discernment is necessary to preserve truth from becoming folly. "This man is not from God," some Pharisees said of Jesus, "because he does not keep the sabbath" (John 9:16). Wrong! Wrong! Wrong! Having abstracted the truth of the sabbath into a formal principle, they failed to discern that Jesus was "Lord of the sabbath" (Mark 2:28). As a result, as Peter was later to accuse, they "killed the Author of life" (Acts 3:15)! What utter folly! Defending, so they thought, the truth of God, they were led to the point of absurdity.

When truth is pushed to the point of absurdity, it becomes foolishness.

Theology that cannot stand the "absurdity test" is likely to be a poor theology, if not a dangerous theology. I once participated in a debate sponsored by college students over the issue of divorce and remarriage. My counterpart in the debate argued his position strongly. It was absolutely impossible to permit the remarriage of a divorced person on the grounds that Jesus forbid it by his teaching. Even the so-called exception clause in Matthew 19:9—"except for unchastity"—he argued was a later addition to the teachings of Jesus. There could be no exception, he stated, because the word of Jesus was final.

My argument that the actions of Jesus were as authoritative as his teaching did not cause him to waver. Finally, a student raised his hand and asked: "Professor, you say that the sin of divorce, while it can be forgiven, allows for no remarriage; is that correct?" The answer was yes.

"Then is it not also true that in the case of the death of one's spouse the surviving spouse could remarry, as that would not violate the teaching of Jesus?" Again, the response was affirmative. I quickly saw where the good professor was being led, and remained silent as the lamb was led to slaughter!

"Then what about this," the student asked, "in Bakersfield there was a pastor who became angry with his wife and shot and killed her. When he gets out of prison, is he now free to remarry, seeing that instead of divorcing his wife he killed her?"

It was too late. The branch has been sawed off, and the professor, consistent with his formal logic to the end, had to admit that, "yes, this man could remarry!" The laughter of the students over the absurdity of this case reduced his argument to folly in their eyes. He, of course, expressing deep discomfort over the logical outcome of his position, remained unmoved.

What is my point? It was the ministry of Jesus, not merely his teaching, that revealed the character and purpose of God. Over and over again, Jesus appealed to his listeners to practice discernment in evaluating his ministry.

"What do you think?" was a favorite gambit of Jesus. "What do you think, Simon? From whom do kings of the earth take tribute? From their children or from others?" (Matt. 17:25; see also, 18:12; 21:28; 22:42). In each case, Jesus sought to draw his listeners into an inner logic contained within a life situation that revealed a truth concerning the nature and purpose of God.

Theological Discernment:
A Case Study

There may be one theologian prior to Moses, and it is a woman named Rebekah. We remember her as the wife of Isaac, the son of Abraham who is the heir of the promise through whom God's Word would come to pass.

As it turned out, when Rebekah became pregnant she suffered some physical distress and went to the local priest for a diagnosis and "Word from the Lord." She received both. "There are two nations in your womb," said the priest, thus indicating that she was bearing twins. This was at least a partial answer as to her physical difficulties. But there was more. "The two peoples born of you shall be divided; the one shall be stronger than the other, the elder shall serve the younger" (Gen. 25:22–23).

As it turned out, she gave birth to twin boys; the firstborn was named Esau and the second, Jacob. The custom of that culture and times was that the firstborn son automatically inherited the blessing reserved for the one who would carry on the family line. This way of thinking is what I have called formal logic. It is a rule and principle that binds all who belong to that particular people. To what extent Rebekah shared the revealed Word of the Lord concerning the fate of the two boys with her husband Isaac, we are not told. It would be natural to assume that she did, but in any event, when it came time for Isaac to pass on the blessing to the firstborn, he made plans for the ritual. Esau was summoned and asked to prepare for the event (Genesis 27).

It is perhaps not without some significance that when Moses told the story he wrote, "When Isaac was old and his eyes were dim so that he could not see, he called his elder son Esau . . . " (27:1). While this appears to be a description of Isaac's physical condition, it might also point to his spiritual blindness!

Rebekah, however, seeing what was about to happen, created a ruse whereby Jacob presented himself to his father disguised as Esau. Isaac was easily deceived by his failing eyesight and, acting out of what appeared logical and right, gave the birthright to Jacob as an irrevocable blessing. Too late, Isaac discovered that he had been deceived by his wife and too late Esau discovered that he had been cheated out of what he considered rightfully his.

Judged by a code of ethics assumed to be universally binding, we might charge Rebekah with an untruthful act—she deliberately deceived her husband. Why? Out of favoritism? One might think so, seeing that Jacob was her favorite among the twins. "Isaac loved Esau, because he was fond of game; but Rebekah loved Jacob" (Gen. 25:28). But this would be to ignore an even more significant fact.

Rebekah demonstrates in her life and action what every theologian must do and what every minister must know. She had God's Word as to the relationship of Jacob to the promised blessing, and she was the only one in a position to implement it, even though it required an act of deception. Her action turned out to be a ministry of God's Word prompted by her theological discernment.

Such theological discernment as a form of ministry requires two things. First, one must have insight into God's revealed purpose for the outcome of a situation. It was not only that her pregnancy was an answer to prayer (Gen. 25:21), but that the outworking of the lives of all concerned was to accomplish God's purpose at the end. She was given what we might call an "eschatological" insight into what God intended to bring about in the future.

Second, theological discernment must be open to the direction of the Holy Spirit in order to interpret any given situation in terms of the eschatological preference of God rather than merely conform to historical precedence and principle. Rebekah's action, ambiguous though it might be considered from a human level, had theological integrity as a ministry of God's Word.

We will return later in this book to the importance of eschatological preference as against historical precedence when dealing with practical matters of ministry and its implication for biblical interpretation. For now, it is sufficient to take note of Rebekah as a woman of extraordinary theological discernment in the ministry of God's Word in the face of Isaac's apparent passivity and sheer impotence.

Asking the Questions Again

Now let me return to the twofold question presented at the beginning of this chapter.

"Does not your view of ministry reduce the command and Word of God to pure subjective content so that each person can decide for himself or herself what the Bible teaches? Does not the text of Scripture provide us with an objective truth that we can discover by reading and interpreting it in an attempt to determine the single intent of the author?" My response was, not necessarily so.

In answer to the first question, I have suggested that it is not one's own subjective mind or experience that determines the truth of God. Rather, the mind is challenged to discern the truth of God's Word within the event of God's Word. This truth is objective to the subjective human mind. As it turns out, there is nothing more subjective than abstracting away from the concrete situation and judging the Word of God on the basis of a human concept or principle. Concepts are not finally objective at all; they are a projection of human subjectivity out of time and space and thus dangerously devoid of real content.

Experience itself is not the criterion for what is the truth of the Word of God. But the truth of the Word of God must be discerned in terms of its effect when applied to humans in their life situation. When the effect of a truth extracted from the Word of God contradicts the effect of the Word, then it becomes absurd, and to follow it consistently is folly. This was as true of the people in the Old Testament who turned the law of God into a law that dehumanized as of those in the New Testament who resisted the ministry of Jesus.

This leads into an answer for the second question. I have attempted to demonstrate from Scripture itself that the Word of God is not a textbook of doctrinal truths that can be stated in so-called objective propositions. Rather, Scripture is a revelation of God's nature and purpose through its faithful proclamation and teaching. While the biblical text must be taken as an authoritative Word of God, discerning its meaning is related to its application in a contemporary context with the Holy Spirit as a guide.

"This is very subjective," my students usually protest. My response is that there is nothing more subjective than consulting scholarly commentaries on the text and then making a decision as to which one provides the best interpretation before preaching it as the Word of God! The objectivity of the Word of God is not secured by abstracting principles or general truths from the text. Rather, the Word of God remains objective as a command to carry out God's ministry faithfully and completely in the context in which we seek to apply it.

The baptism of uncircumcised Cornelius by Peter was not based on a point of doctrine drawn out of the Old Testament. Rather, it was based on the objective phenomenon of the manifestation of the Holy Spirit that came upon Cornelius through the preaching of the gospel of Christ (Acts 10). Peter had earlier received a vision that led him to discern that God had the authority to suspend his own rules! When he saw that the uncircumcised Cornelius had received the Holy Spirit he said, "Can anyone withhold the water for baptizing these people who have received the Holy Spirit just as we have?" (Acts 10:47).

This is ministry as theological discernment!

In this chapter I have explored the difference between a concept of truth as abstract knowledge and truth as a disclosure of reality through experience. *Formal logic* was defined as a way of thinking in accordance with concepts that are timeless and contentless with regard to personal being. *Inner logic* is discovered as one discerns the relation between the invisible and visible as an objective structure of reality in which one participates. When we look at the Word of God from the perspective that discernment of the effect of the Word is as crucial to our understanding as its source, we see the practical necessity of discernment.

Jacob was the exception to the rule. Isaac attempted to safeguard the promise by laying his hand on Esau. Our temptation today is the same, whether it is the head of John Calvin, Martin Luther, or Karl Barth. The exception is more likely to bear the blessing of God than the normative principle. What scholars cannot decide, ministers must discern. What theologians cannot bear, ministers must bless.

Let those who think theologically listen to what God says about what his Word intends as it comes to pass, and let those who minister not be satisfied with conformity to what God has said, but press on to participate in what God is doing!

3

Ministry as
Theological Innovation

"One puts new wine into fresh wineskins," Jesus reminded his disciples, when they were stunned by his seemingly radical actions and teaching (Mark 2:22). Accused by the Pharisees of breaking the law of the sabbath, he replied, "If a man receives circumcision on the sabbath in order that the law of Moses may not be broken, are you angry with me because I healed a man's whole body on the sabbath?" (John 7:23).

Jesus ministered to human need and so performed the ministry of God, even on the sabbath. When his ministry was challenged, he responded, "The sabbath was made for humankind, and not humankind for the sabbath; so the Son of Man is lord even of the sabbath" (Mark 2:27–28).

The new wine is the ministry of God; the new wineskin is the theology that must expand and be shaped by the ministry. Healing on the Sabbath is an act of ministry that teaches something about God, and reveals God's purpose for humanity. The older law of the sabbath established by Moses must give way to the newer law of the Messiah. Jesus is the Christ, the Messiah, and as such, is the Lord of the sabbath.

Tasting the New Wine

The theological formulation comes *after* the ministry to humanity on the sabbath. "The sabbath is made for humankind," said Jesus. This is a prime example of theological innovation.

Let me give you another.

When Peter witnessed the Holy Spirit coming upon the Gentiles in the house of Cornelius, he baptized them immediately. When he returned to Jerusalem, he defended his actions by saying, "who was I that I could hinder God?" (Acts 11:17). The baptism of uncircumcised Gentiles was performed on the basis of the manifestation of the power of the Spirit of Jesus in the context of the ministry of preaching. Peter, however, was apparently ambivalent about the theological significance of this event. So were James and John who, along with Peter, constituted the leaders of the church in Jerusalem. Peter was later to be publicly rebuked by Paul for siding with the Jewish Christians who insisted that baptized Gentiles still needed to be circumcised (Gal. 2:11–14).

When Saul of Tarsus was converted through his encounter with the risen Jesus Christ on the road to Damascus, he resisted strenuously the attempt by certain of the Jewish Christians based at Jerusalem to require circumcision of baptized Gentile believers. Paul too experienced the presence of the Holy Spirit among uncircumcised Gentiles through his ministry of preaching. The difference was that Paul put this "new wine" in "new wineskins." He took the next step by formulating a new theology of membership in the kingdom of God.

Paul's opponents argued that circumcision was a command of God binding for all time. Paul responded by asserting what was utter theological innovation. "Circumcision is nothing, and uncircumcision is nothing; but obeying the commandments of God is everything" (1 Cor. 7:19). "For in Christ Jesus neither circumcision nor uncircumcision counts for anything; the only thing that counts is faith working through love" (Gal. 5:6). "For neither circumcision nor uncircumcision is anything; but a new creation is everything!" (Gal. 6:15).

The commandments of God, as Paul understood them, were to be interpreted by the presence and ministry of the resurrected Christ. The basis for all of the commandments, Paul argued, is love. Thus one who fulfills God's law of love through love of the neighbor has fulfilled the commandments (Rom. 13:8–10). The kingdom of God is not food and drink, said Paul in response to those who insisted upon strict observance of the Old Testament regulations, but "righteousness and peace and joy in the Holy Spirit" (Rom. 14:17).

This was theological innovation!

In the case of Jesus we find a new theology of the sabbath resulting from God's ministry on the sabbath. In the case of Paul, we have a new theology of circumcision following the ministry of the Holy Spirit in bringing the uncircumcised Gentiles into the kingdom of God. With Jesus, the ministry of healing was the new wine, and the new theology of the sabbath was the wineskin. With Paul, preaching a resurrected Jesus Christ accompanied by signs and wonders wrought by the Holy Spirit was the new wine, and a new theology of circumcision as being "of the heart" rather than "in the flesh" was the new wineskin (cf. Rom. 2:29).

Circumcision and the sabbath were no doubt the two anchor points for the Jews of Jesus' and Paul's day. To treat either of these as old wineskins that need to give way to the new wine was more than many could tolerate.

Jesus suffered more resistance and outright persecution because of his ministry on the sabbath than any other aspect of his ministry. "This man is not from God, for he does not observe the sabbath" (John 9:16). It was these same people that concluded that he must be put to death for the sake of preserving the status quo (John 11:50–53).

Paul was constantly hounded by the Jewish Christians who sought to undermine his ministry by insisting that without circumcision, Gentile Christians could not enter the kingdom of God. He was, by his own account, treated inhumanely for his theological stance (2 Cor. 11:23–27). At one point, a band of his accusers, more than forty, took an oath not to eat or drink until they had killed him (Acts 23:12).

Theological innovation is dangerous to your health!

Are There No Absolutes Left?

"It still seems to me," the reader might well ask, "that what you call theological innovation is nothing more than theological relativism. There are no longer any absolutes, but everything is relative to what works best. Why is this not simply theological invention?"

Let me respond by making two points. First, the concept of what is absolute regarding the command of God is connected to the ministry of God. And second, there must be a theological antecedent for what becomes theological innovation. The Word of God, as originally revealed through God's ministry, bears within it the clues to what later will appear as theological innovation.

In the previous chapter, I explored the difference between formal logic and inner logic. *Formal logic* is grounded in concepts of the mind for which one claims universal validity. To tell a lie violates the universal principle that one is bound always to tell the truth. Formal logic in the case of ethics demands that one should always act in such a way that the action can be willed as a moral imperative for all persons, regardless of their situation, as Immanuel Kant argued.

Inner logic, on the other hand, shifts the center of gravity, so to speak, from the formal principle as an abstract mental assertion to the inner structure of reality as it is encountered through relation to others and to the world in which one lives.

For example, when I was a high school student one question on my physics final exam was the following: Define the atom. I wrote what turned out to be the correct answer: An atom is the smallest indivisible particle of nature. I received an A in the exam. What my physics textbook held to be true and by which I was examined was later to be radically revised when the atom was split and the new inner world of atomic physics discovered. What was true according to principles of physics held by the mind at one time was later radically changed when the physical nature of reality turned out to be quite different!

The point is this. The physical universe is itself the *absolute* truth. The principles of physics are relative to the physical world itself and are rightfully changed and corrected as the inner logic of the physical reality is discovered.

When we ask, "Are there any absolutes?" we can answer, "only what *is* absolute!" Our concepts and principles formulated by abstraction from what exists as a created world are surely not more absolute than that world itself! It is true, we live by basic laws of nature that appear to be fixed and unchangeable. But these laws are themselves grounded in the deeper truth of nature that lies beyond our comprehension, to some degree. We call miracles "supernatural" because we have no way of explaining these phenomena in terms of our formal logic. But if what we call "nature" is itself an interactive continuum including both visible and invisible reality, then we cannot *absolutely* rule out phenomena that we cannot control or for which there is no "logical" explanation.

With regard to the sabbath, for instance. The commandment of God to "keep the sabbath" as a holy day is put in the context of God's mighty act of liberation from Egypt. "I am Yahweh your God, who brought you out of the land of Egypt," reads the preface. The commandments follow as precepts intended to regulate the religious, civic, and social life of the redeemed people (Exodus 20). The inner logic of the people's relation to God as a living God whose purpose is to restore their humanity as originally intended leads us toward the absolute truth of the commandment as grounded in the objects of God's grace. For the Israelite, *the absolute* is located in God's action, which embodies God's being.

When the Jewish people later took the commandments out of this living relation to a redeeming God and made of them an abstract rule of righteousness, they destroyed this inner logic. The commandment of the sabbath, for example, became a formal principle with absolute authority, permitting no exception.

When Jesus healed on the sabbath, along with other actions that were conducive to human health and wholeness, he understood that the inner logic of the sabbath had to do with God's work on behalf of humanity. Thus he taught, "the sabbath is made for humankind, not humankind for the sabbath" (Mark 2:27). This is theological innovation because it overturned centuries of theology that taught that the principle of sabbath-keeping was more important to God than the welfare of humans. The *absolute* is the nature of humanity as created in the divine image. The law of the sabbath is relative to that absolute reality. This is not "relativism" in the sense that most people think of it, any more than the principles of physics being relative to the absolute reality of the physical universe is "relativism." The exception to the formal principle, as said in the previous chapter, may often be the truth.

We can say the same thing about circumcision. The practice of circumcision was instituted by God in the context of God's gracious promise to Abraham. Circumcision was a sign of God's faithfulness in keeping the covenant that he established with Abraham. The inner logic of this covenant relation was grounded in the power of God to produce "out of nothing," as it were, a seed for Abraham. Sarah, as the barren wife, conceived a son who was created out of the possibility of God, not out of the possibilities of human flesh. The "cutting off" of the flesh involved in circumcision pointed to the inner logic of this relation between a gracious God who makes and keeps promises and a people who represent all humanity under both judgment and hope (Genesis 12, 15, 17).

When the Jewish people abstracted the principle of circumcision from its purpose as a sign and seal of God's covenant promise, they made of it an absolute criterion with no exceptions. As Paul rightly saw, the absolute reality in circumcision was not in the sign itself, but in the covenant relation established through Abraham for all humanity and completed through Jesus Christ in his death and resurrection. When Jesus as the "seed" of Abraham was "cut off" in the flesh through his crucifixion and raised again from the dead, Paul understood that baptism into Jesus Christ is now an absolute satisfaction of what circumcision was only a relative and temporary sign (Galatians 3).

The Rule of the
Theological Antecedent

The second point that I wish to make in response to the charge that theological innovation constitutes theological relativism and compromise is this: For every instance of theological innovation there must be a theological antecedent.

This will lay to rest, hopefully, the charge that theological innovation *invents* new options out of "whole cloth." We must remember that the reshaping of theology is like the response of new wineskins to new wine. The new wine is the dynamic power of the ministry of God revealed through God's actions on behalf of the restoration of humanity into the fullness of the divine image and likeness. Theology is always bound to interpret and set forth the inner logic of God's ministry as it occurred in the beginning and continues to take place today through the presence and power of the Holy Spirit.

By an antecedent, I mean some aspect of God's earlier ministry that can now be seen in a new and liberating way through God's continuing ministry.

Let us look at the question of the law of the sabbath again. What is the theological antecedent for the innovative way in which Jesus understood the sabbath as made for humankind?

When we understand that Moses was the first theologian, as has been asserted in the first chapter, and that the liberation of the people from four hundred years of bondage and oppression in Egypt was the context, we can then discover the antecedent for the sabbath.

The fall into slavery and bondage on the part of the covenant people was seen by Moses as the theological paradigm for the original creation and fall of humanity. Life in Egypt under the taskmaster was brutal and oppressive to both the body and the spirit. Generation after generation were born and died under the relentless determinism of this bondage. Remembrance of the covenant promise made to Abraham and the land of their inheritance was transmitted by story from one generation to another.

The liberation from this bondage through the mighty act and power of God brought forth a new name—Yahweh—and a new sacrament of covenant promise. "Remember the sabbath day, and keep it holy," was the commandment. "Six days you shall labor and do all your work. But the seventh day is a sabbath to the Lord your God; . . . For in six days the Lord made heaven and earth, the sea, and all that is in them, but rested the seventh day; therefore the Lord blessed the sabbath day and consecrated it" (Ex. 20:8–11).

Let me stir your imagination for a minute! Picture the Israelite, liberated from Egypt but still struggling against the brutal forces of nature in order to survive. Day after day, life goes on, fighting the elements, suffering from physical fatigue and spiritual depression. Then, at the end of the sixth day, as the sun sets, that same Israelite can suddenly stand erect and turn away from that same task and say, "For twenty-four hours you have no power over me! For twenty-four hours I am liberated from this bondage and determinism of an unfriendly world. For the next night and day I am under Yahweh's presence and power, and his will is to restore my health and heal my bruised humanity."

Can you imagine the feeling? The sabbath was a gracious law that terminated temporarily the relentless law of being under the power of the dust from which each person came and to which each person must return (Gen. 3:19). While the exodus happened only once, every seventh day was a sacrament of this divine deliverance and a theological paradigm that Moses inserted into the creation story.

Jesus clearly understood the sabbath as designed by God for the good of humanity. When the law of the sabbath took precedence over human concern, Jesus scolded the Pharisees for their blindness. While they permitted kindness to animals on the sabbath, they refused to allow healing for humans (Luke 13:15; 14:5). The theological antecedent for Jesus' ministry on the sabbath was clearly established by the original purpose for the sabbath. The sabbath was, in the beginning, God's ministry for the good of humans, and Jesus' ministry on the sabbath recovered that purpose in the form of theological innovation.

Paul, likewise, appealed to a theological precedent for his innovative theology regarding circumcision. The Jewish Christians argued that circumcision was necessary for admittance to the kingdom of God. Paul disagreed and found an antecedent for his position in the case of Abraham. First of all, Paul reminded the Jews, the law of Moses only entered four hundred years after Abraham received the promise by faith (Galatians 3). Therefore righteousness comes through faith, not by keeping the law. Furthermore, Paul argued by asking a rhetorical question: When was righteousness reckoned to Abraham? "Was it before or after he had been circumcised?" (Rom. 4:10). Abraham was declared righteous *before* he was circumcised, Paul responded. Thus circumcision could not be a requirement for right standing with God.

The theological antecedent is there! What appeared to be theological novelty in setting aside circumcision as "counting for nothing" is theological innovation. Cutting through the underbrush of a thousand or more years of theological tradition, Paul breaks out into the clearing with the discovery that Abraham was declared acceptable to God on the grounds of his faith in God's promise without circumcision being a condition. If Christ is the seed of Abraham, as Paul argued in Galatians 3, circumcision has been completed in his own death as a "cutting off" of the flesh. The resurrection of Christ by the power of the Spirit of holiness (Rom. 1:4) now has established the absolute ground for all to inherit the promise to Abraham. This promise, as Paul reminds his readers, was that "all the families of the earth" should be blessed, thus indicating again that there is a theological antecedent for the inclusion of Gentiles in the covenant (Gen. 12:3; Rom. 4:17). Christian baptism is a baptism into this death and resurrection, making circumcision unneccessary (Romans 6).

Some have charged that ministry as theological innovation is frivolous and that it abandons the absolute character of truth for a relativistic and pragmatic theology based on expediency. I have attempted to answer this charge by pointing out that the absolute nature of God's truth is grounded in God's Word as a living and active reality rather than in abstract principles or doctrines. Furthermore, I have argued that there is the "rule of the theological precedent." This provides a check against an arbitrary shift from the authority of God's Word to a convenient or cultural principle of expediency. Conformity to the authority of God's Word may require non-conformity to a theological tradition as well as nonconformity to contemporary culture and ideology.

"We are the aroma of Christ to God," Paul asserted, and then, clapping his hand over his mouth said, "Who is sufficient for these things?" We are, responded Paul, answering his own question, "For we are not peddlers of God's word like so many, but in Christ we speak as persons of sincerity, as persons sent from God and standing in his presence" (2 Cor. 2:16–17).

This is the kind of confidence that ministers need when their ministry demands theological innovation. This is the kind of confidence that comes from God, "who has made us competent to be ministers of a new covenant, not of letter but of spirit; for the letter kills, but the Spirit gives life" (2 Cor. 3:6).

How does God's ministry come alive in the praxis of our ministry? Turn the page and we shall see!

4

Ministry as
Theological Praxis

"Why is there no mention of any ministry of Jesus prior to his baptism?" I put this question to the pastors in my seminar on theology of ministry. "Certainly," I added, "Jesus did not become a caring and ministering person only after presenting himself to John for baptism. How do you account for that?"

When there was no response, I suggested that Jesus had no ministry of his own. His ministry was to do the will and work of the Father (John 4:24; 9:4; 17:4). The only reference to his activity prior to his baptism was the brief appearance in the temple at the age of twelve. While he demonstrated a precocious knowledge of the law, he was gently rebuked by his mother and, as Luke tells us, he went home and "was obedient to them" (Luke 2:51).

No, none of the kind words, none of the sympathizing tears, none of good deeds done by Jesus prior to his baptism were remembered and noted. There is a good reason for this. In retrospect, the disciples understood that it was the anointing by the Spirit of God at his baptism that confirmed him to be the Messiah and revealed his life and work as the ministry of God and the power of the kingdom of God. It was not by his own power, nor by the power of the evil one that Jesus performed signs and wonders. But, as he said, "if it is by the Spirit of God that I cast out demons, then the kingdom of God has come to you" (Matt. 12:28).

Only that ministry of Jesus performed in the power of the Spirit of God was noted and certified as the ministry and work of God. Jesus was driven by the Spirit into the wilderness following his baptism (Mark 1:12). Immediately following that trial, he began to proclaim the coming of the kingdom of God (Mark 1:15). Luke tells us that his first appearance in the synagogue at Nazareth following his baptism was marked by his reading from the prophet Isaiah, "The Spirit of the Lord is upon me, because he has anointed me to bring good news to the poor. He has sent me to proclaim release to the captives and recovery of sight to the blind, to let the oppressed go free, to proclaim the year of the Lord's favor." Sitting down, he announced, "Today this scripture has been fulfilled in your hearing" (Luke 4:16–21; Isa. 61:1–2).

At his baptism, Jesus became the Messiah—the Christ—the long-awaited anointed one. It is as the Christ, the anointed one, that he will perform the ministry of God through the power of the Spirit of God. The "day of the Lord," as God's promise of future blessing, is now present in a provisional, and yet powerful, form through the person and work of Jesus Christ as the presence and power of the Spirit.

This is how God's ministry comes alive in the praxis of Spirit. First through Christ's ministry, and then through those who are empowered by the Spirit of Christ.

Praxis Is not Practice!

Why do I introduce a technical term like *praxis?* Because it is necessary to distinguish the *practice* of ministry from ministry as the *praxis* of the Spirit of God. Give me a chance and I will show that it is not mere theological jargon!

Most of us were taught that truth is discerned as a primary intellectual or mental task. Through abstraction away from the uncertainty and ambiguity of the experiential world, we are led to believe that reality can be secured with some degree of certainty as "timeless truths." Once these truths have been mastered, then one can apply them as a "practitioner."

Theological schools quite often divide the curriculum into "practical theology" and "pure theology." *Practical theology* often means the acquiring of skills through experience. We are taught the truths of the Bible by scholars and how to preach and teach it by those who have some experience in the practice of ministry. Is that not too often the case?

Praxis, then, is quite different from the mere application of truth or theory. Let me explain.

Aristotle once described two quite different ways of viewing an action. The first kind of action he called *poiesis,* which means an action that produces a result, like a carpenter constructing a cabinet, or a contractor building a house. The end product completes the action regardless of what the future use may be of the product. This future use or purpose, what Aristotle called a *telos,* does not enter into the process of making something (*poiesis*).

For example, a builder might be asked to build a house according to a specific design and blueprint. When the house is finished, the contractor is paid in full if the building has been constructed according to the design. If, after several years, persons living in the house commit illegal or immoral acts, the builder of the house cannot be held liable for these actions. In other words, the ultimate use of the house, or its *telos,* was not part of the builder's responsibility. This is what Aristotle meant by *poiesis.* The product completes the action (see figure 1).

Figure 1

There is another kind of action, which Aristotle called *praxis*. While this includes some elements of *poiesis*, it goes beyond merely producing a product according to a design. With praxis, the *telos*, or ultimate purpose and value of an action, becomes part of the action. While the design serves to orient the action toward its goal, the ultimate purpose, or *telos*, informs the action so as to correct the design, if necessary, in order to realize the ultimate purpose. One involved in praxis, therefore, is not only accountable to implement the design with skill, but to discover the *telos* through discernment (see figure 2).

In figure 2 the action stands between the design and the *telos*, with the *telos* reaching back into the action from the future. The one who performs *praxis* must have discernment of the ultimate purpose or goal that is becoming evident through the action. It is also the case that only in the process of the action are certain truths concerning the final purpose and goal discovered. The action itself can reveal these truths. This is what makes praxis quite different from practice as the application of truth through a skill or technique.

John the Baptist, for example, was "practicing" baptism with the purpose of producing repentance on the part of those who submitted to the

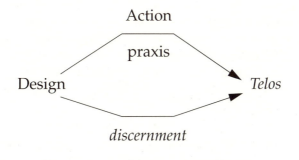

Figure 2

ritual. Suddenly he recognized Jesus standing near him asking to be baptized. Discerning even then that Jesus was "the lamb of God which takes away the sins of the world," John was reluctant. When Jesus prevailed, John realized that the future had entered into the present. What began as a practice, became praxis (Matt. 3:13–17; John 1:29–34)!

If he had not been practicing the ministry of baptism, he would not have discovered the praxis of the Spirit! As it was, John pointed to the future that had even then become visible in the present. He did not merely predict the future as the prophets had done, he pointed to it and announced its presence! He exercised the spiritual gift of discernment.

Let me use another example.

Consider the task of constructing a sermon from the Bible. If the sermon manuscript is the product, based upon exegetical methods that are faithful to the text, then the preacher has fulfilled her or his responsibility when the manuscript is completed and the sermon read. This is *poiesis*. But if, when the sermon is preached, no person's heart is convicted of sin and turns to God, then the *telos* of the sermon as an event of the Word of God preached is not reached. The sermon manuscript by itself is not the praxis of God's Word. Praxis includes the effect of the Word as well as a presentation of it.

If the sermon manuscript were sent back to the homiletics professor in seminary, an "A" might be awarded! But from the standpoint of the purpose of the Word of God, the sermon has not realized its *telos* until the Word of God has had an effect. "So shall my word be that goes out from my mouth," says God through the prophet Isaiah, "it shall not return to me empty, but it shall accomplish that which I purpose, and succeed in the thing for which I sent it" (Isa. 55:11).

The preparing and preaching of a sermon from the Word of God ought to be praxis, not *poiesis*. The *effect* of the Word of God is bound to the authority and power of the Word in the same way that its source is inspired by the Spirit of God. It might also be said at this point that there are some truths in Scripture that are only revealed through the living, preaching, and teaching of the text. This has enormous implications for how we interpret the Bible, an issue that I will discuss later in the book.

The Praxis of the Spirit:
A Case Study

Our theme in this chapter is ministry as theological praxis. Christ's ministry was the ministry of God working through him by the power of the Spirit of God. Our ministry is the ministry of Christ continuing through us by the presence and power of the Spirit of Christ. Theological praxis means that truths of God are discovered through the encounter with Christ in the world by means of ministry. This is what I call Christo-praxis. Much more will be said about this in part 2.

My concern is to uncover the inner logic of what is meant by the praxis of the Spirit. Here is a biblical example.

Consider once again the case of Peter, who was led by the Spirit to the house of Cornelius, a Roman soldier (Acts 10). Cornelius was apparently a "God-fearer," the term the Jews used to describe Gentiles who believed in the God of Israel but who were uncircumcised. In a vision, Cornelius was instructed to send for Peter, who was staying in a nearby village called Joppa. At the same time, Peter was praying on the rooftop of the house in which he was staying. In a vision, Peter saw something like a large sheet descending with various kinds of animals. Peter was told to rise, "kill and eat" some of the animals. As they were "unclean" animals by the Jewish law, Peter protested. At this point, the voice said, "What God has made clean, you must not call profane." When this happened three times, the vision suddenly was over and Peter was left perplexed as to its meaning.

The servants sent by Cornelius arrived at that very moment. The Spirit of God spoke to Peter and instructed him to go with them without hesitation. Arriving at the house of Cornelius the next day, Peter began to proclaim the gospel message of Jesus' ministry, death, and resurrection.

"While Peter was still speaking, the Holy Spirit fell upon all who heard the word. The circumcised believers were astounded that the gift of the Holy Spirit had been poured out even on the Gentiles . . . " (Acts 10:45). Peter ordered Cornelius and his household to be baptized on the basis of having received the Holy Spirit. Upon returning to Jerusalem, he gave account of his vision and the ministry to Cornelius, arguing, "Who was I that I could hinder God?" (Acts 11:17).

The importance of this event is marked by Luke's extensive account, marking a transition from the early ministry of the disciples in and around Jerusalem to Paul's ministry that began at Antioch (Acts 13).

The theological implications are staggering. The prompting of the Spirit of God in the heart of the Gentile, Cornelius, is understandable, for he was a God-fearer, though not a circumcised Jew. Most Jews of that time would have allowed for this, even providing a space near the temple for such persons. What astounded them was that the Holy Spirit came upon this uncircumcised Gentile! This was obviously unheard of and unthinkable prior to this event.

But what is even more astounding is the Spirit's instructions to Peter. When urged in his vision to kill and eat unclean flesh, Peter protested on the basis of the Scripture itself. The law of Moses clearly forbade what the Spirit was asking Peter to do. When Peter arrived at the house of Cornelius and heard the story Cornelius told of his own encounter with the Spirit, Peter responded: "I truly understand that God shows no partiality" (Acts 10:34). This theological discernment led Peter to theological innovation, and he baptized Cornelius, which is theological praxis!

At a later date, when Paul's ministry to the Gentiles was challenged by the Jewish Christians in Jerusalem, in the meeting of the council, Peter came to Paul's defense by citing the episode in the house of Cornelius. Peter reminded the council that "in the early days God made a choice among you, that I should be the one through whom the Gentiles would hear the message of the good news and become believers. And God, who knows the human heart, testified to them by giving them the Holy Spirit, just as he did to us; and in cleansing their hearts by faith he has made no distinction between them and us" (Acts 15:7–9).

Again, the theological truth that God considers both Jew and Gentile as equal and that no distinction exists between them with regard to the blessings of the promise made to Abraham is an incredible theological innovation. This is exactly the kind of innovation that we discussed in the previous chapter. Now we see more clearly how such an innovation is discovered.

Let us mark these steps clearly.

First, the presence and working of the Holy Spirit is considered to be a criterion of God's truth that takes precedence over all former teachings and laws of God. The Holy Spirit is the objective reality of the very being of God revealed through the Spirit's own presence in a concrete event, such as we saw in the house of Cornelius. This is the praxis of the Spirit that takes precedence over the practice of the law. Where the Spirit acts in such a way as to reveal God's presence and purpose, obedience is required. Not to obey by acting in accordance with the Spirit's direction is to resist God's own truth. Thus Peter defended his action by saying, "Who was I that I could hinder God?" (Acts 11:17).

Second, the task of theological discernment belongs to those who experience the praxis of the Spirit in the context of ministry. In our case study, Peter is on a mission when he received the vision concerning Cornelius. It is Peter who drew the astounding theological conclusion that "God shows no partiality, but in every nation anyone who fears him and does what is right is acceptable to him" (Acts 10:34–35). Need I remind you that this was the opening part of his sermon to Cornelius?

Later, the church leaders in Jerusalem do acknowledge that this theological assertion came first of all from Peter (Acts 15:14). There is no mention of a vision coming to these leaders and no indication that they had any theological discernment of their own! In fact, as Paul was later to discover, there continued to be a great deal of opposition to his ministry to the Gentiles coming from these same people. Paul reported that even Peter was swayed by their insistence on making distinctions between Gentile and Jewish Christians (Gal. 2:11–12).

Third, there is a search for a theological precedence to establish continuity between God's Word from the beginning and his later revelation. This is documented by James at the Jerusalem council when he said, "Simon has related how God first looked favorably on the Gentiles, to take from among them a people for his name. This agrees with the words of the prophets, as it is written,

> After this I will return, and I will rebuild the dwelling of David, which has fallen; from its ruins I will rebuild it, and I will set it up, so that all other peoples may seek the Lord—even all the Gentiles over whom my name has been called. Thus says the Lord, who has been making these things known from long ago. (Acts 15:16–18)

The importance of a theological precedent for theological innovation was discussed in the previous chapter. Now we see it in action as part of authentic theological praxis. This again should lay to rest concerns that theological innovation is sheer novelty. The necessity of a theological precedent demonstrates the continuity of God's self-revelation through redemptive history. At the same time, the new wine must be placed in new wineskins. The form must give way to the substance.

What was once designed by God as a sign and seal of covenant relation—circumcision, for example—must give way to the new covenant reality. The "shadow of what is to come," as Paul noted, must give way to the "substance," which is Jesus the Christ (Col. 2:17). What the Holy Spirit innovates is nothing less than the reality of Jesus Christ. When the Spirit comes, he will not speak on his own, Jesus said, "but will speak whatever he hears, and he will declare to you the things that are to come. He will glorify me, because he will take what is mine and declare it to you" (John 16:13–14).

The innovative action of the Spirit requires innovative theology, obedient to the praxis of Christ as a contemporary witness to God's ultimate purpose for humanity.

The Praxis of Discipleship

The disciples of Jesus were drawn into his own praxis of discipleship. Jesus was clearly a student of the Scriptures but was also a servant of the Spirit. The inner relationship that he experienced as the Son of the Father grounded all that he did in love. It was the assurance of the Father's love for him that empowered him to face the hostility of his enemies, the disenchantment of his followers, and finally the betrayal by Judas. It was his own love for the Father that directed him to love all that were loved by the Father, especially those marginalized and minimized by society.

Dietrich Bonhoeffer has reminded us that true discipleship is conformity to Jesus Christ as a contemporary presence leading us into the world. Ministry is thus grounded in the praxis of following Christ. The theological task is incumbent on those who are first of all disciples involved in Christ's mission to the world.

Too often we attempt to build our discipling programs on conformity to rules, disciplines, and control-minded religious personalities. Jesus will have none of that! His discipleship is grounded on the obedience issuing from love, servanthood growing out of sonship, and freedom grounded in fulfillment of God's purpose for his life.

We began by standing at the burning bush with Moses. The ministry of Moses led to the discovery of God's ministry of redemption and creation. We end sharing with Paul, the liberating Spirit of Jesus Christ poured out into the world through Pentecost. The beginning and end of all theology is the burning bush and the baptism of the Spirit.

Ministry continues, and so does theological discernment and innovation through the praxis of discipleship. What follows in this book is the beginning of the discovery of the depth and height, and the length and width, of the glory of God's ministry of creative love and covenantal grace. Walk with me as a fellow disciple of God's revelation in Word and deed.

II

God's Ministry in Covenant and Creation

5

The Word of God
Which Creates the Response

Imagine, if you will, this scene. The bleak and lonely landscape of Sinai flows endlessly around a solitary figure, trudging wearily in front of a flock of sheep. Looking closely, we see that it is an old man. His weariness is worn like a seamless garment. His face is weathered, his beard flecked with gray, and his steps are measured, so as to last the day. Yet his posture is erect and, despite his eighty years, his eyes are bright and there is something princely in the way he holds his staff.

We have discovered Moses, a fugitive from Egypt, an outcast from Pharaoh's house, a sheepherder these past forty years. This is the man who once had access to political and personal power but who lost it all in an impulsive act. He killed an Egyptian who was beating a Hebrew, one of his own kinsmen, and hid the body in the sand. When Pharaoh discovered the deed, Moses fled for his life into the wilderness of the Arabian desert (Ex. 2:11–15).

This is the man who turned aside to see the bush that burned but was not consumed. This is the man who heard the voice of God call to him out of the burning bush. This is the man, a fugitive and failure, eighty years old, powerless and penniless, whom God called to lead the Hebrews out of their bondage and oppression back to the land of promise (Exodus 3).

Here it is, I have suggested, that we find the theological beginning point in the Bible. Here it is that we find the first theologian. Here it is that we discover the core paradigm for the ministry of God that will reveal a new name—Yahweh—an ancient mystery—covenant love—and a future glory—life emerging out of death.

The inner logic of this paradigm of God's ministry can be summed up in one phrase: The Word of God creates the response out of nothing.

The Power of the Word: A Case Study

The scenario described above deliberately stresses the frailty, futility, and finitude of Moses. Let us list what we know of the situation:

Moses is a fugitive from Egypt, with an execution order issued by Pharaoh that one assumes is still in effect. His life is in danger.

Moses was rejected by his own people in his early attempt to intervene in a quarrel (Ex. 2:14). His leadership is in question.

Moses is eighty years old when God called him to go back to Egypt (Ex. 7:7). His life is virtually over.

Moses has no followers and no resources with which to mount a campaign against Pharaoh in order to liberate the people. His pockets are empty.

Moses has a severe speech impediment that causes him to seek to be excused from the mission (Ex. 4:10). He has an inferiority complex!

The people have been slaves for four hundred years and are powerless—emotionally, politically, economically, and militarily. The situation is hopeless!

All of this leads us to the conclusion that, from a human standpoint, what God requires and expects of Moses is an impossibility (see figure 3).

Figure 3

Is this merely an unfortunate situation that requires extraordinary resources and power from God? Or, is this the *necessary* condition that must exist in order that the theological truth be revealed—God's Word creates the response out of nothing?

It is the latter. Our case study clearly reveals that the attempt by Moses to come to the aid of his own people when he had every advantage and opportunity utterly failed. Not only that, the forty years of lapsed time stripped Moses of any hope of serving his people or of ministering for God.

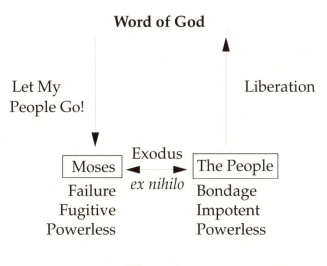

Figure 4

If we take this to be the critical element in the paradigm, then we must place it at the very center, which marks the intersection of the power of the Word with the need of the people (see figure 4).

In figure 4 the power of Pharaoh is displaced by the power of the Word of God. The apparent hopelessness of the situation is dramatically transformed when the Word of God is uttered as a creative power. The effect of this Word is produced solely from the Word itself. The point at which the Word of God enters is marked by powerlessness from the human side. Moses is drawn into the center as a powerless figure along with the people. The Word of God creates the response out of nothing.

The Latin phrase is *ex nihilo*—out of nothing. When theology textbooks set forth the doctrine of creation, the expression is often used: God created the world *ex nihilo*, out of nothing. There is an *ex nihilo* located at the very core of the paradigm that portrays the ministry of God. The fact that the *ex nihilo* was first of all revealed through God's ministry as Redeemer leads us to understand that as Creator, God created *ex nihilo*. This does not mean that "nothing" is itself something out of which God creates something! Rather, the *ex nihilo* indicates that the *only* antecedent for that which does exist is the Word of God.

The author of Genesis first knew of God as Redeemer before knowing him as Creator. We are not surprised, then, to find within the opening chapters of Genesis the story of creation, out of nothing, as it were.

There is also a suggestive use of language that ties the exodus event to the creation story. In the beginning, we are told that, when God created the heavens and the earth, at each successive stage the words used are "And God said, 'Let there be. . . .'" In verse two of Genesis chapter one we are told that the earth was a "formless void." It was only when God spoke and said, "Let there be light," that creation emerged out of this formless void—this nothingness. This is reminiscent of the words spoken at exodus: "Let my people go!" It is by the power of the Word of God that the people were redeemed from bondage, and it is by the power of that same Word that all things were created out of nothing.

Karl Barth has suggested that the structure of these opening verses deliberately create the condition of a void in order to show that only when God speaks is there a response. The Word of God creates the response. The void—the *ex nihilo*—is the necessary condition for the Word to bring forth God's creation.

The *Ex Nihilo* as Interpretive Model

Does this same paradigm serve as an interpretive model for other aspects of the creation story? Indeed it does.

Look at the story of the creation of the first humans, for instance. Is there an *ex nihilo* also present in this account? Indeed there is.

We must remember that Moses experienced personally the power of the Word of God in bringing the redemption of the people out of bondage. In this event he discovered the inner logic of God's ministry of redemption and used it to expound the inner logic of creation, especially that of the origin and nature of human persons.

Following the overall depiction of creation as issuing out of the Word of God, and the creation of the man and the woman in the image and likeness of God, the second chapter of Genesis inserts the core theological paradigm into the narrative. The focus is upon the human in this second account. But suddenly we are confronted with a problem! The creation of the man occurs as the Lord formed him from the dust of the ground and placed him in the garden to care for it. There are apparently no animals as yet formed, nor is there any other human.

Viewing this situation, God said, "It is not good that the man should be alone; I will make him a helper as his partner" (Gen. 2:18). But then the animals are formed out of the ground and brought to the man to "see what he would call them." Finally, the divine verdict upon this attempt is given, "but for the man there was not found a helper as his partner." The man was put into a deep sleep, and out of his side the woman was created. Then the man said, "This at last is bone of my bones and flesh of my flesh" (Gen. 2:23).

Twice in this story we see the *ex nihilo* strategically placed. First, the solitary human creature is presented as a pathetic figure. He is described as "not good" and when given command of the animals that are placed before him, could not create a response. His naming of the animals indicates the exercise of the power of Word, but in the end it remains powerless. The counterpart (partner) for the man cannot be found in the dust of the ground. Even God cannot find it there. Not because God lacks the power, but because the ground itself has no possibility for producing the image of God. The divine image and likeness is endowed directly by God, *ex nihilo*, one might say!

Second, the man is put to sleep and rendered inoperative in the situation. Sleep is a metaphor for death in the Bible, and, in a sense, the suspension of the power of the human is like a death out of which life will come. The creative power of God is brought to bear in this *ex nihilo* situation, and the result is the completion of the human in the image of God— "This at last is bone of my bones and flesh of my flesh." Now for the first time in this second account the terms for male and female are used. This indicates that human sexuality itself is more than a biological capacity. Human sexual differentiation as male and female is an expression of the image of God.

Why is the creation of the first humans portrayed in this way, and why was it so meaningful to the Hebrew people when first told by Moses? Let me suggest a reason.

Remember that the people who came out of Egypt had suffered for four hundred years under intolerable conditions where the males were forced to work as slaves in Pharaoh's public works program. The loss of identity and personal dignity was no doubt communicated from generation to generation as a sense of shame and isolation. One of the deepest wounds to the human spirit is the isolation and fragmentation that occurs when self-dignity and self-worth are systematically eroded. This is the pervasive effect of any form of human bondage and oppression, whether it be due to race, economic factors, political control, or marital and family abuse. The story of human origins in the Bible needs to be read from the perspective of redemption from this loss of personal being.

Writing under divine inspiration, Moses intended the creation story to be a radical reminder of the inherent dignity and worth of each person by revealing the divine image and likeness as the foundation of personhood.

We read the account of the creation of the first humans as intended to heal contemporaries of Moses of the shame and fragmentation of the life of the self that centuries of slavery produced.

The first account, in Genesis chapter one, grounds humanity in the mutual differentiation and relation of male and female as expressive of the divine image (1:26–27). With the male and female split apart by the ravages of slavery that penetrated to the very core of their existence, the Hebrew people, to whom the story was told, needed to find healing, unity, and hope. If it is true that the Hebrew women preserved a sense of identity through connectedness with their children of the covenant, the males needed to discover their own being and connectedness to this "stream of consciousness" embodied by the women and children. The mutual empowering that God intended in the original relation was felt as a loss when the identity of the male was obscured. The recovery of self-identity as both male and female is thus grounded in the divine image as a mutual and complementary empowering.

For the Hebrew male, who has suffered loss to his communal identity through the isolation and fragmentation of being an anonymous slave, the pathetic figure of the first man (Adam) as alone and unfulfilled is a powerful reminder of that experience. Moses depicts the solitary man (Adam) as having no partner to complement his own humanity and constitute true selfhood. This is a replica of the male's situation as a slave in Egypt. It is not only one of absolute individuation, but carries the connotation of shame. For when the man attempts to complete what is lacking through relation with the earth and the animals God created, he ends in failure and frustration.

Only when God creates woman separate from and yet complementary to the man do we find the first expression of self-conscious personhood in the creation account. "This at last is bone of my bones and flesh of my flesh; this one shall be called Woman, for out of Man this one was taken" (2:23). Up to this point in the narrative, there is not a single instance of self-reference and self-expression on the part of the human. Now human selfhood is complete and the shame of estrangement is healed. "And the man and his wife were both naked, and were not ashamed" (2:25).

Why Do Our Words So Often Fail?

Moses doubted that his own words would be adequate when confronting the formidable power of Pharaoh. He had failed once through his actions, now he feared failing again through his inadequate speech. Adam failed to find the counterpart to the promise of his own humanity in calling forth the creatures by name.

Written deep into the paradigm of the Word of God as the ministry of God is the memory of this primeval failure. We feel it as an unspeakable threat that lies behind every word we speak. We raise our voices in a vain attempt to cross over this chasm and produce by sheer volume what the words themselves will not bring forth. Words become weapons that are intended to hurt and destroy that which resists our coaxing and refuses our command.

The response we seek is not a response that we can create by our own efforts.

Why do our words so often fail? Because our words are not themselves a creative power, but rather a response to the divine Word that calls us into being. When Moses realized that his own speech would be inadequate to confront the terror of Pharaoh's wrath, God responded, "Who gives speech to mortals? Who makes them mute or deaf, seeing or blind? Is it not I, the Lord? Now go, and I will be with your mouth and teach you what you are to speak" (Ex. 4:11–12).

The human word is itself a response created by the divine Word. Without the divine Word there is no possibility of a human word. Without the divine speech there is no possibility of human hearing. The speaking creates the hearing.

There is no mention in the Bible of God speaking to any creature other than the human. God curses the serpent (Genesis 3), but does not speak to the serpent so as to produce a response. God has spoken to the human who bears the divine image and thereby creates the possibility of hearing.

It is not as though there is a latent possibility of hearing the Word of God within creaturely being, which humans have managed to bring forth by their own power into a word of response to God. No. The speaking creates the hearing. And whatever God addresses by his Word will be given the capacity of response. "My word shall not return to me empty," says the Lord through the prophet, "but it shall accomplish that which I purpose, and succeed in the thing for which I sent it" (Isa. 55:11).

Does this mean that all humans will of necessity hear and respond to God in a positive way? No, but it does mean that every person bears the responsibility of hearing, because the Word of God summons each one into response. The only way of voiding the Word of God is to hear but not be willing to hear, to see but not be willing to acknowledge what one sees.

This is the judgment pronounced by Isaiah when he himself had his lips touched with a coal from the altar. "Go and say to this people: 'Keep listening, but do not comprehend; keep looking, but do not understand.' Make the mind of this people dull, and stop their ears, and shut their eyes, so that they may not look with their eyes and listen with their ears, and comprehend with their minds, and turn and be healed" (Isa. 6:9–10).

The Word of God creates the response, which will either lead to repentance and life or lead to resistance and death. The Word that brings a sentence of death is the same Word that creates the possibility of life.

As the apostle Paul said, "For we are the aroma of Christ to God among those who are being saved and among those who are perishing; to the one a fragrance from death to death, to the other a fragrance from life to life. Who is sufficient for these things?" (2 Cor. 2:15–16).

Why do our words so often fail us? It may be because our lips need to be touched with the coal from the altar. We have the power to hurt and destroy when we use words to control others and to compensate for our own sense of shame and powerlessness.

Like Moses, we too can end up on the barren landscape of our own futility and failure. There is nothing that can make up for what we have lost and nothing that we can do to gain what we most desire. Nothing? Are we ready to acknowledge that? Then we are in exactly the right place. The bush burns only for those who have burned their own bridges, and the voice speaks only to those who pause to listen.

"Speak Lord, for your servant is listening" (1 Sam. 2:9).

6

The Grace of God
Which Presupposes Barrenness

The cry of Abraham's lament overshadowed the pain of Sarah's burden. "O Lord God, what will you give me, for I continue childless, and the heir of my house is Eliezer of Damascus?" (Gen. 15:2). Indeed, Abraham had a reason for concern! He was seventy-five years old when the Lord appeared to him and made a promise, "I will make of you a great nation . . . " (Gen. 12:2). To complicate matters, his wife Sarah was barren, and already beyond the normal age of childbearing.

The failure of a Hebrew woman to bear a son so that her husband might perpetuate his line was so bitter that it could only be understood as due to the Lord's displeasure. The mystery of conception was hidden from these people, and it was conventional wisdom that the Lord opens and closes the womb at his will. Not to conceive, for a woman, was not only to fail her husband but to live under the burden of failing to please the Lord.

Can Blessing Come Forth
from Barrenness?

Conception is a metaphor as well as a biological event. Failure to conceive and bring to birth what we desperately long for and what we believe to be God's promise is an affliction of contemporary persons for which modern science has little explanation. One person's lament is usually another's burden, if not a curse attributed to divine displeasure, or at least indifference.

The metaphor of barrenness is a powerful insight into the psyche of our contemporary society. Blaming God is still one way of deflecting self-accusation for failing to conceive and give birth to our hopes and desires. Without a God to blame, failure to bring forth what we expect or hope for is a cancer that has no cure.

It is the barrenness of Sarah that catches our attention. Her inability to conceive is a formidable barrier to the realization of Abraham's dream and God's promise.

But why are Abraham and Sarah chosen in the first place? I mean, not chosen by God, but chosen by Moses?

Inspired by God, Moses has the task of tracing the mystery of Yahweh's redeeming love back to the very beginning of human origins. Surely he has a wealth of oral tradition and a thousand stories from which to choose. Why Abraham and Sarah? Indeed, why Sarah?

The answer: It is Sarah who is the key to the mystery, not merely Abraham. It is Sarah's barrenness that is the indispensable key that will unlock even further the mystery, the inner logic, of Yahweh's grace already demonstrated in redeeming the people from bondage in Egypt.

Moses' Hermeneutic

When Moses sorts through the ancestral stories and combs the tradition for clues as to which stories teach the theological truths that he has learned through the exodus, he knows he has found the answer in Sarah. What he is looking for, under divine inspiration of course, is that which will replicate in the history of the people what now has been revealed through God's ministry of liberation and redemption of the chosen people from Egypt.

Why indeed were they ever chosen in the first place? And what does it mean to be "chosen of God?" If Yahweh is now the only name by which the ancient name of Elohim is to be understood, where are the clues that will connect the inner meaning of Yahweh's name to the history of Yahweh's people over the previous centuries?

As I have said, Sarah is the key, not Abraham. This will surprise and alarm some. For we have been taught to revere Abraham as the "father of faith," and so he is. But you cannot be a father without a child, and the miracle of God's grace is not that Abraham could disseminate his seed, but that a barren woman could conceive from it!

Even the commentary on this story by Peter stresses the role of Sarah in the gracious work of God. "Thus Sarah obeyed Abraham," Peter says, "and called him lord. You have become her daughters as long as you do what is good and never let fears alarm you" (1 Peter 3:6). The obedience of Sarah was not abject submission to his authority role as husband, but to the promise of God that came to him, but that only she could fulfill! Without Sarah, the life of Abraham would have no theological content!

The Inner Logic
of Barrenness and Grace

This is what Moses saw when he looked deeper into the story of Abraham and Sarah. The inner logic of the exodus event as a demonstration of Yahweh's gracious power of deliverance was the *ex nihilo* that we considered in the previous chapter. Why did the Lord wait until Moses was eighty years old, a failure and fugitive, with no possibilities? Because the element of human possibility must be removed. The people were power-less and helpless. They cried out to the Lord. Moses was chosen to be the redeemer because he was also without power on the human level. Moses understood that this "powerlessness" is itself a necessary ingredient in the chemistry of divine grace.

The barren womb of Sarah represents the *ex nihilo* that corresponds to the impotence and powerlessness of Moses and the people of God. The inner logic of barrenness and grace replicates the same core paradigm as Moses discovered through the exodus. Ishmael is set aside in the same way that the early attempt by Moses to liberate his people failed to accomplish God's purpose. Figure 5 portrays the inner logic of barrenness and grace.

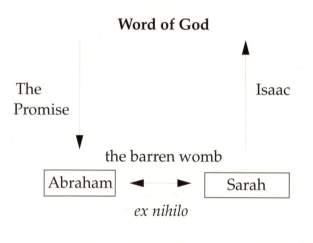

Word of God

The Promise   Isaac

the barren womb

Abraham ◄ ► Sarah

ex nihilo

Figure 5

With the birth of Isaac, we see what Thomas Torrance once called the "scandal of particularity." The choice of Isaac over his elder brother Ish-mael appears as a "scandal of grace," viewed from the perspective of nat-ural rights and common law. Let us return to the story of Abraham and Sarah for ourselves and trace out a theology of divine grace.

The promise comes to both Abraham and Sarah, which becomes clear as the story unfolds. Sarah is to bear a son who will become the heir through which the covenant promise is to be fulfilled. Abraham will have so many descendants that they can scarcely be counted, as many as the stars in the heavens (Gen. 15:5), indicating that God's promise will extend infinitely. Not only that, through this promised seed "all the families of the earth shall be blessed" (Gen. 12:3). This is the promise, and Abraham believes and it is reckoned unto him as righteousness (Gen. 15:6).

We have already mentioned the fact that Sarah is barren. What now occurs is further development of the inner logic of grace. Sarah concludes that she is the obstacle and says to Abraham, "You see that the Lord has prevented me from bearing children; go in to my slave-girl; it may be that I shall obtain children by her" (Gen. 16:2). According to custom, this is both morally and legally permissible. The paternity of the child is the key to the inheritance of the blessing. This was also true in the case of polygamous marriage at that time.

To Hagar, the slave girl, a son was born, who was named Ishmael (Gen. 16:15). It is worth noting that Moses identifies her as an Egyptian slave girl (16:3)—a thinly veiled reference to the fact that the child born represents the slave status of the Hebrew people when they were in Egypt, a condition from which the Lord graciously redeemed them.

Abraham is now eighty-six years old (16:16), and is apparently satisfied that they have successfully appropriated the promise of God by circumventing Sarah's barrenness. Several years go by and the Lord again appears to Abraham, who is now ninety-nine, and reiterates the covenant promise. He also announces the astounding news that Sarah, who is now eighty-nine years old, will conceive a child in her barren womb, thereby fulfilling God's promise (Genesis 17).

No wonder Abraham fell on his face and laughed (17:17)! The birth of a son through Sarah was not only impossible but unnecessary.

Let me elaborate, if I may. I picture Abraham protesting strongly and pointing to his son Ishmael. "I already have a son," he might say. "There he is. He is already thirteen years old. He is almost as tall as I am. I have taught him every night by the campfire that he is the very embodiment of the promise of God. He is the one who will be chosen to carry on the promised blessing."

"Then unteach him," the Lord might have replied.

"O that Ishmael might live in your sight," cried Abraham (17:18)!

"No," replied the Lord, but your wife Sarah shall bear you a son, and you shall name him Isaac" (i.e., *he laughs*, 17:19).

While Ishmael will also be provided for, he is set aside as the chosen one to bear the promise. As much as Abraham has invested in Ishmael, he must now set him aside and trust God to enable barren Sarah to conceive. "O that Ishmael might live in your sight!"

Ishmael represents thirteen years of Abraham's ministry. Ishmael was an act of faith and obedience on Abraham's part, interpreted by his own

context and culture. Ishmael was not produced out of unbelief and disobedience, as far as Abraham was concerned. And yet, Ishmael, along
with thirteen years of ministry, must be canceled out.

This reminds us that the issue is not so much obedience as contrasted
with disobedience, but true obedience as compared with false obedience.
It is not so much an issue of unbelief as it is of right belief contrasted with
wrong belief. True obedience and right belief are based on apprehension
of God's purpose and conformity to God's will. False obedience and
wrong belief result from a human way of thinking.

Jesus rebuked Peter for his wrong belief when Peter attempted to persuade Jesus not to go to Jerusalem. "You are a stumbling block to me;"
Jesus said to Peter, "for you are setting your mind not on divine things but
on human things" (Matt. 16:23). Peter believed that he was acting in accordance with what seemed right, but he was wrong!

When we take up the Word of God on our own lips and proclaim the
mystery of God's grace and love, we are not preaching and witnessing to
those who have no belief and to those who are disobedient—in their own
eyes. When we preach the Word of God, we are speaking to those who believe in something dear to them, and to those who rely on their own way
of obedience. This belief must be stripped away as was Abraham's belief
in Ishmael. No wonder Paul exclaimed, "Who is sufficient for these
things?" (2 Cor. 2:16).

What is difficult, as we hear it in the plaintive cry of Abraham, is the
death of our own Ishmaels. The grace of God must first kill before it can
make alive. The grace of God requires barrenness, not our own belief, as
a precondition. True faith and true obedience come as a gift of God's grace,
and the inner logic of that gift requires that where we have inserted a human possibility the grace of God must remove it. This was true for Moses
as he experienced his own failure and futility, only to witness God's
power and grace through that weakness.

But what about Sarah?

It is, after all, Sarah who must consent and cooperate with divine grace
in order that her barrenness be overcome and she conceive.

How does Abraham convince Sarah that they must now turn toward
each other and embrace that barrenness with hope and faith? I could well
imagine Sarah's reaction.

"You have no right to ask that of me. Thank God for the day that I
passed the age of bearing children. Yes, I had finally to surrender the
hope and dream of producing a child, but that hope is itself a curse.
Each morning when I awakened and realized that I had failed again to
conceive, I felt the sharp edge of the Lord's disapproval and the openly

expressed scorn of my friends. And, yes, Abraham, you too were disappointed in me. I felt it."

"I have long since given up hope," Sarah continues, "but I at least have accepted my fate and find it comforting and secure. In asking me to hope again you are asking me to risk despair and disappointment again."

It is not hard to write the script for this conversation which is not recorded in Scripture. For there is a burden to hope that tears away at the spirit when failure occurs. "Hope deferred makes the heart sick," the proverb reminds us (Prov. 13:12). Self-blame is only one part of hope deferred. The failure of God to respond as we pray and petition strikes at the core of our faith and trust.

There is a kind of peace that comes when one settles for the inevitable. Surely Moses felt it and used it to smooth over the old wounds and try to forget failed dreams.

But the grace of God will not permit that. As Moses was summoned out of his anonymity and silence to speak the Word of God to Pharaoh, so Sarah is summoned out of quiet resignation to her fate to conceive what had never been possible for her, and to hope for that which had always eluded her.

The Burden of Hope

Hope is sometimes a burden too great to bear. Those who have the courage and faith to bear forth the seed, as the Psalmist reminds us, also bear the burden of the seed.

> He surely toils along weeping,
>   carrying the burden of seed;
> he surely comes in with rejoicing,
>   carrying his sheaves.
>   (Ps. 126: 5–6; literal
>   translation of the Hebrew)

The burden of the seed is to hope again. Hope is the burden that one must bear in order to live by faith and the promise of God.

The burden of hope is the anguish over what has already been lost. Hope always emerges out of the ruins of some failed dream, some unfulfilled desire, some loss that must be grieved.

There is a kind of hope that is childish and immature. It is short-term and short-lived. It flickers for an instant and then just as quickly dissolves with the first tears of frustration over the loss of some simple pleasure. Hope is not a wish or desire that can be washed away with the first summer storm. That hope is merely a fantasy of the mind, an illusion that shares the same bed with fear—both are ghosts in the night and cannot survive the bright light of day.

Hope was first expressed in the Bible following the first murder. Eve was the mother of two sons, Cain and Abel. When Cain killed Abel, we read, "Adam knew his wife again, and she bore a son and named him Seth, for she said, 'God has appointed for me another child instead of Abel, because Cain killed him'" (Gen. 4:25). I can hear her whisper to herself, "Will Cain slay him? Will I lose this son too?"

There are those who would not have risked another child, another tragic loss. There are those who prefer never to try again rather than to suffer the anguish of bearing hope.

Hope requires risk, so much that it hurts. Hope makes us vulnerable to future and even greater loss. Hope exposes us to disappointment, frustration, and betrayal. Faith plants the seed and promises a harvest, and so creates hope. But with the promise of a harvest comes the possibility that the promise will fail. That is the burden that hope must bear.

To take up the burden of hope one must not only accept the yoke of life and enter into partnership with the creative power of God, but also engender the trust of others in the process. Both Abraham and Sarah must share the risk, though Sarah bears the greater burden of hope.

The gift of faith is not the burden. Rather, faith is the empowerment of God to bear the burden of hope and to sow and tend the seed. This seed is an investment of something precious to us in utter dependence upon the promise of a harvest through a power over which we have no control.

To have faith is to be a sower, and not only a reaper. But in that we come face to face with our helplessness.

The burden of hope is the weakness of the seed and our own helplessness to care for it in the face of the unpredictable storms of life. Without rain the seed will not grow. But with every raincloud there looms the possibility of a ravaging and cruel storm. The apostle Paul reminds us that the created world was subjected to futility in hope that creation itself would be set free from bondage to decay and would obtain the freedom of the glory of the children of God (Rom. 8:19–21).

Not every rain will produce a flood, nor will every cloud produce some rain! Not every sickness leads to a death, but death does occur, senseless and outrageous to the human spirit. Having lost one child, will you bear the burden of hope and risk another one? Will the burden of anguish and responsibility be too much? How will one survive through the inevitable childhood sicknesses that follow the birth of every child, when sickness has already produced one death?

Not all jealousy and hatred leads to murder. But violence and murders do occur. Eve has chosen to have another child. There will be jealousy and anger again. Can one bear the burden of helplessness in the face of such uncertainty?

Having lived her life under the burden of hope and then having that burden removed through the natural process of growing too old to bear children, can Sarah hope again? This is the astounding fact of Sarah's "obedience to her husband," as Peter noted. This is her willingness to "bear the burden of hope" again so that the Word of God can perform its work.

Ministry as Our Part in the Work of Grace

Some have misunderstood the inner logic of grace and barrenness. They rightly suggest that all ministry is by the grace of God, and not of works. They have heard well the biblical witness to grace as the sole cause of our salvation and the only basis for faith. The misunderstanding comes with pointing to the priority of God's grace to the neglect of the human share in that work of grace.

The righteousness reckoned to Abraham was not based on his passivity, but on the fact that he actively grasped the promise as coming through sexual union with his wife, Sarah. Isaac did not drop down from heaven, but came through the cooperation and participation of both Abraham and Sarah. Abraham's faith was not believing in an absurdity but believing in the power of God to do what is impossible for humans. "Is anything too wonderful for the Lord?" Abraham and Sarah are told (Gen. 18:14). The faith of Abraham and Sarah in the Word of God was demonstrated as they embraced the barrenness that lay between them. Without that act there would have been no Isaac!

What then is the difference between the conception of Ishmael and that of Isaac? From the standpoint of human involvement, virtually none. In both cases an act of physical intercourse took place, one with a young slave girl named Hagar, and another with Sarah, the barren wife. In both cases, Abraham was the male partner in the act, and in both cases a conception and a birth occurred.

The point is this. The difference between that which is produced through the grace and power of God and that which is not cannot be located in the degree of human participation and effort, but solely in that which grace produces through the human act.

Move with me through time. It is now thirty years later. You have heard that God has given Abraham a son who is the promised seed through

whom the blessing shall come to all people. You are told that both sons of
Abraham are working in a nearby field. As you approach, you see the two
men. One will be about thirty years of age and the other forty-three. Both
appear about the same size, and it is difficult to determine which is the
younger Isaac and which is the older Ishmael.

As you draw near, you ask each of them in turn: "Tell me about who
you are and where you came from." One answers, "My name is Ishmael,
Abraham is my father, and my mother was a young and fertile woman."

The other answers, "My name is Isaac, and I too am a son of Abraham,
and my mother is a barren, old woman." You protest. "That cannot be
true. If your mother was barren you would not be here. In that you were
conceived and born, your mother could not be barren."

"But it is true," he responds, "my mother is barren and I am her child."

It is now quite clear which one is the son of promise. It is Isaac, whose
mother is barren. The inner logic of barrenness and grace is the clue. What
the exodus event revealed as the paradigm of God's ministry through the
ex nihilo of powerlessness and impotence is now replicated in the history
of Sarah and Isaac.

Suppose that Sarah had other children following the birth of Isaac. Is it
still true that, for Isaac, his mother is barren? Of course! For Isaac the barrenness of his mother is a reality that accounts for his own identity as the
child of promise. Subsequent children born to her cannot void the fact that
he was conceived in a barren womb.

If one were to ask Jesus the question, "Is it true that your mother is a
virgin, even though she may well have conceived and given birth to other
children following your birth?" his answer would be the same. "My
mother is a virgin."

Once again, the virgin womb of Mary, the mother of Jesus, is the *ex nihilo*
that grace presupposes in order that the ministry of God be authentic.

What have we learned in this chapter? We learned that the grace of God
presupposes barrenness, not fertility; that impossibility from the human
side is the condition that demonstrates most clearly the inner logic of
grace. We also have learned that humans have a share in the ministry of
God; that human obedience and faith are not set aside by grace, but are
drawn into the grace of God as an indispensable aspect of God's ministry.

Sarah's burden of hope and her cooperation with the promise of God
made what otherwise would have been a story of human tragedy and tri-
umph into a theological paradigm through which we can see even greater
depths of divine love. The covenant was made with Abraham but was
consecrated through Sarah. What exactly is this covenant and why is it the
clue to God's creation? This is another chapter in our story.

7

The Covenant of God
Which Precedes Creation

"It's hard to follow your thinking," my students tell me. "You think backward and not logically. Now you are trying to tell us that even though creation occurred prior to the exodus event, God's covenant with Israel actually preceded creation. It doesn't make sense!"

At this point I like to read them a quotation from Karl Barth: "We must understand that God is the measure of all reality and propriety, understand that eternity exists first and then time, and therefore the future first and then the present, as surely as the Creator exists first and then the creature. He who understands that need take no offense here."

I then remind the students that the creation story was written by a person who first experienced God as redeemer and only then discovered the theological framework for creation. It was Moses who installed the explicit covenant relation between God and the redeemed people. Through this theological paradigm in which the *ex nihilo* was revealed as the critical core, Moses did "think backward," so to speak, and discovered the clues to the covenant in all that had gone before, even in the very heart of the creation narrative.

For example, when Moses asked for the name of God he received the cryptic answer, "I am who I am," or, "I will be for you as I am." This was immediately followed by a further designation, "I am Yahweh, the God of your ancestors, the God of Abraham, the God of Isaac, and the God of Jacob" (Ex. 3:14–15). While the name Yahweh was only revealed in the exodus event, Yahweh is the name of the God who is the God of the ancestors and also the name of the God who is the Creator.

Covenant as the
Inner Logic of Creation

While the technical term for covenant (*berith*) is not found in the creation account, the ingredients of the covenant relation that exist as the presupposition of this account can be found there.

When God created by speaking the Word: "Let there be," this is remi-

niscent of the words that were given to Moses to say to Pharaoh, "Let my
people go." The covenant was instituted solely through the Word of God as
a gracious and creative event, *ex nihilo*. The powerlessness and impotence
of both Moses and the people are at the critical center of the covenant.

This aspect of covenant is also found in the creation account. The Word
of God appears suddenly as the sole power and source of creation. The
"void" in Genesis 1:2 corresponds to the vacuum in the life of Moses and
the people. God's creative Word is the single word spoken by which all
other words and speech come into existence. Creation is not only placed
in its own existence by this Word, but it is related back to the creative
Word in a reciprocity of relation, marked by the setting of boundaries for
the human and the subsequent obedience demanded.

The covenant is *unilateral* and not *bilateral* in its inception. This means
that it was established solely by God's initiative and power, without any
conditions on the side of the Hebrew people that brought it into being.
This unconditional covenant required unconditional obedience. But the
obedience was not demanded as a condition upon which the covenant
was originally enacted. Obedience follows grace; it does not precede it.

Grace is thus the presupposition of nature, not the reverse. Love is the
inner logic of the covenant, and is the ground of creation as well as its purpose, with the human as the focal point. Moses instructs the people who
have experienced God's gracious love by saying, "When your children ask
you in time to come, 'What is the meaning of the decrees and the statutes
and the ordinances that the Lord our God has commanded you?' then you
shall say to your children, 'We were Pharaoh's slaves in Egypt, but the
Lord brought us out of Egypt with a mighty hand'" (Deut. 6:20–21).

Moses reminded them, "It was not because you were more numerous
than any other people that the Lord set his heart on you and chose you—
for you were the fewest of all peoples. It was because the Lord loved you
and kept the oath that he swore to your ancestors, that the Lord has
brought you out with a mighty hand, and redeemed you from the house
of slavery" (Deut. 7:7–8).

This is what is meant by saying that the covenant was enacted unilaterally by Yahweh alone. The only precedent for his action was his prior
Word. This same Word was spoken at creation. All things came into existence *ex nihilo*, out of the void. The author of the book of Hebrews captures
this exactly: "By faith we understand that the worlds were prepared by
the word of God, so that what is seen was made from things that are not
visible" (Heb. 11:3).

The God who creates and sustains the world by "speaking," corresponds
to the covenant-making God whose Word brought forth the liberation of the

people from bondage. The covenant as theological paradigm revealed through the exodus event constitutes the theological framework for the creation story. This is reflected in the very structure of the narrative, as the seventh day is placed at the end of the chronological sequence so as to orient all that has gone before to God's purpose and goal. The seventh day is itself a sign, and even a kind of sacrament of the covenant, to remind the people who were redeemed that their destiny is not determined by their past but by their future. While the seventh day follows the sixth day in the chronological sequence, the seventh day "precedes" the first day in the same way that covenant precedes creation. This "precedence" is what Karl Barth earlier referred to when he said that "eternity exists first, and then time."

God's act of reconciliation and healing precedes and provides the context for understanding creation's purpose and goal. For the human, nature is not absolutely determinative of personal existence, for nature is itself grounded in grace. Figure 6 shows the inner logic of covenant and creation.

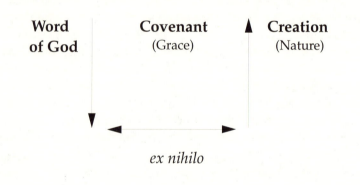

Figure 6

Note that the *ex nihilo* is at the core, showing that the basis for covenant is not in nature but in grace. This has immense significance for us when we consider God's ministry of redemption from the effects of the fall of the human into sin and death.

Grace as the
Inner Logic of Sin

There is a version of grace that defines it as God's special form of unmerited mercy extended to those who have violated God's law and fallen into sin. In this view, grace is God's response to human sin. The creation story is read as though the first humans were related to God originally by their own obedience and observance of God's law. "You may freely eat of every tree of the garden; but of the tree of the knowledge of good and evil you shall not eat, for in the day that you eat of it you shall die" (Gen. 2:16–17). The specific command gives space for human choice but sets limits backed up by the threat of death. In violating this limit, Adam and Eve suffer the fatal defect of separation from God as a consequence. Nonetheless, in this version God shows mercy and restraint, and makes provision for them to continue to live, though now under conditions that reflect their original fall from innocence.

Why is this version not acceptable? Why should we not find in the story of creation the fundamental definition and description of human nature as God intended it and as humans violated it?

Let me suggest two reasons.

First, the name Yahweh is the revealed name by which the generic name Elohim is to be understood in speaking of God. This is made clear through the exodus event and the special nature of the covenant as the inner logic of God's Word. The content of the name Yahweh is first of all understood as revealing God's grace as creative and all-powerful—grace is the very heart of the divine Word, not an added dimension necessitated by human sin. To say that grace emerges as God's response to sin is to consider sin as that which prompts God's grace. This is untenable, because it leads to the conclusion that grace is not an essential aspect of God's being. Theoretically, in this view, if sin had not occurred, there would have been no need for grace.

When we read the creation account through the paradigm of the God who expresses covenant love and grace as the very core of divine being, we must understand the creation of the first humans, as well as all else in creation, to be grounded in God's grace and freedom.

Second, the creation story by which the first humans came into existence liberates human nature from biological determinism through the insertion of the *ex nihilo* between their creaturely nature and their human nature. The image and likeness of God does not emerge out of the simple fabrication of humans out of the dust of the ground, as the second creation account makes clear (Genesis 2). The first creation account tells us what the "fact of the matter" is, that humans were created after the animals on the sixth day, and "in the image of God"—male and female (Gen. 1:26–27).

In the second account (Genesis 2), the story is retold as a theological case study. In this account, what has already been revealed as "the fact of the matter" is now given theological content. The fact is that the image of

God resides in humans as "male and female" (1:27). The fact is that the animals were created first and then the humans (1:24–25).

What are we to understand then by the second story, which begins not with two humans, but with only one—Adam—and by the animals created *after* this person and not before? This second account, as I have suggested, can be considered "as if" the Creation took place in this form, for the purpose of expounding more clearly the theological content of the "facts" as given in the first account.

It is as though God is saying, "I know what your question is. Can the image and likeness be possessed autonomously by a single person? Can the man be fully human and complete without the woman?" The answer is provided by the case study.

When the man—Adam—is created, he is given a space in which to live, with responsibilities to assume and a command that he is to obey. It is apparently a perfect and idyllic environment. Yet God suddenly said, "It is not good that the man should be alone; I will make him a helper as his partner." Note that this was not a complaint by Adam! Adam did not approach God and say, "I don't want to appear ungrateful, but there seems to be something missing!"

No, it is God who informs Adam of this distressing news. I am sure that Adam must have said, "I'm sorry that you told me! It seemed good enough before."

Nonetheless, God says in effect, "Don't worry, I'm going to fix it." With that, God created out of the ground creatures (animals and birds) and brought them to the man to "see what he would call them" (2:19). Adam was given the words to say, "Let this be . . . some such thing." Does Adam's word produce a response and locate the missing element of his own being? Apparently not, for the narrator says, "but for the man there was not found a helper as his partner" (2:20). Nothing can be found in the dust, and Adam's words return to him as if out of the void. Is this not reminiscent of the *ex nihilo?*

At this point, Adam is cast into a deep sleep, which indicates the total suspension of his participation in what will follow. The Lord created out of his side (not out of the dust of the ground!) another being to be alongside him. When Adam awakens he cries out, "This at last is bone of my bones and flesh of my flesh; this one shall be called Woman (*'ish*) for out of Man (*'ishshah*) this one was taken" (2:23).

What was earlier stated as "the fact of the matter" is now shown to be true in a deeper sense. Between the human and the nonhuman there is an *ex nihilo* that only the grace of God can overcome. While the humans are taken out of the same dust of the ground and on the same day as the animals, there is an absolute difference between them.

For all but the humans, the physical nature of each determines their destiny. For the humans, though taken from the dust, their human nature is determined by the gracious Word of God and marks their destiny as formed in the image and likeness of God. For the humans, then, there is a sabbath, a purpose and goal that lies beyond the capacity of earthly desire and duty to attain.

Bear in mind that in this story we have a judgment of God—"not good"—as well as a virtual death—a deep sleep—and a resurrection to shared life—this at last! And all of this is prior to the introduction of sin in Genesis chapter three!

Grace must first kill before it can make alive, as I suggested in the previous chapter. This dramatic statement is meant to capture the radical nature of grace as that which brings judgment against any possibility that is inserted into the *ex nihilo* from the human or creaturely side. Moses experienced this judgment in terms of his own failure. Abraham experienced it in the rejection of Ishmael, and we find the same theological axiom in the creation story.

The Human Dilemma
and the Divine Deliverance

The motif of life out of death is central to the story of God's redemption and the inner logic of grace. Sin is a devastating problem for humanity, resulting in acts of murder, violence, and, not least of all, idolatry and estrangement from God. Yet sin is not the terrible human dilemma that death is.

The author of Hebrews expresses this fact when he writes of Abraham, "Therefore from one person, and this one as good as dead, descendants were born . . . " (Heb. 11:12). Sarah's womb was "dead," and yet the grace of God enabled her to conceive life.

The creation story points to this terrible dilemma in stark terms. "In the day that you shall eat of it you shall die," is the warning, not "you shall become a sinner" (Gen. 2:17). Yes, sin infects the human race as a result of this act, but that is not the dilemma itself. It is death that creates the dilemma, not merely sin. Even if sin is forgiven, without resurrection from the dead this forgiveness is null and void. "If Christ has not been raised, your faith is futile and you are still in your sins" (1 Cor. 15:17).

This death is not an instantaneous termination of physical life, but rather an immediate severing of the human from the grace of God that is the only source of life. To sin against this grace is to fall back into the *ex nihilo*. It is to slip out of the seventh day into the sixth day, where nature

determines destiny. The sentence of death came following the sin against
grace: "you are dust, and to dust you shall return" (Gen. 3:19). This is as
much a descriptive statement as a prescriptive one. In other words, it was
not necessary for God to "put to death" the first humans, but their action severed them from the *ex nihilo* life-sustaining relation that had originally lifted
their human nature out of the determinism of their biological origin. Without grace, their mortal nature became determinative of their human destiny.

In somewhat the same way that the Israelites were prone to slip back
into slavery and even, at times, longed to return to Egypt (Num. 11:5), so
the first humans could be tempted to sever the connection with grace that
was their only deliverance from the inevitability of death due to their mortal bodies. This deliverance from the dilemma of death was graciously
provided *prior* to their original sin. Having sinned, they forfeited that deliverance and were dependent upon God's grace to restore it as a possibility. In this way, the doctrine of salvation is already grounded in the doctrine of creation as deliverance from the dilemma of death.

In covenant language, grace means the recovery of a relationship with
the living God, not merely atonement from sin. The blood sprinkled on the
altar cannot of itself create life, it can only cover (*kaphar*) the sin. The blood
represents the pouring out of life on the part of the victim so that the *ex nihilo* is once again created as the condition necessary for God to grant life.
"For the life of the flesh is in the blood," says Yahweh, "and I have given
it to you for making atonement for your lives on the altar; for, as life, it is
the blood that makes atonement" (Lev. 17:11).

Blood is life, the Scripture says, and it is life that is poured out not
merely as an offering that removes sin, but in order that new life may be
created. The atonement is thus grounded in a new, "life-giving" relation
with God. This life must be "given" in the context of the *ex nihilo* in order
to restore persons to God and to their own true humanity. The foundation
for the atonement is thus grounded in the creation account itself, for it is
out of the "deep sleep" of Adam that human life emerged as relation to
God and to others. We shall have more to say about this atonement later
in the book when we consider the death and resurrection of Christ.

For now, it is important to note that the covenant relation is one that is
life-giving and life-sustaining. It is this covenant structure that is
grounded in the original creation of the human. Before there is any mention of sin, there is the human dilemma of death prefigured in the "deep
sleep" of Adam, which represents the *ex nihilo* out of which human life in
the divine image emerges.

Human nature can never become merely a "sin nature." While sin corrupts every aspect of human nature, the *ex nihilo* protects human nature

from becoming "inhuman nature." The tendency to equate "sinful nature" with "human nature," as though human nature is intrinsically and essentially sinful, is an unfortunate one. Essential human nature is endowed with the divine image and likeness. Though that image has been affected by sin in such a way that every aspect of human nature is subject to distortion, the essential nature of being human remains under the determination of God, not of sin.

It is not the degree of sin that constitutes the seriousness of the human condition, but that the essential human nature has come under the power of death. The reason that removal of sin by whatever means cannot liberate humans from this dilemma is that "the wages of sin is death," as Paul states. Thus the gift of salvation is eternal life (Rom. 6:23). This is also why Paul spoke of ministry as one of bringing life to those who are dying. "Death is at work in us," Paul reminded the Christians at Corinth, "but life in you" (2 Cor. 4:12).

In this chapter we have discovered that the inner logic of grace is grounded in the covenant love of God that came to expression through the Word of creation and continues through the Word of redemption. Liberation from the human dilemma of death is the grace by which human life is upheld so that it cannot slip back into the abyss of the *ex nihilo* (death). God's ministry has its source in the eternal covenant of love, its beginning in the creation of human life, its continuation in the history of redemption, and its consummation in the sabbath rest reserved for the people of God. God works on the sabbath day. This is good news!

8

The Sabbath of God
Which Renews and Restores

No one who has been a parent needs to be reminded that children hate to stop playing and take their rest. Children fight going to sleep with a passion, even as fatigue and frustration drive them to a frenzy of activity. This is but one small indication of the compulsive drive to pursue the goal of self-fulfillment beyond what is healthy or wise.

What is there in us that takes the gift of rest and renewal and makes it into rule and regimen that we resist, even at great cost to ourselves? Thankfully, we eventually learn to go to bed at reasonable hours without compulsion. But by that time we have already acquired other outlets for our need to "keep going" until we drop. And we find other ways of defying the gifts that are meant to promote our well-being and heal our spirit.

There is a "slave master self" lurking at the edges of the human psyche. At one time we thought it was the taskmaster parent, the tyrant boss, or the tormenting job. Like the children of Israel who thought they had left the slave master in Egypt, we, like them, discover that we have carried it with us as a hidden virus with an insatiable appetite for healthy flesh.

Moses observed this virus in the attitude and behavior of the people, and understood then the significance of the sabbath commandment. While the people had been redeemed from the slave master in Egypt, they had not yet been delivered from the slave driver within. Not only would the people need to learn the discipline of the sabbath for their own mental and physical health, they would need to learn the theology of the sabbath in order to fortify their faith and harvest their hope.

Without a theology of the sabbath, the discipline of the sabbath would itself become a slave master as, in fact, quickly happened. By the time of Jesus, the sabbath discipline had become a law more severe and sacred than any moral imperative. Paradoxically, liberation from the taskmaster of the sabbath law was a primary occasion for the condemnation and execution of Jesus. That which was to be a sacrament of liberation, of renewal and restoration, had become a rigid and inhumane rule from which liberation was effected by the ministry of Jesus!

For this reason, the theology of the sabbath must be put in place in order for the ministry and discipline of the sabbath to achieve its purpose.

The Theology of the Sabbath

The biblical concept of the seventh day lies close to the center of the inner logic of the covenant in its relation to creation. It is the only one of the Ten Commandments that is directly used in the creation story. It marks the end of God's creative work and the beginning of God's renewing ministry. We need to remember that it was revealed in the command given at Mount Sinai before it was written in the creation account. Exodus is prior to Genesis, I have said, and in this case the sabbath as commandment is prior to the sabbath as creation story.

This priority, I hasten to add, is one of revelation. Moses received the name of God as Yahweh only at the exodus event. The name is related to God's covenant relation with the people and revealed the inner logic of love and grace that binds the Redeemer God (Yahweh) to the Creator God (Elohim). As we discovered in the previous chapter, the name of Yahweh is not the revelation of a new and different God, but of the same God who was known to Abraham. For this reason, Moses is able to identify Yahweh's presence through Word and deed at the very beginning of creation.

In the giving of the fourth commandment, therefore, we find the sabbath day of redemption related to the sabbath day of creation. "Remember the sabbath day, and keep it holy. Six days you shall labor and do all your work. But the seventh day is a sabbath to the Lord your God [Yahweh your Elohim]; . . . for in six days the Lord [Yahweh] made heaven and earth, the sea, and all that is in them, but rested the seventh day; therefore the Lord blessed the sabbath day and consecrated it" (Ex. 20:8–11).

In the same way that covenant is prior to creation and grace prior to nature, the seventh day is prior to the sixth day, as figure 7 now shows.

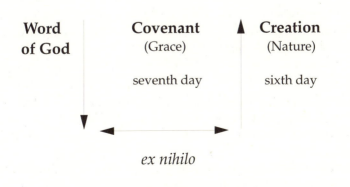

Figure 7

The *ex nihilo* separates the covenant from creation so that one cannot find within creation a logical antecedent for covenant. Nor can one find within nature an antecedent for grace. The covenant and the grace of God issue solely from the divine creative purpose so as to *place* humanity within the created order, but also to *free* humanity from creaturely determinism and fatalism.

So it is with the seventh day. There is no logical antecedent and no *telos* within the first six days that will point to the seventh day as the "last" day. If I should start counting with number one and ask you to stop me when I come to the last number, we might as well both go home! The concept of the seventh day as the "last" day is known only through divine intervention and revelation. There is thus the same *ex nihilo* between the sixth and the seventh day.

The sixth day represents creaturely possibility as well as impossibility. The barrenness of Sarah is of the sixth day even as the birth of Ishmael to Hagar is of the sixth day. Possibility and impossibility are twins, conceived simultaneously during the first six days.

The birth of Isaac, like the selection of Jacob his younger son, represents the inner logic of the seventh day. There is nothing to account for either Isaac or Jacob other than God's gracious determination.

The theology of the sabbath, therefore, is related directly to a theology of covenant and grace. The inner logic of the *ex nihilo* as the necessary presupposition of grace connects the impotence and powerlessness of Moses and the people to the barrenness of Sarah and to the determinism and fatalism of the sixth day. Even as redemption from slavery in Egypt and the birth of Isaac from the barren womb demonstrates the inner logic of grace, so does the seventh day serve as the sign of liberation from the tyranny of the sixth day.

The fatalism of biological origin is captured in the description of human life under the conditions of death: "By the sweat of your face you shall eat bread until you return to the ground, for out of it you were taken; you are dust, and to dust you shall return" (Gen. 3:19).

A theology of redemption is woven into the creation account before there is a theology of sin and death. The second creation account begins with the statement, "Thus the heavens and the earth were finished and all their multitude. And on the seventh day God finished the work that he had done, and he rested on the seventh day from all the work that he had done" (Gen. 2:1–2).

It is noteworthy that the text does not say that God finished his work on the sixth day, but "on the seventh day God finished the work that he had done." The seventh day is the day of completing the work. The sixth day represents the culmination of creaturely possibility, while the seventh day represents the possibility and creative conclusion that God provides.

A theology of the sabbath, therefore, is a theology of God's sabbath ministry of completion of his work. This is the ministry of renewal and restoration set forth as the theme of this chapter. The author of the book of Hebrews elaborates on this theology of the sabbath in the context of the exodus event. This shows once again the theological significance of the exodus event as a theological paradigm.

In this account, the author depicts the sabbath rest as synonymous with the completion of the journey of the Israelites from bondage in Egypt to the land of promise. This land is always presented to the Israelites as a land "flowing with milk and honey" (Ex. 3:8; 3:17; 13:5; 33:3). These metaphors create an image of a place that will satisfy every desire and fulfill every need.

Entry into this promised land is described by the author of Hebrews as "entering into God's rest" (Heb. 3:11, 18; 4:3). The seventh day is specifically identified with entering into this land using a quotation from the creation account cited (Heb. 4:4; Gen. 2:2). Because the people who came out of Egypt did not enter themselves, because of disobedience, the author of Hebrews suggests that entry into this "sabbath rest" has not yet been completed. "So then, a sabbath rest still remains for the people of God; for those who enter God's rest also cease from their labors as God did from his" (Heb. 4:9–10).

The sabbath rest of God can be understood as the continuing ministry of God "completing his work" on the seventh day. The seventh day is the *eschaton* of the sixth day. This *eschaton* represents the last, or final work of God. The seventh day, therefore, provides an eschatological orientation for the sixth day. As the "last day" (the *eschaton*), the seventh day now casts its light back into the sixth day, the next to the last day.

Dietrich Bonhoeffer spoke of the last day as the ultimate, and the next to the last as the penultimate. One does not know what is next to the last (penultimate), until the last has been revealed. The theology of the seventh day gives special meaning to the sixth day. Bonhoeffer was also careful to say that the ultimate does not evacuate the penultimate of its own time and meaning. The sixth day as the place in which humans live out their earthly existence has value and meaning for humans in its own right. Human life under the limitations of the sixth day is still fully human, and even its burden and pain cannot be dismissed as meaningless. But the meaning and purpose of life in the penultimate has significance only because the ultimate has already been revealed. Anticipation of the seventh day, even from the first day of the week, makes what would otherwise be unbearable something that can be accepted as having only limited power and duration.

Without this eschatological reality represented by the seventh day as the day in which God completes and finishes his work, the six days would appear relentless and endless. This is what is meant by the determinism and fatalism of the sixth day. While the sixth day does end by returning to the dust, this fate is intolerable for the human spirit. As Ernest Becker has so brilliantly said in his book, *The Denial of Death,* the human spirit cannot bear the knowledge of its own mortality, but instead evades this reality through projection of self-identity on persons and events that seem to be "larger than life."

The sabbath represents God's ministry of renewal and restoration. This is the ministry of God's continued working on the sabbath as he completes his work. The ministry of the sabbath is thus God's ministry issuing out of the heart of covenant and creation.

The Ministry and Discipline of the Sabbath

Jesus consistently referred to his own ministry as the work of the Father who dwelt in him: "The words that I say to you I do not speak on my own; but the Father who dwells in me does his works" (John 14:10; cf. John 9: 3, 4). I have suggested that the sabbath rest does not mean the cessation of God's activity, but the "finishing" of his work, the bringing to completion of the original Word of creation.

For this reason, Jesus taught that the "sabbath is made for humankind, not humankind for the sabbath." He then added, "so the Son of Man is lord even of the sabbath" (Mark 2:27–28). Jesus understood the theology of the sabbath clearly and so expected that the "work of the Father" would continue on the sabbath to bring healing to the sick, restore sight to the blind, recover the use of limbs, and grant relief and comfort to suffering and needy humanity.

Jesus, as the lord of the sabbath, continues the ministry of the sabbath through his presence on earth as persons receive and exercise the gift of the Holy Spirit. Paul saw this as an extension of the sabbath ministry of God through every day of the week. "Some judge one day to be better than another, while others judge all days to be alike. Let all be fully convinced in their own minds. Those who observe the day, observe it in honor of the Lord" (Rom. 14:5–6; cf. also Col. 2:16).

The original consecration of the seventh day as the sabbath left the other six days unconsecrated, as it were. Only on the eve of the sixth day could the Israelite stand with his or her back to these days and step across the *ex nihilo* into the day consecrated by the renewal and restoration of the Lord. On this day they were to celebrate life as a gift of Yahweh, with no efforts of their own needed beyond the necessary chores. The point was that they were to leave behind the struggle to live by their own efforts and live out of the gracious provision of God.

Those who attempted to carry over into this consecrated day some tasks related to their own purpose were severely judged. Some were even put to death for this violation. Even so small a matter as gathering sticks for the fire on the sabbath caused the death of one man (Num. 15:32–36). The enormity of the violation was not determined by the scale of the incident, but because it served to undermine the entire fabric of the covenant grounded in grace alone. The "slave driver" within must be exposed and removed before we can experience the full deliverance of our humanity from bondage. Grace does not stop with the removal of external conditions of oppression and pain, but seeks deep inner healing and recovery.

This again shows how strategic the sabbath was as the inner logic of the covenant and why, along with circumcision, it became the defining criterion for a relationship with God for the Hebrew people.

With the fall of Adam and Eve out of the sabbath rest through their disobedience, the natural destiny (death) of the sixth day became their fate. The sabbath had already been attached to creation so that the *ex nihilo* was not an abyss that separated the creature from the Creator, but was the "axis," as it were, on which creation spun. The fall threw creation off its course and exposed the *ex nihilo* as the terrifying void of nothingness toward which it was plunging. The sabbath was reinstalled as a sacramental bridging of this abyss, offering immediate relief from the powers of nature and the peril of death. The six days would remain under these powers, but on the seventh day there was to be relief, renewal, and restoration as an eschatological "jubilee," a provisional, but promising, hope of complete reconciliation.

Even the cosmos itself, as Paul later saw, was affected by the exposing of this *ex nihilo* at the core of all creation. "For the creation waits with eager longing for the revelation of the children of God," wrote Paul. The futility to which the creation was subjected in this fall tilted it toward ultimate decay and brought it under bondage. But this was also "in hope that the creation itself will be set free from its bondage to decay and will obtain the freedom of the glory of the children of God" (Rom. 8:19–21).

Along with the groaning of humans who also await this final restoration, the "whole creation has been groaning in labor pains until now," wrote Paul. But through Jesus Christ the promise has already begun its glorious work. In Paul's mind, Christ plunged into this *ex nihilo* and destroyed its power through resurrection. Now, as the *Logos* through whom the world first saw the light (John 1:1–5), the risen Christ has disarmed the powers of the sixth day and destroyed the power of death (1 Cor. 15:54–57).

Paul's triumphant hymn of praise to this victory over the powers of the sixth day is a litany of sabbath rest: "For I am convinced that neither death, nor life, nor angels, nor rulers, nor things present, nor things to come, nor powers, nor height, nor depth, nor anything else in all creation, will be able to separate us from the love of God in Christ Jesus our Lord" (Rom. 8:38–39).

This is the sabbath ministry of Jesus Christ that now consecrates *every* day with sabbath rest and renewal. No longer is it just one day out of the week, but each day has sabbath consecration as it was in the original creation. The *ex nihilo* is no longer an abyss that separates the sixth day from the seventh with a flaming sword. Rather, the consecration of life out of nothing has become a gracious gift of grace to be appropriated and experienced every day.

In my judgment it is just as mistaken to call the first day of the week the only sabbath as it is to claim the seventh day and leave the other six days with no sabbath consecration. The day we choose to celebrate the "Lord who is the sabbath," is left to us and to our conscience, if I understand Paul correctly (Rom. 14:5–6).

Through the history of the sabbath, the language of "keeping the sabbath" has often been used. This suggests that setting aside activity ordinarily done and maintaining an attitude of passivity toward the mundane sphere while focusing upon the spiritual sphere is something that humans "do" in keeping the sabbath.

This concept is quite foreign to the inner logic of the sabbath as grounded in the grace and covenant love of God. It is God who "keeps Israel," and who "neither slumbers nor sleeps" (Ps. 41:2; 121:3–4). The ministry of God as sabbath ministry is constant and without interruption. Sabbath does not mean the cessation of human activity alone, but the bringing of all activity under the blessing of God's ministry.

The discipline of the sabbath can be better understood as conformity to Christ as the Lord of the sabbath than as the "keeping" of rules and regulations. Such regulations, as Paul reminds us, "refer to things that perish with use; they are simply human commands and teachings" (Col. 2:22).

The ministry of the sabbath is God's ministry now expressed through Jesus Christ that seeks to relieve humans from oppression, pain, abuse, injustice, and everything that dehumanizes persons. The discipline of the sabbath is our conformity to Christ as disciples who have ourselves experienced the firstfruits of sabbath rest in our own healing, and then seek the renewal and restoration of others as those whom God loves and seeks to redeem from the abyss.

All ministry is now Christ's ministry. And with that we are permitted to peer even deeper into the mystery and miracle of the divine heart.

III

Jesus' Ministry to the Father on Behalf of the World

9

The Baptism of Jesus
into Messianic Ministry

The baptism of Jesus was his burning bush. For some, Nazareth in Galilee was too insignificant to produce a prophet, and innuendoes concerning his birth were sufficient to cast a shadow over any aspirations of greatness.

"Can anything good come out of Nazareth?" appeared to be conventional wisdom (John 1:46). Questions concerning his paternity were used to cast aspersions against Jesus' character. "We are not illegitimate children; we have one father, God himself" (John 8:41). Until his baptism by John in the Jordan, Jesus had only the secret knowledge kept in the heart of his mother as an unanswered question (Luke 2:51).

With his baptism, we have the entry point into the life and ministry of Jesus. Contrary to the chronology of his life, the theological significance of Jesus does not begin with his birth, but with his baptism.

Why the baptism of Jesus? Because, as the burning bush commissioned Moses to initiate the redemption of his people, so in the baptism by John, Jesus was anointed with the power of the Spirit to fulfill God's messianic promise.

Earlier in this book I suggested that there is virtually no reference to any ministry performed by Jesus prior to his baptism. In retrospect, of course, the story of his birth and one incident at the age of twelve is recorded. But the coming of the Spirit of God upon Jesus at his baptism is where the voice from heaven is heard saying, "This is my Son, the Beloved, with whom I am well pleased" (Matt. 3:16–17). As Moses heard the voice of God calling out to him from the burning bush, so Jesus heard, apparently for the first time, the voice of his Father calling him Son, and recognized the coming of the Spirit upon him.

Baptism as the *Ex Nihilo*
of Barrenness and Exodus

For the Hebrew people, circumcision of males signified the special election to be God's covenant people. Instituted following the covenant made with Abraham, circumcision was itself a physical sign of the *ex nihilo* that marked the power of God to create out of nothing a people to carry the blessing of the covenant to all humanity. This sign that designated the descendants of Abraham as a chosen people was not so much a mark of an exclusive people but of God's exclusive and sovereign grace in light of human attempts to fulfill the Word of God on their own terms. The rejection of Ishmael as the promised seed was a judgment against the insertion of a human possibility as a contributor to divine grace. The fact that Ishmael was circumcised was itself a sign that he too must bear the mark of the *ex nihilo* in order to receive the blessing that was to come through his brother Isaac (Gen. 17:23).

During the centuries that followed, Gentiles who accepted Yahweh as the true God and who wished to become members of the covenant community not only had to be circumcised as Abraham was, but had to participate in ritual baptism as a sign of passing through the sea with Moses in the exodus. This "proselyte baptism" reenacted the exodus event along with circumcision, making it possible for Gentiles also to become children of the kingdom of God.

The baptism by John, therefore, represented a symbolic reenactment of the *ex nihilo* in the exodus where the people passed through the sea, preserved by the power of God's intervention. But it was not Gentiles who were invited to be baptized. Rather, John called circumcised Jews to undergo this baptism as a sign of repentance. This summons to baptism by John was a shattering critique of the self-righteous assurance of the Jews that they could rest upon their circumcision and keeping of the law as a sufficient claim upon God. It was an innovative theological praxis!

For circumcised Jews to accept John's baptism was to acknowledge a spiritual separation from God equivalent to being a Gentile. The call to repentance was not only a negative judgment against self-righteousness and human effort to merit God's promise, but it was a positive step into the *ex nihilo* of God's grace. It was, in a sense, a re-entry into the barren womb of Sarah in order to become descendants of Isaac rather than Ishmael. This baptism was an experience of God's grace and the acceptance of God's gift as children of the covenant.

As Paul was later to say, the self-righteous Jews who sought to preserve circumcision and the law as a claim upon God's promise no longer were children of Sarah, but children of Hagar, the slave woman. "Now Hagar is Mount Sinai in Arabia and corresponds to the present Jerusalem, for she is in slavery with her children. But the other woman corresponds to the Jerusalem above; she is free, and she is our mother" (Gal. 4:25–26). This is exactly the indictment contained in the baptism by John. The descendants of Abraham and Sarah by human genealogy had virtually become children of Hagar in a dramatic reversal of roles! In order to become children of Sarah, and true descendants of Isaac and Jacob, they needed to pass again through the *ex nihilo* of baptism.

Jesus understood this, and he had the theological discernment to know that the baptism by John was not his confession of being a sinner, but an affirmation of his being "born from above." He sought through baptism the grace of God in the *ex nihilo* of Sarah's barren womb even as he had learned from his mother the mystery of the *ex nihilo* of his mother's virgin womb. At the same time, Jesus identified with all who stood outside the covenant, both Jew and Gentile, and took his place with them in an act of vicarious repentance. He thus laid the foundation for human faith and repentance in his own gracious act on behalf of all.

The baptism of Jesus points backward as well as forward. It points backward to his birth and forward to his death and resurrection. Later he was to say concerning his death, "I have a baptism with which to be baptized, and what stress I am under until it is completed" (Luke 12:50)! In the conversation between Jesus, Moses, and Elijah on the Mount of Transfiguration, Luke tells us that they "were speaking of his departure [exodus] which he was about to accomplish at Jerusalem" (Luke 9:31). The Greek word *exodus* was used by Luke in recording this conversation. This is a remarkable reference backward to the exodus event at which Moses was present and forward to his "baptism" through death and resurrection.

Jesus as the Son of the Father

The baptism of Jesus also points us backward toward his birth as the very incarnation of the divine *Logos*. Only when Jesus was recognized as the very presence of God through his ministry did the story of the virgin birth have significance. It is the incarnation of God in the person of Jesus the Messiah that is the great mystery (*mysterion*) of our faith (1 Tim. 3:16). We are not asked to believe the miracle of the virgin birth, Karl Barth reminds us, until we have confessed the mystery that Jesus Christ is God incarnate.

When Jesus declared the forgiveness of sins to the paralytic, it was noted by the Pharisees and acknowledged by Jesus that only God could forgive sin (Mark 2:5–10). His act of ministry revealed his authority as that of God himself. "I have come down from heaven," testified Jesus, and so claimed to be the living bread in contrast to the bread that Moses gave, which perishes (John 6:26–51). The miracle of God's work manifested through the presence and person of Jesus pointed to his origin in God and his special relation to God as the Son of the Father.

"All things have been handed over to me by my Father," said Jesus, "and no one knows the Son except the Father, and no one knows the Father

Inner Logic

except the Son and anyone to whom the Son chooses to reveal him" (Matt. 11:27). This inner relation between Jesus and God is the inner logic of the story of the virgin birth. One upholds the other.

The *ex nihilo* of virgin birth connects the baptism of Jesus to his conception by the Spirit of God. The incarnation by the Spirit anchors the messianic ministry of Jesus in his authority as the Son of the Father. The ministry of Jesus as Son of God is empowered by his anointing by the Spirit. Figure 8 depicts this reciprocal relation.

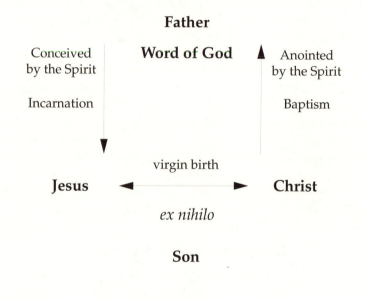

Figure 8

The special relation that Jesus experienced with God as his Father is suggested at his baptism and only further developed by John in his gospel. The language of divine sonship is ambiguous, so biblical scholars say. There may have been several meanings denoted by the phrase, "son of God." What became undeniable, however, was that Jesus did claim to have a special relation with God. In his prayers, he spoke to God as *Abba*, which is Aramaic for "father" in a very familiar and intimate sense (cf. Mark 14:36, where the Aramaic word "Abba" is preserved in the text).

The story of Jesus' conception by the Holy Spirit in the virgin womb can now be understood as the *ex nihilo* that corresponds to the barren womb of Sarah. Thomas Torrance, in his lectures at the University of Edinburgh, used to stress the point that the virgin birth was not only a biological fact attested by Scripture, but a theological necessity. If Jesus is not conceived directly by the Holy Spirit without the role of a human male, then the inner logic of the covenant has been destroyed and Jesus' relation with God as the Son of the Father has been severed at the core.

The baptism of Jesus was his burning bush. It marked the critical beginning of his inauguration as the Messiah of God, the anointed one who was commissioned by God to carry out the ministry of God on behalf of the world.

Spirit-Empowered Ministry

Beyond the significance of John's baptism was the baptism by the Spirit descending upon Jesus, representing the fulfillment of the promise that the Spirit of God would anoint one to usher in the Day of the Lord wherein salvation would come to the people of God. The popular name for this expected savior was Messiah, taken from the Hebrew word for anointing (*mashach*, to anoint; *mishchah*, anointed).

A typical passage from the Old Testament prophecies of this event can be found in Isaiah 61, a passage that Jesus read following his baptism in the synagogue in Nazareth. "The spirit of the Lord God is upon me, because the Lord has anointed me. . . . " (61:1; Luke 4:16–19). By identifying himself as the anointed one intended by this prophetic word, Jesus for the first time accepted the designation as Messiah. The Greek translation of the Hebrew word Messiah is *Christos*. Jesus of Nazareth from this point can also be called the Christ, the Messiah, one anointed by the Spirit of God to carry out the ministry of God.

To say "Jesus Christ" is to acknowledge that Jesus is the one anointed by the Spirit of God in fulfillment of the prophecy. It is by the power of the Spirit of God that Jesus now undertakes the ministry to which he is called.

The twofold ministry of Jesus in the power of the Spirit has been called the ministry of revelation and the ministry of reconciliation by Thomas Torrance. Jesus is the mediator of all that God is toward humans (revelation), and all that humans are called to be in relation to God (reconciliation).

Jesus reveals the inner being of God as the love of the Father for the Son. At the same time, Jesus takes hold of humanity in its condition of disobedience and estrangement from God and binds humanity back into relation with God through his own love as the Son to the Father.

Jesus not only speaks the Word of God, he opens up the ear of humanity to hear that Word in his own hearing and obedience. Jesus is not only a messenger who brings the Word of God, he is the message as the very embodiment of that Word. And, at the same time, he is the one who hears and obeys that message in his own obedience as the Son of the Father.

All of this is possible because Jesus is the very expression of God in his own being. The Spirit has no incarnation of his own. The Spirit has no humanity of his own, but enters the humanity of Jesus and takes residence in that humanity, "becoming accustomed to humanity," as Irenaeus once said, so that the Spirit can dwell within the humanity of others.

The Spirit of God does not come to us "unclothed," as it were, but comes clothed with the very humanity of Christ. Every feeling and every sensation that Jesus experienced as a complete human person became an expression of the divine being, revealing the truth of God through the humanity of God. Every feeling, need, and aspiration of the human spirit has its correspondence in the humanity of Jesus, which bears all human experience directly into the divine heart.

The Spirit of God mediates the reality of God to us through the humanity of Christ and, through that same humanity, mediates us to God. This twofold mediation can be expressed as the humanity of God and the humanizing of humanity in the image and likeness of God. These two aspects of the mediation of Christ are interrelated and interdependent.

The Humanity of God

With the assumption of humanity on the part of the divine *Logos* (John 1:14), created humanity has been taken up into the very being of God. This has been a standard formula for orthodox theology since the fifth century and the counciliar decree at Chalcedon. Karl Barth has suggested that the concept of the eternal humanity of God in the form of divine humility and divine condescension is the antecedent of the assumption of created humanity in the person Jesus of Nazareth.

In any event, to say that the humanity of God is one aspect of the essence of God is certainly possible, as God must possess the same qualities represented by humans created in his image. The incarnation of the divine as the very form of God is the incarnate form of the divine *Logos* that has been raised from the dead and has ascended to God as the exalted Jesus Christ. As mediator, the continuing humanity of Christ is the objective basis for our knowledge of God (revelation) and our approach to God through Christ (reconciliation). The concepts of God that encourage us to think of God as possessing human qualities that we desire are not projections of our desires, but are manifestations of God's own humanity, of which we are the image and likeness. That in God of which we are the image is not the deity of God, but the humanity of God.

The humanity of God assures us that God has entered into our own sphere of temptation and trial. Driven by the Spirit into the wilderness following his baptism, Jesus brought divine being to the side of those tempted. "For we do not have a high priest who is unable to sympathize with our weaknesses," writes the author of the book of Hebrews, "but we have one who in every respect has been tested as we are, yet without sin" (Heb. 4:15). Jesus brought the reality of God to the side of those tempted, though God himself cannot be tempted (James 1:13). In the incarnation, God assumed the capacity to be tempted in the form of the temptation of Jesus.

The humanity of God as expressed through Jesus Christ makes God an ally of those who are bereft of love, who are betrayed, and who are stricken and oppressed. Wherever Jesus was found, there the humanity of God was found on the same side as humanity under distress. As James Torrance has eloquently said,

> "Christ does not heal us by standing over against us, diagnosing our sickness, prescribing medicine for us to take, and then going away, to leave us to get better by obeying his instructions—as an ordinary doctor might. No, He becomes the patient! He assumes that very humanity which is in need of redemption, and by being anointed by the Spirit in our humanity, by a life of perfect obedience for us, by dying and rising again, our humanity is healed *in him*."

Recently I was asked what my approach was as a pastor officiating at the funeral service for a person who was not known to have made a profession of faith in Jesus Christ. My response went something like this.

"We believe that God became human through Jesus Christ, and that Christ brought the presence and reality of God not only into life, but into death. When God became a human person in the form of Jesus Christ, God came to those who were bereft of faith as well as those who professed faith. God came to those who were sick unto death as well as those who possessed the strength of health and life. Through Jesus Christ, God entered not only into the dying of humanity, but into the grave of humanity. The tomb of Jesus became the tomb of God.

"Our belief in Jesus Christ as God in the form of humanity means that no one goes to his or her grave alone. No longer does the grave represent the terror of godlessness, for God had his own grave here on earth. Our hope is not in heaven as something that we have earned, but our assurance is that our own dying and our own grave have been entered by God through his Son, Jesus Christ. It is this God that we turn to in our own hour of need and grief."

In saying something like the above, I do not intend to imply that the person who has died is in heaven, for I have no authority or power to do that, regardless of who the person is. What I intend is to put God in the grave through the humanity of Christ as a faithful proclamation of God's solidarity with humans in their own darkest hour.

Of course there is also a word of hope expressed through resurrection. But I have found that resurrection does not offer the deepest revelation of God to people who are caught in the throes of death and the grief that it brings. It is the humanity of God that takes hold of human suffering, pain, and grief. When this God is proclaimed, the Holy Spirit mediates the reality of Christ as God with us, a positive basis for grief to find a resting place in faith and hope.

The Humanizing of Humanity

If it seems strange to express the second aspect of the Spirit's mediation of Christ as the "humanizing of humanity," then we have not yet understood the dehumanizing nature of sin. What satisfies God is not a sacrifice to appease the dishonor done to him by sin, but the recovery of full humanity on the part of those who are the objects of God's love. The medieval doctrine of the atonement developed by Anselm went astray at this point. What Anselm did not consider was the effect of sin upon humanity and how the incarnation of God in Jesus Christ restores humanity to its intended health and wholeness. I shall have more to say about this later in the book.

Through Jesus Christ we see the anger of God expressed at that which dehumanizes humanity, whether it be disease, demons, or misuse of the law itself. When the Pharisees sought to trap Jesus by flinging a woman caught in adultery at his feet, demanding she be put to death in accordance with the law, Jesus became her advocate (John 8). Refusing to condemn her to death, Jesus instead restored her to the freedom of recovering her full humanity by releasing her from the demand of the law and binding her to himself.

If indeed she became a follower of Jesus, with the support and enablement of the other disciples, she began the journey toward her full humanity as given through the life, death, and resurrection of Christ as savior and Lord.

Where there was demonic possession with its devastating consequences, Jesus not only delivered the victim from the power of the demons, but restored the person's humanity through reentry into the community. When Jesus found the man possessed of demons in the region of the Gerasenes, the man was naked, dragging pieces of chain, and living among the tombs. These are all indications of severe dehumanization.

When the demons were exorcised, Luke tells us that the man was "sitting the feet of Jesus, clothed and in his right mind" (Luke 8:35).

I have always wondered where the man received the clothes! It is one thing to drive out the demons, one thing to heal a person's mind, but quite another to clothe the person. Clothes, as contrasted with the man's tortured nakedness, is a sign of his humanization. We tend to focus on the supernatural miracle of demonic exorcism and miss the natural ministry of clothing the man's nakedness and, we hope, offering readmission to his family and the community.

All ministry is baptism into Jesus' ministry as the one anointed by the Spirit of God for the ministry of God. Where there is no Spirit, the bush does not burn. Where the bush burns, the baptism begins. Where the Spirit moves, the call to servanthood comes. Jesus heard that call, and began to serve the Father on behalf of the world.

Jesus as the Servant of the Father on Behalf of the World

The conversation on the airplane became somewhat more intense when my seatmate discovered that I was a teacher of theology at a Christian seminary. "You Christians are always trying to get converts," he said. "I served for six years in the Peace Corps helping people learn how to grow their own food using more effective farming techniques. We contributed directly to the physical welfare of these people. As I recall, Jesus called himself a servant too. What's the big difference?"

"If you are a servant," I replied, "it might make a difference who it is that you are serving. Servants have masters. Who is your master?"

"I knew it," he said, shaking his head, "You are trying to convert me!" He was good-natured about it and, as the plane was beginning its descent, we settled back, each in our own thoughts.

My own thoughts carried over into the pastors' seminar I was teaching. I broached the subject to them, each of whom was a seminary graduate. "When you think of Jesus' ministry as a servant, what is the most distinctive aspect of that ministry?" I asked. The responses were what I expected. His service was done in love; it was indiscriminate with regard to race and religion; it was entirely without regard for his own needs, and it ended up costing him his life.

"What was the primary motivation for his service?" I prodded. Again, the answers were predictable. He was moved with compassion for those in need; he had a mission to accomplish and, as the scripture says, "Having loved those who were in the world, he loved them to the end" (John 13:1). I was reminded that the towel with which he girded himself as he assumed the role of the servant in washing the feet of his disciples was the primary biblical metaphor of servanthood.

"Would you then agree," I said, "that Jesus was the servant of the world on behalf of God?" The agreement was unanimous, and I noted several writing this statement down in their notes, assuming that this was the first point in the lecture.

"Well, I don't agree," I replied. "I think that way of stating it misses the crucial point in the servanthood of Jesus. It is not the ministry of Jesus to the world on behalf of God that made him a servant, but his ministry to the Father on behalf of the world." What follows in this chapter is the substance of my argument for what seemed to these pastors a novel interpretation.

The World Does Not
Set the Agenda

A theology of ministry based on the concept of being a servant is at the heart of the New Testament. "I am among you as one who serves," Jesus told his disciples (Luke 22:27). When the disciples were sent out "as sheep among wolves," Jesus reminded them, "A disciple is not above the teacher, nor a slave above the master; it is enough for the disciple to be like the teacher; and the slave like the master" (Matt. 10:24–25).

While the disciples were arguing among themselves as to who would occupy the higher positions in the kingdom, Jesus reminded them, "Whoever wishes to be great among you must be your servant, and whoever wishes to be first among you must be your slave; just as the Son of Man came not to be served but to serve, and to give his life a ransom for many" (Matt. 20:26–28).

Many such Scripture texts may be cited in support of the concept that ministry is primarily a service to others on behalf of God. What is missing from this popular version of ministry is the fact that Jesus was not, first of all, one who served the world, but one who served God.

"Find a need and fill it," is a popular maxim meant to motivate Christians for a ministry of service. But the needs of the world did not set the agenda for the ministry of Jesus.

It is true that wherever the needs of the world impinged upon him, he reached out to heal the sick and feed the hungry. But hunger, sickness, and even death did not set the agenda for his ministry.

Let me cite a biblical example.

When Lazarus was sick and dying, his two sisters, Mary and Martha, sent word to Jesus. "Lord, he whom you love is ill" (John 11:3). The context is clear and compelling. Mary and Martha, along with their brother Lazarus, had often provided hospitality for Jesus in the little village of Bethany. As the sisters indicated, there was an unusual bond of love between Jesus and Lazarus.

If we could place their request in the vernacular of today's language, we might hear them say, "Jesus, Lazarus your beloved friend is deathly ill, and you have the pills in your pocket to cure him." Indeed he did! He had earlier interrupted a funeral and raised a widow's son from death (Luke 7:12), and had healed many from various diseases and infirmities.

Yet we are told, "Accordingly, though Jesus loved Martha and her sister and Lazarus, after having heard that Lazarus was ill, he stayed two days longer in the place where he was" (John 11:5–6).

What do we make of this? Some commentators hold that the chronol-ogy suggests that Jesus knew that Lazarus was already dead by the time he received the message, and that this accounts for his delay. From the perspective of the sisters, however, any delay was unforgivable. Each of them in turn accused Jesus when he arrived, "Lord, if you had been here, my brother would not have died" (11:21, 32).

This much is clear. The love of Jesus for Lazarus and the desperate plea of the two sisters did not set the agenda for the ministry of Jesus. This need from the side of the world did not take precedence over his commitment to serve the Father. It is the Father who loves the world and sends his Son (John 3:16). Jesus does not have to love Lazarus more than the Father.

The inner logic of Jesus' ministry is grounded in his obedience as the Son to the Father. Consequently, the first priority of Jesus is to serve the Father who sends him into the world.

When Jesus did arrive and found Lazarus had been dead for several days, he asked that the stone be removed. The sisters protested, and at-tempted to stop his ministry! Martha said to him, "Lord, already there is a stench because he has been dead four days" (11:39). Jesus replied, "Did I not tell you that if you believed, you would see the glory of God" (11:40)? And Lazarus came forth.

The sisters had a concept of Jesus' ministry that was based on response to human need. They knew that as long as their brother was only sick, he might still be healed if only Jesus could arrive in time. Death, however, is not a need that a physician can meet. Death, to their minds, was a reality that required its own ministry—respect and care for the one who had died, and sealing the tomb as a boundary between life and death.

This is why they attempted to stop the ministry of Jesus. The boundary of death set limits to their expectation. Jesus crossed that boundary as one sent by the Father in order that the glory of God might be revealed in the raising of Lazarus. Lazarus was restored to life and to other needs that would demand attention. The difference between a ministry founded on the meeting of needs and one that is directed by the will and wisdom of God is worth discovering.

The one who attempts to minister by meeting human needs will, at some time or other, arrive too late. When need is the master, the servant becomes a slave.

Need Is a Relentless and Unforgiving Slave Master

"Who is your master?" was the question I posed to my seatmate on the airplane. He had argued that his service to humankind was equivalent to the ministry of Jesus without having to accept the theological baggage that Christianity required. He interpreted my question as an attempt to convert him. Actually, my question was an attempt to trap him in the logic of despair to which his concept of servanthood would inevitably lead.

I have asked the same question of pastors who have accepted much the same concept of ministry as my non-Christian acquaintance. If human need is the defining element in one's sense of calling and commitment to ministry, the same logic of despair lurks beneath the surface.

Human need is an insatiable and unforgiving slave master, as many pastors have found. Those who seek help from ministers as well as from other Christians will inevitably create a burden too great for any one person to bear.

The double bind in using need to define one's ministry as a servant is complicated by the concept of a "calling," or vocation. My own sense of calling to be a minister was directly linked with a pastoral role that I understood as being available and on call for any person who had expressed need for counsel, comfort, advice, or simply a listening ear.

The exhilaration that came from being needed and viewed as a resource for others was quickly tempered by the frustration of limited resources and time. Those who were quick to seek help were sometimes the same ones to blame: "Pastor, if you had been here. . . !" Human need has no concept of a sabbatical! Needy persons do not have discernment and instincts for the well-being of the caretaker.

Some years ago I was approached by a medical doctor who was doing research on clergy morale. His concern was that pastors were resistant to reasonable suggestions for taking care of their emotional and physical health. He was probing me for some clue as to why clergy were often reluctant to take time for exercise and to show responsibility in their eating habits so as to promote better health. "The typical person in Christian ministry is on a collision course with a fatal heart attack, if not other physical problems," he reported to me. "And I can't understand why there is such resistance to good health management."

My response was that, in retrospect, I could well understand some of the dynamics. I suggested that many pastors have a secret "death wish." The double bind is that one's faithfulness to the calling of God means being available to meet the needs of people. At the same time, it is just this ministry to human need that is draining the life out of those who minister. To withdraw from meeting need for the sake of one's own well-being appears to be self-centered and failing God's calling. At the same time, being available to meet these needs on demand is to define one's ministry as God's servant.

"The ministry is killing me," such a pastor secretly knows, "but the only way to escape with honor is to go down in flames." The so-called burnout phenomenon among pastors is not so much due to over-investment in one's work as it is a symptom of theological anemia. The problem is not that one is overworked, but that one is serving the wrong master, and this reflects an anemic, or sick, theology. A healthy theology based on the inner logic of Jesus' ministry to the Father rather than to the world will go a long way toward healing the sickness of pastoral burnout.

Jesus knew who his master was. He was a servant of the Father, not of the world. The needs of the world did not set his agenda. He did not have to love the world more than the Father who sent him into the world.

Careful to preserve that inner relation of love that existed between him and the Father, Jesus often withdrew from the active ministry of meeting human need. Over and over again, he stopped healing and teaching to withdraw with his disciples (cf. Matt. 8:18). On one occasion he called his disciples away from the ministry of teaching and healing because, as Mark tells us, "For many were coming and going, and they had no leisure even to eat. And they went away in a boat to a deserted place by themselves" (Mark 6:31–32).

How, in good conscience, could Jesus stop meeting the needs of people when he had such incredible resources to heal the sick and even raise the dead? The answer is that, while he had compassion for the needs of people, his conscience was governed not by human need but by the Father's will and purpose.

Jesus' Ministry:
Service Grounded in Sonship

The ministry of Jesus to the Father on behalf of the world is the inner logic of all ministry. Every aspect of the ministry of Jesus is grounded in the inner relation of mutual love and care between the Father and the Son. On behalf of the world, Jesus offers up to the Father a ministry of prayer, worship, obedience, and service. His ministry is first of all directed to God and not to the world. The needs of the world are recognized and brought into this ministry, but they do not set the agenda.

There is a kind of *ex nihilo* between the ministry of Jesus to the Father and his ministry to the world. We saw this in his ministry at the tomb of Lazarus. The sisters expected Jesus to respond out of human compassion and the bond of love. Surely he will respond because he cares. However, the real ministry of Jesus was not to prevent Lazarus from dying as a demonstration of the possibilities that he carried within himself. Rather, his ministry was to demonstrate the power and glory of God through the *ex nihilo* of death.

In the incident with Lazarus we can see the inner logic that is present in every act of Jesus' ministry. For the most part, the *ex nihilo* was hidden to all but Jesus. He understood clearly, however, that he could only do what the Father sent him to do. "Very truly, I tell you," said Jesus, "the Son can do nothing on his own, but only what he sees the Father doing; for whatever the Father does, the Son does likewise. The Father loves the Son and shows him all that he himself is doing" (John 5:19–20).

Figure 9 shows how the ministry of Jesus issues out of the *ex nihilo* and draws human need into his ministry to the Father.

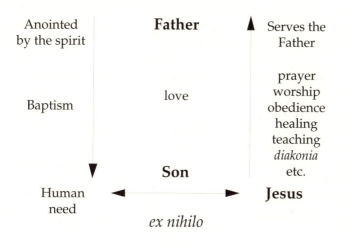

Figure 9

The world is represented by human need in this diagram. Jesus draws human need into his own ministry of service to the Father. In this ministry to the Father, all ministry on behalf of the world is taken up and fulfilled. There is no ministry that belongs to the church or to members of the body of Christ that is not already grounded in the ministry of Jesus.

For example, the ministry of discipling those who have become believers is not based on methods of discipleship drawn from the early disciples as much as it is on Jesus as the true disciple of the Father. This grounds discipleship in the love that Jesus has for the Father. Discipling programs based on methods alone can produce religious robots, who may lack the true motive for discipleship, which is love.

The same can be said for obedience. Obedience itself is at best neutral

and at worst demonic. One can assume that the demons are perfectly obedient to the devil. Obedience can be demonic and inhuman. We have all
witnessed the tragedy of those who have come under the power of some
person or program of discipling, often to their own harm and destruction
in the end.

It can also be the case that specific ministries, such as discipling programs, evangelism, or healing, for example, can become detached from
the overall ministry of Christ. Some who become rabid disciples never
worship. Some who are content to worship are never involved in *diakonia*.
In his ministry Jesus united all of these discrete ministries around the primary motivation and core of love. This provides for a healthy motivation
for ministry as well as integrating the various forms of ministry around a
holistic and mutually supportive structure.

Our Calling to Ministry: Participation
in the Ongoing Ministry of Christ

There is a sense in which one can say that baptism into Christ is ordination into the ministry of Christ. As Christ was called and ordained to his
messianic ministry through baptism, so the baptism of every person can
be viewed as a calling into the ministry of Christ. The special ordination
that sets baptized persons apart as representative of the ministry of Christ
through the church is still grounded upon baptism.

If, for example, I should renounce my baptism into Christ, there would
remain no longer a basis for ordination as a member of the clergy. As we
shall see later in the book, this provides the foundation for a theology of
the ministry of the laity. For Christ's ministry is, first of all, that in which
every member of his body has a share. The office of ministry, in this view,
is subordinate to the function of ministry and receives its authority from
Christ's ministry as the ministry of the whole body.

There is surely a place for the office and role of the clergy in Christ's
ministry. But this comes under the heading of the order of ministry. The
order of the church's ministry is the strategy by which the church carries
out the ministry of Christ. This allows for a variety of different forms and
orders of ministry grounded in the single ministry of Christ. As Paul said,
"There is one body and one Spirit, just as you were called to the one hope
of your calling, one Lord, one faith, one baptism, one God and Father of
all, who is above all and through all and in all" (Eph. 4:4–6).

We often speak of a church "calling" a minister to serve as pastor. Typ-
ically, when a church issues a "call," it has determined its needs through
some kind of ministry profile, and then seeks to find a pastor who

"matches" that profile in terms of experience, competence, and willingness to serve. Churches that operate under this polity tend to use the concept of "call" as part of the negotiation between a candidate for the position and the "call committee." The assumption that prayer and the
guidance of the Holy Spirit are involved, of course, is not to be discounted.
But the fact remains that such a view of a call to ministry can have some
unfortunate problems.

Let me present another way of looking at the concept of a call to ministry and to a church.

Strictly speaking, the calling of a minister is first of all to participate
in Christ's calling to serve the Father and, secondarily, to go where one
is sent, as did Jesus. A congregation in need of pastoral leadership calls
out to God, preparing its self-study and specifying its needs. The "call"
is thus not directly to the candidate for the position, but directly to God
and only indirectly to the candidate. The assumption is that God hears
the "call" of the people (as in the case of the people in Egypt) and
"sends" a pastor to lead the people in the ministry of God (as in the case
of Moses).

This allows for an *ex nihilo* to exist between the call and the response.
While much of the preparation and work in seeking a pastoral candidate
remains the same, the theological understanding of the relation of the people to its pastor/leader is quite different.

The candidate, in reviewing the opportunity and assessing the need
along with his or her own strengths and weaknesses, searches for signs of
"being sent" by God rather than merely answering the call of the church.
Again, the mechanics of determining where one is sent by God will look
very much like responding to a call. The difference is the *ex nihilo* that is
assumed to be at the very heart of this relationship on the part of both the
people and the candidate.

The practical value of this *ex nihilo* in the call to ministry depends upon
the awareness of the church and the candidate of a theology of ministry
that holds human possibilities and needs in tension with God's power and
purpose. There are many churches who are seeking an Isaac and end up
with an Ishmael. Equally important with the ministry profile that a church
compiles based on its needs is a ministry theology based on its understanding of Christ's service to the Father and the Father's sending him to
the world.

How did Jesus know when and where he was sent? In the end, he was
sent further into the desperate need of the world than he ever thought possible. But it was there also that he had the deepest confirmation of divine
blessing on his life. " . . . [T]he one who sent me is true," said Jesus, "and

I declare to the world what I have heard from him. . . . And the one who sent me is with me; he has not left me alone, for I always do what is pleasing to him" (John 8:26, 29).

Perhaps it is time we think not so much of where we are called to minister, but where we are sent to be servants. Then we will know who the master is!

Jesus as Sent to the World on Behalf of the Father

Jesus was sent into the world on behalf of the Father to create a true form of humanity in the midst of the world. In the face of all that is inhuman, whether it be in secular or religious form, Jesus lived a truly human life.

As he was sent into the world, Jesus took up both sides of the ministry of the Father. Jesus brings to the world the good news of the gospel of love for the world. At the same time, Jesus came forward from the side of the estranged and broken world in need of healing to reconcile humanity to God.

Thomas Torrance says it eloquently when he writes:

> The Church cannot be in Christ without being in Him as He is proclaimed to men in their need and without being in Him as He encounters us in and behind the existence of every man in his need. Nor can the Church be recognized as His except in that meeting of Christ with Himself in the depth of human misery, where Christ clothed with His Gospel meets with Christ clothed with the desperate need and plight of men.

The vivid language of Torrance captures the double movement I have stressed as the inner logic of revelation and reconciliation. Jesus is the incarnation of the divine *Logos* and, as such, stands with humans offering up to God the true ministry of service on their behalf. At the same time, Jesus stands among humans as the very presence of God bringing to bear the reality of divine mercy, grace, and love for persons in their need.

The two movements in the ministry of Jesus can now be depicted in their mutual inter-relatedness (see figure 10). The movement from below to above is shown on the left side, and the movement from above to below on the right side. Both movements are grounded in the person of Jesus Christ as the Son of the Father. Both movements are conceived and empowered by the Spirit of God. This grounds all ministry in the trinitarian relation and actions of God as Father, Son, and Holy Spirit.

Jesus serves the Father, and the Father sends him into the world. The relation of the serving and the sending is vital to our theology of ministry.

Figure 10

Many have confused the serving with the sending, resulting in a ministry that makes human need the criterion and motivation for turning toward the world. The reconciliation of the world to God does not occur through solidarity with the world alone, but in the bringing of the world into the reality of God's love and grace through Christ's ministry to the Father on behalf of the world.

The ministry of Jesus to the world on behalf of the Father took place through the obedience of the Son to the Father, an obedience that had as its inner motivation love, and as its outer form solidarity with humanity under sentence of death. This solidarity, as Karl Barth has reminded us, means sharing the common humanity of all who are under distress and estranged from God.

Being Found in Human Form

In the christological hymn that Paul included in his letter to the church at Philippi, the assumption of humanity on the part of Jesus is described as an experience of "self-emptying." Christ Jesus, "though he was in the form of God, did not regard equality with God as something to be exploited, but emptied himself, taking the form of a slave, being born in human likeness.

And being found in human form, he humbled himself and became obedient to the point of death—even death on a cross" (Phil. 2:6–8).

Theologians have speculated over the centuries as to the nature and extent of the humanity of Jesus. The fact that Jesus was without sin is the clear testimony of Scripture (John 8:46; 2 Cor. 5:21). Does this mean that Jesus was exempt from the consequences of Adam and Eve's sin and free from the temptation of sin? It does not.

The fact that Jesus was tempted clearly indicates that he had assumed a human nature capable and susceptible of temptation at his conception and birth (Heb. 2:18). The consequence of sin is death, according to the creation account and Paul's reiteration of this fact (Gen. 2:17; Rom. 6:23).

The human nature that belonged to Jesus was "flesh and blood," according to the author of Hebrews, "so that through death he might destroy the one who has the power of death, the devil" (Heb. 2:14). This point is further emphasized by the author when he adds, "Therefore he had to become like his brothers and sisters in every respect, so that he might be a merciful and faithful high priest in the service of God, to make a sacrifice of atonement for the sins of the people" (2:17).

Jesus was not sent to the world as only a messenger, delivering good news and urging persons to repent and believe the gospel. No, he was sent to become the "bad news," as it were. He was sent to bear in his own humanity the consequence of sin in order to draw that consequence into the very being of God.

What am I saying?

Does this mean that Jesus was a carrier of the fatal consequence of sin from the very moment of his conception and birth? Am I saying that Jesus, though he did not have a "sinful nature," nonetheless had a "death nature?" And that Jesus assumed the death of humanity as well as the life of humanity in being sent to the world? Indeed I am saying this.

How else can we understand the reconciliation of humans to God except that God has assumed the very worst that could befall humanity in order to transform that into the best?

It is not only sin that is the great human dilemma, but it is death. It was not just that Adam and Eve became "sinners" when they disobeyed and suffered estrangement from God. It was far more serious. Their mortal bodies became subject to the fate of all that is mortal—death. The inevitable physical death that resulted from their sin only sealed the spiritual death that occurred in their turning away from God by their act of self-determination. Because both body and soul comprise the spiritual reality of humanity as created in the divine image, the death of the body as the consequence of sin must be reversed in order for spiritual life to be restored.

The Father sent the Son into the world to assume that death, to experience that death, to die that death, in order that the death of humans might become the death that God dies. God, who has no death to die because God is the source of life itself, assumed human death as the consequence of sin in order to die that death.

Jesus, thus, had his own death to die. He did not simply die the death of others vicariously. He died the death that was part of his humanity assumed at conception and birth. I stress the point that it was a human death that God assumed in becoming human.

This means two things. First, it means that the inhumanity of death is overcome as it is brought within the humanity of God in Jesus Christ. This provides a basis for a theology of death and dying. Ministry to those who are dying in the name of Christ can now be understood within the context of a "human ecology" of the death experience. The humanizing of death enables us to integrate our own dying and death with our human life. While death is still the "enemy," its sting has been removed, as Paul tells us (1 Cor. 15:56).

Second, the assertion that it was a human death that God assumed through the incarnation means that human death has been brought back into the *ex nihilo* that constituted the original relation of humanity to God. The original nature of Adam and Eve was "from the dust," and as such mortal and subject to death. Death is therefore not something that was unknown to God's good creation. What kept death from becoming an inevitable fate for the humans was the *ex nihilo* that preserved human life in relation to God through the power and presence of God's grace.

This was the basis for Paul's confidence that, while he continued to experience the reality of death and dying, the power of life through Christ delivered him from that death as an inevitable fate (2 Cor. 4:16; 6:9). The resurrection of Christ completed the atonement for sin, and created the basis for a new humanity into which those who receive the Spirit of Christ are given a share. This will be the theme of the next chapter.

My concern in this chapter is to show how the sending of Jesus into the world constituted the basis for all Christian ministry. As Jesus was sent into the world, so too are Christians sent as a continuation of the ministry of Christ. From this comes what I call a manifesto for Christian ministry.

A Manifesto for Christian Ministry

In his prayer on behalf of his disciples, Jesus prayed: "As you have sent me into the world, so I have sent them into the world" (John 17:18).

The *as* and the *so* constitute the hinge on which Christians turn toward the world for the sake of Christ's ministry of healing and hope. As we explore the content of the *as*, we will begin to develop the content of the *so* and the profile of an authentic ministry.

Several aspects of the humanity of Christ reveal to us what it means to say he was sent into the world to reveal and recover true humanity. Jesus demonstrated authenticity, integrity, love, and maturity. He saw people as individual persons, and yet called them into community.

Each of these dimensions of the humanity of Christ can be used to form a "manifesto for Christian ministry." Let us peer into each in order to discover what it means to minister humanly. The format of this manifesto will be to discuss each aspect of Christ's ministry under three sections. First, the *as* Jesus was sent will be described. Then the *so* we are sent will be articulated, followed by a brief statement as to what our commitment should be in light of the *as* and the *so*.

Authenticity

As Jesus was: In the midst of a religious culture that prized appearance and cultivated form, Jesus appeared among us clothed simply in grace and truth. He refused to recognize as spiritual that which was artificial and affected. He valued the truth of being and doing over the righteousness of words and prayers. He told it like it was—both in the street and in the temple. He had one language for both the saint and the sinner. He stated divine realities in terms of human experience. His lifestyle was that of a human person living among humans. Because he *was* the truth, he had no fear of exposure, nothing to defend.

Because he was *human*, he had no fear of humanness, in himself or others. Because he came in love, he had no fear of love. He was open to all who were open to him, closed to all who closed themselves to him.

So we should be: A real Christian must also be a genuine human being. Spiritual growth is manifested in those who demonstrate the fruit of the Spirit in relationship with others (Gal. 5:22–23). The Christian is to be related to his or her own society in the same way that Christ was related to the world (John 17:18). The test for truth in a Christian is what the world sees in us of Jesus Christ, not what other Christians see in us as a Christian.

We are *committed* to live a transparent life, willing to be known for who we really are, not only by who we say we are.

We are committed to live in openness toward others, accepting them as Christ has accepted us, having a spirit of tolerance toward others who do not share our concepts or convictions. And we know that openness is not permissiveness, and tolerance is not compromise.

We are committed to acknowledge the fact that a Christian does have anxieties, temptations, moods, doubts, frustrations, and problems—that we are still human!

Openness
≠
Permissiveness

Tolerance
≠
Compromise

We are committed to have no ulterior motive or religious device in our love for God and our love for our neighbor: that is, to be authentic.

Integrity

As Jesus was: In the person of Jesus there was a spiritual integrity that revitalized the spirit of persons amid the dead weight of tradition and legalism: where Jesus was there was life. In the life of Jesus was a moral integrity that brought an absolute sense of right to specific human situations: where Jesus was there was truth. In the truth of Jesus there was a personal integrity that spoke with authority against the enslaving influences of religious formalism and demonic delusion: where Jesus was there was freedom.

So we should be: Jesus Christ is the truth of God for persons. One whose life is centered on Jesus Christ thereby has spiritual integrity (Col. 2:18–19). There is no Christ other than the Christ of Scripture as present to us in the power of the Holy Spirit. The integrity of Christ exists in the integrity of Scripture as the Word of God written (John 5:39). The integrity of Christian fellowship rests in the person of Jesus Christ as the object of personal faith and the ground of mutual commitment: where Jesus is, there is the church (Matt. 18:20).

1. We are *committed* to include all in fellowship who seek to know Jesus Christ as Savior and who honor the integrity of Christ between us.
2. We are committed to keep good faith between one another and so preserve the unity of Christ in fellowship. Within this integrity of fellowship there is room for disagreement but not divisiveness. It is the wisdom of the Spirit and the patience of love to know the difference.
3. We are committed to allow Jesus Christ perfect liberty in the creating of his church in the world. Our concepts, prejudices, traditions, successes, and failures constitute no obligation upon his will.
4. We are committed to so live, in word and deed, that our motives are perfectly clear and our methods consistent with the message: that is, to have integrity.

Love

As Jesus was: Jesus revealed the heart of God to be most loving toward us. He brought God's Spirit of tolerance to the sharp edge of divine justice. His love held back the law long enough for people to discover *why* they were law-breakers, and to receive mercy (John 8:1–11). His liberating love loosed the dehumanizing bonds of a religiously structured society. He taught that the sabbath was made for the restoration and renewal of humans, not humans in bondage to the sabbath. Everything doesn't have to be perfect to please God, and pleasing God is easier than pleasing others.

He brought a new dimension of practicality to the word love. Love from God can be worn on the back, put on the table, and sat down beside you—it is human as well as divine, tangible as well as spiritual. It is Jesus.

So we should be: Love is something you do. The feelings, expressions, and words of love have little substance apart from being "incarnated" into an act (James 2:15). Clothing is love to the naked; food is love to the hungry; you *being there* is love for the one in prison, and a seat beside you is love for the stranger. Love is common to both God and human persons.

When God loves it means the same thing as when we love. The difference is that it is God loving, not a separate kind of love. Therefore, our love for God is evidenced by our love for one another (1 John 4:8, 12). Love is the point of contact in the world for Jesus Christ. The love of the Christian for the non-Christian is the bridge by which persons come to God.

1. We are *committed* to create a fellowship that embodies as much of the Spirit of Christ as the truth of Christ.
2. We are committed to be tolerant of all that seems contrary to us and intolerant of all that is contrary to Christ, and to be willing to learn the difference! Where the Spirit of the Lord is, there is freedom (2 Cor. 3:17).
3. We are committed to allow people in the world to see the interior life of our Christian fellowship; and, in knowing us, leading them to know God: where love is, there is God.
4. We are committed to make no discrimination in our love between the body and the soul, the spiritual and the personal, between mine and yours: that is, to have love.

Maturity

As Jesus was: Jesus Christ fulfills the greatest potential and God's highest purpose for human persons. He liberated the spirit from the law and created children of God out of slaves. He lifted the burden of the law by fulfilling it, not by breaking it, and pointed beyond it to a higher fulfillment. Those who become his slaves find their freedom (John 6:63; 2 Cor. 3:4–6). In his own life, he brought both body and soul into balance.

Because he understood and accepted his own humanity, he never condemned another for being human. He demonstrated that a holy purpose can only be completed when the spirit and the flesh become one. He was in every sense a mature person:

> His feelings ran deep but they had a bottom
> His love flowed freely and yet within boundaries
> He was sensitive to pain but not easily hurt
> He had a dream, but consecrated his life in duty

So should we be: Growth is a greater value than conformity. This means that there must be room to grow for the immature and reasons to grow for the more mature. When standards become barriers to growth they must be moved. Responsibility is a higher motive than guilt. Instead of exploiting guilt to achieve results, we seek to enlarge responsibility to produce growth.

Love is a better fruit than work. Only the capacity to love engages the whole person and fulfills the complete law. In learning how to love, the Christian brings every part of life into discipleship (Rom. 13:8–10). Freedom is the highest act of personhood. It is achieved by one who is neither slave to self or to the world. Only one who is free can love. It is complete submission to the Spirit of Christ that produces this freedom (Gal. 5:1, 13; 2 Cor. 10:5).

1. We are *committed* to bring each person to his or her highest level of responsibility. With the assumption of responsibility comes the removing of restraints. Responsibility is itself a law of God working within and through the individual's perception of self and God.
2. We are committed to bring each person to his or her greatest capacity to love. This will mean the exposure of each other to the risks of love and the expectation from each other of the fruit of love (Heb. 10:24).
3. We are committed to help each person to become a whole person—effectively able to receive and apply God's grace, fully equipped to live a creative and purposeful life, meaningfully involved in the functions of the body of Christ: that is, to have maturity.

The Individual

As Jesus was: Everyone was a person to Jesus Christ. He ignored the categories established within his own society. For him the despised Samaritan was a woman who could give *him* a drink, the self-righteous Pharisee a man who wanted to talk, the leper a person who needed to be touched. While people came to him in bunches, each need came with a name. A congregation was not a mob to send home to eat, but individuals to be fed with bread broken with his own hands.

In a crowd he was never simply pushed by people, but was touched by someone who hurt. Within the shouting sounds of a multitude he heard the cry of the blind man, the sigh of a sinner, the murmur of a skeptic. He let people be who they were and offered to help them become who they could be. He had no uniforms for his disciples and no masks for his friends. He did not ask for conformity but for commitment. His style was love, his pattern devotion.

So we should be: Love is treating people as persons. People are persons even before they become Christians. Young people are persons even before they become adults. Christians are persons even after they become Christians. Ministry is to relate to people as persons. The church is made for people, people are not made for the church (Mark 2:27). Outreach is to love people as persons. Every person in the world has a right to know that a particular individual loves him or her for Jesus' sake.

1. We are *committed* to help each person find his or her particular gift to the body of Christ (1 Cor. 12:7, 11). Until each individual contributes to our function as a fellowship, we are less than the whole body. Until the body permits each individual the full expression of his or her personality, we are less than a whole person.
2. We are committed to seek unity of spirit without requiring conformity of lifestyle (1 Cor. 12:7, 11). We recognize the bonds of love but make no one a slave to a system. The greatest difference between us is far less than the smallest task shared in Christ.
3. We are committed to see persons as Christ sees them, not as prospects or problems, but as persons who bear a name and a need.
4. We are committed to know that we do not love humankind until we love one person so that he or she comes to know that God loves him or her: that is, to be committed to the individual.

Community

As Jesus was: Jesus called men and women out of estrangement and into a redemptive relationship. He came as a Son and introduced God as the Father. Out of this relationship he coined new words to explain human problems and possibilities: prodigal, enemy, reconciliation, friend, brother and sister, flock.

He defined spiritual values in terms of human relationships. God forgives us as we forgive one another; to hate our brother is to hate God; to give of ourselves to another is to love Christ. He gave himself as the new basis for the community of persons. Those who love Christ become his body, with a common life and one heart.

So we should be: There is no such thing as a solitary Christian. One cannot "come to Christ" apart from coming into the fellowship of his body— the church. This fellowship (*koinonia*) is not only spiritual, but personal and social. It may not always be structured as an organization, but it will always be an organism. The highest act of the individual is to surrender his or her right to exclusive self-existence in order to create a community of faith and love.

Because each Christian retains individuality, even in community, the community of Christ is a continuing creation: community is broken whenever the individual acts exclusive of others or loses individuality in the group. Personal spiritual growth is measured in terms of the individual's contribution to the common good of the entire body. The fruit of the Spirit are relational realities: love, joy, peace, patience, kindness, etc. are evidenced in our relationship with others.

1. We are *committed* to give priority to the organism of the church over the organization. Organization is the servant of the organism to carry through the functions that contribute to growth and life: the life of one person is of more value than the entire organization.

2. We are committed to maintain the integrity and health of the body of Christ through responsible participation and loving discipline. The life and health of the body of Christ is more vital than the demands of one person.

3. We are committed to set no limits on love that are not intrinsic to the nature of love itself as revealed by Christ.

4. We are committed to go as far as Christ would go, to share as much as Christ would share, to live in fellowship with those in whom Christ lives: that is, to be committed to community.

This is the manifesto for Christian ministry. As Jesus was sent into the world on behalf of the Father, so we are sent into the world on behalf of Jesus. "Lord, here am I, send me!"

12

The Resurrection and Justification of Jesus as the Verdict of the Father

In a theological examination for a prospective faculty member, one of my theology colleagues posed this question to the candidate: "What work did Jesus accomplish on the cross for our salvation?" I wanted to interrupt and say, "Nothing! A dead man cannot do any work!" But I held my tongue, and the candidate plunged ahead, giving a traditional and apparently acceptable answer.

There is within our theological tradition a long history that stresses the "work" of Christ in addition to the "person" of Christ. In his dogmatic series, G. C. Berkouwer, for example, divided the person of Christ and the work of Christ into two separate volumes.

The traditional doctrine of the atonement is almost exclusively focused on the death of Jesus on the cross as offering complete satisfaction for the dishonor done to God through human sin. The "work" of Christ, therefore, in this view, is taken to be the offering up of his life as a sacrifice to fulfill divine justice and permit God to pardon freely all who accept the death of Jesus as a substitute for their own death. The forgiveness of sin is offered by God based on the satisfaction achieved by the death of Christ.

The candidate, I should add, provided exactly this kind of response and passed with flying colors, having guessed correctly what the question was meant to elicit. Wisely keeping quiet during the investigation of the candidate's theology, I carried over my concern into my class on theology the following day. It is usually safer to explore innovative theology with students than with faculty colleagues! Even though sooner or later the "cat is out of the bag," so to speak, and one must be prepared to give account of one's own theological convictions. Let this be such an occasion.

What Happened When Jesus Died?

"If Jesus had died of a heart attack in the Garden of Gethsemane," I asked my students, "and the disciples carried him out and placed him in a tomb, would there have been a resurrection?" Only a few hands went up. The rest were stunned by the thought and not prepared to respond.

Some who raised their hands argued that he would have been raised from the dead because he was the Son of God, irrespective of how he died. I then played my trump card. "Assuming that he would have been raised from the dead, would there have been an atonement? Could we still say that he died for our sins?"

Now I saw a flurry of hands, and the consensus was that, no, there could not have been an atonement because he did not die on the cross as one rejected by God. My students too had learned the "correct answer."

Some refused to entertain the hypothesis, feeling that the question was itself irrelevant, if not blasphemous. "Jesus died on the cross in fulfillment of Scripture and as God had determined," one protested. "It couldn't have happened any other way."

At the same time, I could tell that there was growing discomfort with this conclusion. Other students were now beginning to do some theological reflection, and one responded, "It was the resurrection that counted, anyway. Without a resurrection there would be no atonement, even if he died on the cross."

Amazing! Here was a student coming up with a theological insight I had never heard mentioned in the theological exam of the faculty candidate. I read from Paul's letter to the Corinthians, "If Christ has not been raised, your faith is futile and you are still in your sins. Then those also who have died in Christ have perished" (1 Cor. 15:17–18).

It is the resurrection of Jesus, not just his death on the cross, that completed the atonement, I went on to suggest. The reason for this is that it is not just sin that needs to be forgiven, but death that needs to be overcome. The consequence of sin is death, as I have argued in a previous chapter. And the great human dilemma is death, not merely sin.

Furthermore, if Jesus assumed a human nature subject to death in his conception and birth, then death was inevitable for him, regardless of the means. Yes, there was in retrospect, after the crucifixion of Jesus, ample evidence in Scripture that even the means of death had been foreseen by God. But death on a cross was not necessary, only that the death assumed by Jesus be completed and that he be raised from the dead in order for the atonement to be completed and humanity restored to fellowship with God.

The language of Paul is deeply rooted in the metaphors of death and resurrection. "You were dead through the trespasses and sins in which you once lived," wrote Paul to the Ephesians. "But God who is rich in mercy, out of the great love with which he loves us, even when we were dead through our trespasses, made us alive together with Christ—by grace you have been saved—and raised us up with him . . . " (Eph. 2:1; 4–6).

It is strange that a theological tradition that insists we are saved not through any works of our own, but through grace alone, wants to speak of the "work of Christ" on the cross as the basis for our salvation! Paul makes it clear that it was by the power of God, not the work of Christ, that resurrection and forgiveness of sins took place. This Jesus who was descended from David according to the flesh, Paul wrote, "was declared to be the Son of God with power according to the spirit of holiness by resurrection from the dead . . . " (Rom. 1:3–4).

Certainly it is true that Jesus was "obedient unto death," as Paul says (Philippians 2). And it is also true that he shed his blood as an expiation for sin (Rom. 3:25; 5:9). Blood, however, is the bearer of life. To pour out one's blood is to give one's life, to die. Without resurrection of the body of Jesus, the shedding of his lifeblood would not have removed the consequence of sin.

The cross must be viewed backward through the resurrection. Only with the resurrection of Jesus can the claim of Jesus to be the Son of God be verified. Only with the resurrection can one dare to say that death no longer has the power to determine the destiny of human persons. Only with the resurrection can it be said that the giving of his life through the "shedding of blood" was an atonement for sin.

In the resurrection of Jesus, the power of death was "destroyed," to use Paul's language. "The last enemy to be destroyed is death" (1 Cor. 15:26). The resurrection of Jesus broke the power of death over those who became subject to death because of sin. It is now God, the one who raised Jesus from the dead, who determines the fate of all who live and die.

The resurrection of Jesus was the Father's verdict concerning his Son. From his baptism to his death on the cross, Jesus maintained that he was sent by his Father, and that he was doing the will and work of the Father. In the end, the evidence was not good. Having once walked on water, he was now too weak to carry his own cross. Where once he was transfigured by the glory that rightly belonged to him, here on Golgotha he was shadowed by the darkness of being Godforsaken. And so he died, wretched and forlorn, to sink into the abyss that goes far beyond the grave in its power over the human spirit.

The divine *Logos* was sent into the world to go to the lengths of human estrangement and to take that desperate condition upon himself as the very form of God. How far then was Jesus sent into the world?

Far enough to die, one might say. But death is not the final word, and the grave is not the final destination of humanity estranged from God. In order to make atonement, God had to send his Son into the world, to die on the cross, to be buried and—dare we say it—to descend into hell.

On the day of Pentecost, Peter cited David in support of the fact that God had raised his Son, not only from the grave, but from Hades (hell). "He was not abandoned to Hades, nor did his flesh experience corruption" (Acts 2:27, 31; Ps. 16:10).

How far was Jesus sent into the world? The question has something to do with the nature of humanity in its fallen condition, and everything to do with the length to which God would go to recover humanity in its estrangement from God. In reciting the Apostles' Creed, one confesses the fact that Christ not only died and was buried, but "descended into hell." What do we mean when we confess this to be true?

How Far Is Hell from Heaven?

If death is the final fate of those who are estranged from God, it could be considered a comfort to those whose pain and torment in life is close to unbearable. If death really brought the end of life as sheer annihilation, it would be a relief to many people and, I suppose, even a kind of salvation. But humanity as created in the image and likeness of God, according to the Scriptures, faces the judgment of God, a reality that death cannot evade. "And just as it is appointed for mortals to die once, and after that the judgment, so Christ, having been offered once to bear the sins of many, will appear a second time, not to deal with sin, but to save those who are eagerly waiting for him" (Heb. 9:26–27).

There appears to be no clear teaching of Scripture that places Jesus in hell after his death. But if hell is the worst fate that can be described for people estranged from God, as the Scripture clearly teaches, then Jesus must be sent into hell itself if humanity is to be recovered from this terrible fate.

The cross of Christ stands on this side of death. The judgment of God appears to stand on the other side. This may itself be sufficient to postulate a descent into hell for Jesus following his death.

I once drew on the chalkboard a figure (see figure 11) that represented the incarnation of God through the humanity of Jesus. I drew a line from God downward to the point where the humanity of Jesus could be plotted as the furthest point from God. I then placed the sign of the cross between the humanity of Jesus and God, indicating that in becoming human God had moved into the world far enough to grasp death in assuming human flesh.

I then asked my students where they would plot the word "hell" on this diagram. One took the chalk and wrote the word below the words "humanity of Jesus," so as to indicate that hell was a step further away from

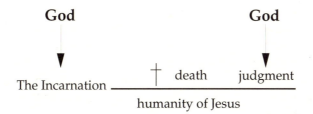

Figure 11

God than even death. I stepped to the board and erased the word and wrote it on the same line as "judgment" (see figure 12).

This shows, I went on to explain, that in becoming human God not only assumed death as belonging to humanity as a consequence of sin, but hell as well. If Jesus "descended into hell," as the Apostles' Creed rightly states, then he was not only raised from the grave in the resurrection, he was raised from hell! Hell is an extension of humanity, not something beyond what is human.

Hands went up all over the room!

The question as to the reality of hell, I reminded the students, is now one aspect of our Christology. If there was a hell for Jesus, there is a hell. The question of the population of hell is not for us to answer. We know that God has been to hell, if Jesus indeed descended into hell. We know that Jesus was raised from hell. We know that hell is within the grasp of God, not beyond his power, if Jesus has been raised from hell.

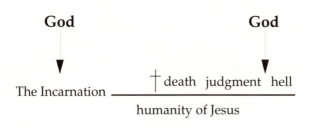

Figure 12

All questions regarding the ultimate destiny of human persons must be asked "through Jesus Christ," as Thomas Torrance once said. We are not permitted to attribute to God motives and intentions beyond what are revealed to us through Christ. Christ is the "alpha and omega," the beginning and the end of our knowledge of God (Rev. 1:8; 21:6).

We know, therefore, that hell has no threat to those who are raised with Christ, as Paul uses the phrase (Col. 3:1; Eph. 2:6). The decisive point with regard to the eternal destiny of humans is not an abstract mathematical number determined by limiting Christ's death only for some, nor by including every human in Christ's death. When Christ died, all died—even as when Adam sinned all sinned, argues Paul (Romans 5). The decisive point is in the power of the resurrection, and the reality of spiritual rebirth into the life of Christ through the Holy Spirit. All have died with Christ, but not all have been raised with Christ.

The point is, in becoming human through Jesus Christ God sent his Son as far from heaven as necessary to provide salvation and reconciliation for humans. In descending into hell, Jesus did not have to take a step beyond what he took in becoming human; he took a step into the abyss that lies within the nature and possibility of every human created in God's image.

How far is hell from heaven? No farther than the span between Jesus and the Father. Jesus "emptied himself" of all self-determination in order to follow the fate of his fellow humans into the deepest crevice of human estrangement. He was fully human, fully prepared to die, fully prepared to descend into hell.

How far was Jesus sent into the world? Farther than any human has ever gone and come back. He assumed the form of humanity, under sentence of death, and took it straight to hell where the Father found him and brought him back to life and glory.

Christ Our Sanctification and Justification

During his life, Jesus claimed to be the Son of God. As such, he assumed humanity in its disobedience to God and bent it back into loving obedience. He assumed humanity estranged from God and consecrated it through the inner holiness of his unbroken relation with the Father in the power of the Spirit. This is the basis for the sanctification of humanity. Sanctification means consecration through relation to God who is the holy One.

In the end, however, the very humanity that he sanctified through perfect obedience and unbroken communion with the Father was destined for death. What justification was there for his claim to be the Son of God?

The outward evidence was not good, as I have suggested. Nonetheless, he trusted the Father to save him from death and to restore to him the glory that he had with the Father before the world began (John 17).

His justification rested with the verdict of the Father and the resurrection from the grave and hell. During his life Jesus believed in the Father's power and promise to grant him life out of death and so to justify his claim to be the Son of God. His justification was therefore in the future, but appropriated during his life by faith. By virtue of his resurrection, Jesus Christ is both the justification and sanctification of humanity. Both justification and sanctification are to be found in Christ.

It is important to note that the sanctification of Christ preceded his justification, even as his life of obedience and unbroken communion with the Father preceded his resurrection from the dead. Figure 13 illustrates the relation of justification to sanctification in the person of Christ.

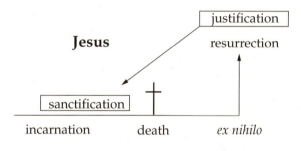

Figure 13

Justification is what I would call an eschatological event. It is connected with resurrection. If Christ had not been raised from the dead, there would have been no justification of his claim to be the Son of God. His life of sanctification would not have saved him, for death and hell would have swallowed up the merits of a good and holy life. The resurrection, like the conception of Jesus in the virgin's womb, takes place out of the *ex nihilo*. The death of Jesus represents a point of absolute discontinuity with historical precedent and continuity.

The circumcised male Jew dies, and this puts an end to circumcision, gender, and race as criteria that can be claimed as the basis for privilege, position, and power with respect to the kingdom of God. The continuity between the historical Jesus and the resurrected Jesus depends entirely on the power of the resurrection. The *ex nihilo* makes it impossible to draw

any historical criteria from the death and resurrection of Christ so as to establish credentials for ministry or full standing in the kingdom of God. Implications of this for the ministry of Christians and the life of the church
are discussed in a later section of the book.

My concern in this chapter is to show how the resurrection of Christ
constitutes the basis for our sanctification and justification, even as his resurrection established the reality of his sanctification and justification.

The eschatological event of resurrection is present to Jesus throughout
his life as trust in the Father's power and promise. He has present assurance of his justification (resurrection), though the reality takes place in the
future. Jesus was, we may say, justified by faith alone. His resurrection
was the verdict of the Father as the eschatological basis for his historical
faith.

In figure 14, we transpose Christ's sanctification and justification as our
own.

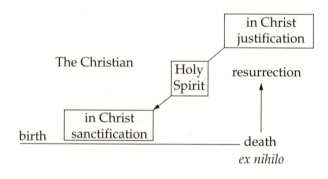

Figure 14

Here too we see that our sanctification and justification both rest in the
reality of "being in Christ." This is fully in accord with the teaching of Paul.
Christ "became for us wisdom from God, and righteousness (justification)
and sanctification and redemption" (1 Cor. 1:30). The righteousness of God
[justification] will be "reckoned to us who believe in him who raised Jesus
our Lord from the dead, who was handed over to death for our trespasses
and was raised for our justification" (Rom. 4:24–25). Justification is connected with resurrection, both for Christ and for the Christian. If our resurrection should fail to occur, not only is the promise of forgiveness of sin canceled (1 Cor. 15:17), but our justification will not come to pass.

Our resurrection is God's verdict that we are truly children of God. The evidence is not always strong in support of this claim. But through the witness of the Holy Spirit we have present assurance of our justification by faith in the God who raised up Jesus. It is important to notice at this point that our faith is not in the objective fact of our justification, but in the God who raised up Jesus and who has given us assurance that we too shall be raised "with Christ."

Justification as well as sanctification are relational aspects of our Christian faith. For Paul, being "found in Christ" at the end is his assurance that God's verdict upon his life will be favorable. He labors hard to be sure that, having preached to others, he would not himself in the end be disqualified (1 Cor. 9:27). As he anticipates the end of his life and ministry, he maintains that he has fought the good fight and finished the race and kept the faith. "From now on there is reserved for me the crown of righteousness [justification], which the Lord, the righteous judge, will give me on that day, and not only to me but also to all who have longed for his appearing" (2 Tim. 4:7–8).

I began this chapter with an anecdote concerning a theological examination of a candidate for a faculty position at a theological seminary. I end with the reminder that there is another kind of theological exam for each of us.

Paul urges the Christians at Corinth to be prepared for this exam! "Examine yourselves to see whether you are living in the faith. Test yourselves. Do you not realize that Jesus Christ is in you?—unless, indeed, you fail to meet the test" (2 Cor. 13:5). Christ in us, and we in Christ.

If this indeed is the criterion for our spiritual life, we should have no fear of the final verdict, and should echo Paul's conviction, "There is therefore no condemnation for those who are in Christ Jesus" (Rom. 8:1).

IV

The Spirit's Ministry
through Jesus
for the Sake of the Church

13

Pentecost as
Empowerment for Ministry

I was just beginning my lecture when a member of the class raised his hand and asked: "I don't understand why my attempts to mobilize the members of the church for ministry do not seem to get off the ground. I have implemented small group training sessions, introduced discipling programs, and used spiritual gifts inventories to help people identify their particular gifts for ministry. I have a lot of well-equipped people but very little ministry going on."

"Is this true for most of you?" I asked the class of well-seasoned pastors. "It is generally true," one responded. "I have read several books on equipping the layperson for ministry and tried to use the principles and programs, but the early enthusiasm soon fades and we are right back where we started."

"What about your own ministry?" I asked the class. "All of you have had professional training and should be well-equipped for ministry. Does ministry effectiveness increase with better methods of equipping?"

The silence was significant. What follows is a version of my response and our discussion.

Empowering Precedes Equipping

Equipping without empowering is like putting Saul's armor on David. Samuel's description of the incident borders on slapstick.

"Saul clothed David with his armor; he put a bronze helmet on his head and clothed him with a coat of mail. David strapped Saul's sword over the armor, and he tried in vain to walk, for he was not used to them. Then David said to Saul, 'I cannot walk with these; for I am not used to them.' So David removed them" (1 Sam. 17:38–39).

David went forth under-equipped by Saul's standards, but empowered by the Spirit of God. "The Lord, who saved me from the paw of the lion and from the paw of the bear, will save me from the hand of this Philistine" (1 Sam. 17:37).

It is not as though David went forth to meet Goliath with his bare hands. He was obviously a good marksman with his rather primitive sling. His bag of stones were the tools of his trade as a shepherd. With the power of the Lord, his own minimal resources proved incredibly effective.

David, however, is only an example. It is Jesus to whom we must look for our own source of empowerment. Somewhat like David, Jesus was well-endowed with spiritual power but rather under-equipped for ministry, measured by our professional methods and techniques.

From his baptism on, the ministry of Jesus was one empowered by the Spirit, as we discussed earlier in chapter 9. His Galilean origin and earlier vocation brought nothing but scorn from the professionals trained in the law at Jerusalem (cf. John 1:46; 7:15). At the same time, the common people recognized in him an uncommon grace and power.

We may well ask, "How was Jesus able to sustain his commitment to ministry in the face of great obstacles and the eventual failure and abandonment of his followers?" It is one thing to be empowered with signs of success, and quite another to be empowered when adversities outnumber the advantages. This man who once walked on water in the end could not even carry his own cross. The one who at one time saw the wine flow miraculously in abundance in the end cried out from the cross, "I thirst!"

The evidence of empowerment is not always in the obvious results, but in the unswerving commitment and the inexplicable devotion to a task. The empowerment of the Spirit did not diminish in the life and ministry of Jesus as he moved relentlessly toward the cross. It was only then that the true nature of empowerment became clear. When the other disciples wavered and abandoned him, his own pathway became clear and compelling (Luke 13:33; 18:31–34).

With the death of Jesus, the disciples concluded that the mission was over and that there was nothing left to do but return to their former lives. Even when they were told of his resurrection, they were unable to translate this good news into personal empowerment. It was the final words of the resurrected Jesus that gave them their clue. "But you will receive power when the Holy Spirit has come upon you; and you will be my witnesses in Jerusalem, in all Judea and Samaria, and to the ends of the earth" (Acts 1:8).

He did not leave with them a manual with techniques and skills gained through equipping. Rather, he promised them the empowerment of the Spirit. This is what began at Pentecost and what continues to this very day as the Spirit's ministry through Jesus for the sake of the church.

"Are you trying to say that we must become Pentecostals before we can be empowered for ministry?" one of my students suddenly asked. I could see that the Presbyterians were uncomfortable while the Assembly of God pastors were smiling!

"Not for a moment," I hastily assured them. "At the same time, I believe that we need to recover both a theology of Pentecost and a new understanding of the experiential purpose and power of Pentecost."

First, we need to place Pentecost in the context of the unfolding of redemptive history through the death, resurrection, and coming of Jesus Christ to the church through the Holy Spirit. Then we will look more closely at the context in which we can expect and experience the empowering of Pentecost for the sake of the church.

A Theology of Pentecostal Empowerment

Pentecost can serve as a compass that performs two functions: (1) *theologically* it orients us to the inner logic of God's incarnational manifestation in the world through Jesus Christ and (2) *experientially* it orients us to the eschatological vision of redemption for the world through Christ's presence and coming. It is as important that we have a theology of Pentecost as an experience of the Spirit which empowers.

With the resurrection of Jesus and the coming of the Spirit on the early believers at Pentecost, the earthly life of Jesus took on new significance. The *content* of the Spirit's work was understood to be a continuation of the ministry of the same Jesus who performed the works of God from his baptism to his death on the cross.

Pentecost is the pivotal point from which we can look back to the incarnation of God in Jesus of Nazareth and look forward into our contemporary life and witness to Jesus Christ in the world. Pentecost is more than a historical and instrumental link between a theology of the incarnation and a theology of the institutional church. Pentecost is more than the birth of the church; it is the indwelling power of the Spirit of Christ as the source of the church's life and ministry.

The nature of the church as the continuing mission of God through Jesus Christ is determined by its relation to Pentecost, not only to the Great Commission, given by Jesus after his crucifixion and resurrection. The Great Commission gives the church its instructions; Pentecost provides its initiation and power. The command, "Go and make disciples of all nations" (Matt. 28:19), anticipates the promise, "you will receive power when the Holy Spirit has come upon you; and you will be my witnesses . . . " (Acts 1:8).

Figure 15 depicts the continuity of spiritual empowerment and the ministry of Jesus. Prior to his death and resurrection, Jesus ministered in the power of the Spirit. Following his resurrection and the coming of the Holy

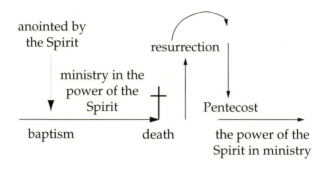

Figure 15

Spirit on the day of Pentecost, the early church experienced the power of the Spirit in ministry.

In Pentecost we see the same *ex nihilo* that lies at the core of the biblical paradigm that we have developed from the beginning in this book. While the disciples and early believers were followers of Jesus and witnesses to his resurrection, they were powerless until the Spirit came upon them at Pentecost. Incarnation without baptism in the Spirit would leave Jesus powerless, even though he was the Son of God. Resurrection without Pentecost would leave believers powerless even though through faith they had become children of God.

A theology of Pentecost is the beginning point for a theology of Jesus Christ, because the Holy Spirit reveals to us the inner life of God as the Father of Jesus and of Jesus as the Son of the Father. To receive the Spirit of God, wrote the apostle Paul, is to "have the mind of Christ" (1 Cor. 2:10, 16). Jesus said, "All things have been handed over to me by my Father; and no one knows the Son except the Father, and no one knows the Father except the Son and anyone to whom the Son chooses to reveal him" (Matt. 11:27). The Holy Spirit is the revelation to us of the inner being of God as constituted by the relation between Father and Son. For this reason, a theology of Pentecost begins with the Christ of Pentecost.

Pentecost is the inner logic of incarnation and resurrection as the beginning and end of God's vision for humanity. This is true because the Spirit which descended at Pentecost is the Spirit of the resurrected Christ as well as of the incarnate Son, Jesus of Nazareth.

Pentecost thus serves to orient both our theology and experience to the inner logic of God's incarnational and eschatological vision of redemption for the world. Through God's embodiment in Jesus of Nazareth (incarnation) the reality of humanity as created by God is grasped by God and retrieved from its fatal plunge into the abyss of eternal separation from God. But in becoming human, God also died and "descended into hell," as the Apostles' Creed tells us. It is in the resurrection from the dead that Jesus Christ puts an end to the power of death and hell. This is the eschatological vision of the redemption of humanity, for the *eschatos*, or "final event," has now already occurred in Christ.

Pentecost, as we now will see, has an experiential function because it occurs in the context of human life and mission. It is the beginning point for our own relationship with God through Christ, for apart from the Spirit we are alienated from the life of God. Paul wrote, "Any one who does not have the Spirit of Christ does not belong to him" (Rom. 8:9). Pentecost is thus both a theological and experiential compass. Without true knowledge of God (theology) our experience can slip into delusion and even become demonic. Without authentic experience of Christ (faith), our theology can become vain and empty speculation.

The Holy Spirit is thus the creative power and presence of Jesus Christ as the "inner *Logos*," or inner logic of God's purpose in creating the church as the missionary people of God sent into the world. The experience of the Holy Spirit at Pentecost was not only an event that Christ promised, but an event in which the same Christ continues to be present as the goal, or *telos*, of history.

The Context of
Pentecostal Empowerment

Christian theology is a contextual theology, as theologian Douglas Hall says, because it is a theology of the living God who continues to be present to the world in the context of the historical reality of the Holy Spirit.

The *context* of the Spirit's ministry was experienced as a community of persons bound to each other and to Christ by a common baptism of the Spirit. This was put succinctly by Paul when he wrote: "For just as the body is one and has many members, and all the members of the body, though many, are one body, so it is with Christ. For in the one Spirit we were all baptized into one body—Jews or Greeks, slaves or free—and we were all made to drink of one Spirit" (1 Cor. 12:12–13).

"Now tell us how we can be empowered by Pentecost without becoming Pentecostals," the Presbyterians asked, with tongue in cheek. "And at the same time," the Pentecostal pastors responded, "tell us how we can be theologically correct without becoming Presbyterians!"

There is nothing like a group of pastors to keep one focused on the subject!

Make Spiritual Empowerment
a Mission Strategy

We begin by understanding that Pentecost has more to do with empowering through the Spirit than being filled with the Spirit. While this may surprise us, let us consider how the New Testament views the relation of the Spirit to empowering.

Luke, in the book of Acts, says that the 120 disciples in the upper room were "filled with the Spirit" on the day of Pentecost (Acts 2:4). Subsequently, certain individuals and gathered people were said to be "filled with the Spirit" (Peter, 4:8; the believers, 4:31; Stephen, 7:55; Saul of Tarsus, 9:17; 13:9; the disciples, 13:52). While these are quite specific instances, they are relatively few considering the importance Luke gives to the Holy Spirit in the book of Acts.

At the same time, Luke made it clear that it was power that the Holy Spirit was to bring, not merely "fullness." "But you will receive power when the Holy Spirit has come upon you; and you will be my witnesses in Jerusalem, in all Judea and Samaria, and to the ends of the earth" (Acts 1:8). Stephen was "full of grace and power" and thus did great wonders and signs, prior to Luke's description of his being "filled with the Spirit" (Acts 6:8; 7:55). Overall, Luke's emphasis is on what I have called empowerment rather than simply an experience of being filled with the Spirit (cf. Acts 2:11, 22; 4:7, 33; 8:10, 19; 10:38).

In a study of Paul's writings, however, it becomes clear that his emphasis was not on the "filling of the Spirit," as such, but on the "power of the Spirit." In only one place does Paul explicitly speak of the filling of the Spirit. "Do not get drunk with wine, for that is debauchery; but be filled with the Spirit" (Eph. 5:18). A better translation of the Greek verb (*plēroō*) used in this verse might be, "seek the fullness which the Spirit gives." The Greek word *pleroma* has more the idea of moving into fullness rather than a container being filled to capacity.

On the other hand, when we read Paul's letters looking for his reference to power and the power of the Spirit, we find more than two dozen references. For example, "I pray that, according to the riches of his glory, he may grant that you may be strengthened in your inner being with power through his Spirit" (Eph. 3:16); "for God did not give us a spirit of cowardice, but rather a spirit of power and of love and of self-discipline" (2 Tim. 1:7; cf. also, Rom. 15:13, 19; 1 Cor. 2:4; 1 Thess. 1:5).

The promise and expectation that led to the Pentecost event was in the context of a community of ministry, not personal edification as an end in

itself. It was for the purpose of sending witnesses of the power of the resurrection "to the ends of the earth" that the promise of spiritual empowerment was given (Acts 1:8). Empowerment for ministry is the express purpose for which one seeks the "filling of the Holy Spirit." Where there is
empowered ministry, there is also the filling of the Spirit. The evidences for
the Spirit's presence are found in the manifestation of the Spirit's power.

This is why Paul appealed to the power of the Spirit manifest in his ministry rather than to his own experience of being "filled with the Spirit" in
defense of his apostolic credentials (e.g., Rom. 15:19; 1 Cor. 1:17; 2:4–5;
14:13; 2 Cor. 12:9).

My impression is that the so-called Pentecostal churches make the Holy
Spirit an almost tangible reality in the worship, preaching, and individual
experience of the Christian. This leads to great expectation of the Spirit's
presence as an edifying experience.

My impression is that the so-called non-Pentecostal churches make the
Bible and biblical doctrine the central aspect of the belief system of both
individuals and the church without much reference to the power and
presence of the Holy Spirit. This leads to an expectation that inculcation
of the truth based on biblical teaching produces edification, interpreted as
"growing in the knowledge of God."

My impressions are caricatures, to be sure, but the Presbyterians and
Pentecostal pastors in my class nodded their heads in agreement!

The context of Pentecostal empowerment is not the Pentecostal church,
but the people as a community of witness and ministry. One does not need
the power of the Spirit unless one is already engaged in the ministry of the
Spirit!

Saul of Tarsus encountered the resurrected Christ on the road to Damascus, and was subsequently "filled with the Spirit." But thereafter,
Saul—now having adopted the Latin form of his name, Paul—experienced the empowering of the Spirit as he left the church at Antioch on a
preaching mission (Acts 13). We read very little in the New Testament
about the power and presence of the Spirit in the church in Jerusalem,
where there is no evidence of a strong mission outreach.

My point is this. When the church baptizes persons into the mission of
Christ rather than merely into the body of Christ, spiritual empowerment
will be the motivation to prayer, the central focus of worship, the aim of
preaching, and the practice of ministry on the part of each Christian. Pentecostals tend to emphasize baptism in the Spirit rather than spiritual baptism into the mission of Christ. Non-Pentecostals tend to stress baptism
into the Word rather than a spiritual baptism into the mission of Christ.

*When spiritual empowerment becomes a mission strategy, ecclesial distinc-
tives and disagreements become softer and sweeter.*

Use What You Have,
Attempt More Than You Can Do

Remember David? His attempt to be equipped by wearing Saul's armor and sword was grotesque and awkward. Nonetheless, he did not retreat from his encounter with Goliath, but advanced with two certainties. He was pretty good with the sling (and he remembered to take along some stones!), and he went forth in the power of the Lord. Note this. He had already had some success against lions and bears. But he did not attribute this to his own prowess but to the Lord. "The Lord, who saved me from the paw of the lion and from the paw of the bear, will save me from the hand of this Philistine" (1 Sam. 17:37).

We need to practice with lions and bears before we go out to fight Goliath! Before we attempt to load people up with methods and equip them with concepts and theories of ministry, we need to empower them by having them learn spiritual empowerment in their daily lives.

We can hardly empower people for ministry when they are not empowered to live their daily lives—to fight with lions and bears! Some of these "lions and bears," metaphorically speaking, are found in our own homes, in the workplace, and in the insatiable demands placed on our time and money. We need, as Robert Banks has reminded us, a "theology of everyday life." Daily life has a way of disempowering people, leaving them discouraged and spiritually depressed. The church makes a mistake in offering them momentary spiritual inspiration through worship without empowering them for daily living.

When the church has difficulty mobilizing its members for ministry, the problem is not with the lack of motivation nor even with the lack of training. The problem is that church members come to church beaten by the "lions and bears" in the daily routine of life.

I suspect that this is also true for many pastors. Most of us are pretty well-equipped for ministry, though some of us have never grown to fit "Saul's armor." What we lack is the kind of spiritual empowerment that comes from using the rather insignificant things that we have and can do to accomplish significant things through the power of God's Spirit.

My suggestion is that we develop strategies of spiritual empowerment that are focused on the context where people live and work before we send them into the world to face Goliath—who appears formidable when measured against our own power and resources. We will discover how to do this when we decide that it is what we want and ought to do.

To paraphrase Paul in a somewhat outrageous way: "Do not imbibe the wine of the Spirit only to get intoxicated, but crave the fullness of the Spirit in every aspect of your life."

14

The Praxis of the Spirit
as Liberation for Ministry

In discussion with South African theologians during a visit to that country in the late 1980s, I was accused on several occasions of espousing a kind of "liberation theology." My use of the word *praxis*, combined with an emphasis on doing theological reflection in the context of the work of the Holy Spirit, raised their suspicions.

I discovered that any theology that raised questions about the practice of apartheid was viewed as liberation theology by many who were defending the concept on theological and biblical grounds. Thankfully, a significant paradigm shift has now occurred among many theologians and church leaders in South Africa today so that the dismantling of apartheid is not only part of a political process but is also the result of a new theological hermeneutic.

The concept of praxis, of course, has become associated with a quasi-Marxist component of some contemporary liberation theology. In this book, I use the concept of praxis more in the tradition of Aristotle, who defined the word as action, taking into account the *telos*, or goal and purpose, of the act. In biblical theology, it is not the *telos* of a historical or human process that constitutes the goal of praxis, but the *eschaton*, or final revelation of God in history through the coming of Christ.

We need not look to the situation in South Africa, however, to discover points of contention and confrontation where the praxis of the Spirit appears to collide with deeply entrenched traditions and theological convictions. In our contemporary situation, for example, the issue of the role of women in ministry, just to mention one instance, can be viewed as a critical matter of biblical interpretation where both a vision of the Spirit's leading and the context of the Spirit's ministry demand a new theological paradigm.

Before we plunge into such an exercise, let us explore a biblical incident where the praxis of the Spirit required a revisioning of a traditional theological paradigm.

Revisioning and Rethinking
Our Theological Paradigm

Theology must be as contextual as it is metaphysical, and it must be as visual as it is cerebral. Another way of putting it is to say that theological reflection must be done in the context of the Spirit's ministry in the world. Theological reflection must also be a "way of seeing" as well as a way of thinking. Let me give an example.

When Peter was visiting in the house of Simon in the seaside village of Joppa, he went up on the roof to pray while waiting for a meal to be prepared. He fell into a trance, and had a vision of a large sheet being lowered with all kinds of animals on it, both clean and unclean. A voice from heaven said, "Get up Peter; kill and eat." But Peter protested. "By no means, Lord; for I have never eaten anything that is profane or unclean." The voice came again, "What God has made clean, you must not call profane" (Acts 10:9–15).

One might account for this vision by the fact that Peter was hungry and that this stimulated his vision. But we are told that immediately when he awakened from the trance, there was a knock on the door, and servants of Cornelius, a Roman centurion who lived in nearby Caesarea, were there asking for Peter. It seems that Cornelius, too, had received a vision in which he was instructed by an angel to send for Peter in order to receive a message from God. For Cornelius, while a Roman soldier, was also a devout man who "prayed constantly to God" (Acts 10:1–8).

The scene now shifts to the house of Cornelius in Caesarea, where Peter said to Cornelius, "You yourselves know that it is unlawful for a Jew to associate with or to visit a Gentile; but God has shown me that I should not call anyone profane or unclean. So when I was sent for, I came without objection" (10:28–29). As Peter began to proclaim the ministry of Jesus under the power of the Spirit, his death, and his resurrection, the Holy Spirit came upon all who heard this good news. With such compelling evidence before him, Peter immediately baptized Cornelius and his household (10:34–48).

It is difficult for us to grasp the significance of this "paradigm shift" in Peter's theology without understanding both the context and the visual perspective. God prepared Peter through the vision by presenting him with what I might call a "visual parable." In much the same way as Jesus attempted to portray the true nature of the kingdom of God by placing a child in the midst of his followers (Matt. 18:1–5), the Spirit of Jesus placed before Peter a visual object that shifted his theological focus from the law to the giver of the law. "What God has made clean, you must not call profane."

But the context was also an important factor in this paradigm shift. Despite his earlier theological training, Peter was obedient to the vision and put himself in the context of the Spirit's ministry to the Gentile household of Cornelius. When Peter confronted the evidence of the Spirit's presence upon these Gentiles, Peter not only made an exception in this case, he made a fundamental shift in his way of thinking, and baptized the uncircumcised Gentiles!

Of course he was challenged for this action by the "theologians in residence" when he returned to Jerusalem! His defense was not based on clever exegetical reading of the Scriptures, but on the compelling praxis of the Spirit revealed through his ministry of witness to the resurrection power of Jesus. Recounting the promise of Jesus, Peter told them, "And I remembered the word of the Lord, how he had said, 'John baptized with water, but you will be baptized with the Holy Spirit.' If then God gave them the same gift that he gave us when we believed in the Lord Jesus Christ, who was I that I could hinder God? When they heard this, they were silenced. And they praised God, saying, 'Then God has given even to the Gentiles the repentance that leads to life'" (Acts 11:16–18).

As a matter of fact, Peter later appeared to have recanted this conversion to a theology of freedom through the Holy Spirit under the influence of the leaders of the church in Jerusalem. This led to his formidable opposition to Paul's ministry at a later time (cf. Gal. 2:11–21).

Paul also had his encounter with the Spirit of Jesus on the Damascus road, and through the praxis of the Spirit's ministry among the Gentiles developed a theology of liberation from the rigid confinement of legal Judaism. Paul's liberation theology, however, was grounded in the praxis of the Spirit, not in historical processes and sociopolitical agendas. It is by "the law of the Spirit of life in Christ Jesus" that we are set free from the law of sin and death, argued Paul. "For all who are led by the Spirit of God are children of God" (Rom. 8:2, 14).

Which Century Is
Normative for Our Theology?

I have suggested that theological reflection is best done where both vision and context inform the interpretation and application of biblical truth. The incident with Peter in the house of Cornelius provided one example of how this was done in the first century.

"Which century is determinative as a context for our understanding of biblical truth?" I ask my students, who are all seminary graduates and practicing pastors. Without fail they respond, "the first century, of

course." They remind me that biblical scholars go to great lengths to recover contextual factors in the period in which the Bible was written in order to aid in our understanding of it.

That is well and good. Accurate exegesis of Scripture requires cultural
and contextual factors as well as linguistic analysis. We are told that
in ancient times where fire was scarce, to give someone burning coals
to carry back to their residence in a basket on top of their head was a
good thing to do. With this information, we can read the proverb quite
differently: "If your enemies are hungry, give them bread to eat; and
if they are thirsty, give them water to drink; for you will heap coals of
fire on their heads, and the Lord will reward you" (Prov. 25:21–22).
Heaping coals of fire is a friendly and neighborly thing to do, even to an
enemy!

Does this mean that the context of first-century Christianity is normative
for our understanding of what it means to live and minister according to
biblical truth? Not at all, as I hope to show. Look at figure 16 (remember that
theological reflection must be visual as well as metaphysical!).

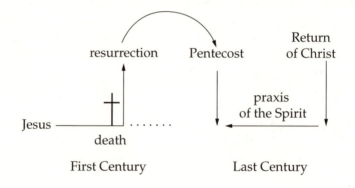

Figure 16

The Spirit that comes to the church comes out of the future, not the past.
The presence of the Spirit is the anticipation of the return of Christ. Paul
makes this clear when he writes to the church at Ephesus reminding them
that in receiving the Holy Spirit they were "marked with the seal of the
promised Holy Spirit; this is the pledge of our inheritance toward redemption as God's own people, to the praise of his glory" (Eph. 1:13–14).
The "pledge" is literally "the first installment, or the "down payment"

(Gr., *arrhabon*) on the inheritance promised as the eschatological fulfillment of God's promise.

When Christ returns to bring to consummation this pledge made by the
gift of the Holy Spirit, it will be the "last century." The Spirit is thus
preparing the people of God for this "last century." While the first century
of the church is normative for the revelation of Christ as the incarnation
of God and the redemption of humans from sin and death, the return of
the same Christ and the resurrection from the dead constitute the normative praxis of the Spirit.

If this century should be the century in which Christ returns and this
age comes to an end, then this will be the "last century." If this return does
not occur until the next century, then that will be the "last century." The
praxis of the ministry of the Holy Spirit can be understood in light of that
which God desires to become a reality at the end, not merely to replicate
that form of ministry during the first century.

This is the perspective that Paul had even during the "first century." He
looked toward the coming of Christ as the final word of approval on his
own teaching and ministry. While the historical Jesus and the cross were
central to Paul's theology of redemption and creation, the Spirit of the resurrected and coming Christ was normative for interpreting the past events
in light of the coming ones.

This was the argument Paul used in defending his own apostolic authority in the face of those who claimed historical precedence based on their relation to Jesus of Nazareth: "It is the Lord who judges me. Therefore do not pronounce judgment before the time, before the Lord comes, who will bring to
light the things now hidden in darkness and will disclose the purposes of the
heart. Then each one will receive commendation from God" (1 Cor. 4:4–5).

Eschatological Preference
and Historical Precedence

The early Christians used the principle of historical precedence to find
a replacement for Judas. As there were originally twelve disciples, so there
must be twelve apostles following the resurrection. As these were all male,
so gender was thought to be a criterion for apostleship after the resurrection as well. Only those who had been followers of Jesus from his baptism
to his crucifixion were eligible, according to historical precedence (Acts
1:21–22). Regardless of what one makes out of the selection of Matthias by
lot as the replacement for Judas, it is clear that the Holy Spirit used the criterion of eschatological preference rather than historical precedence in
calling Saul of Tarsus to be an apostle!

If the same Holy Spirit is active in the world today as then, should we not expect the praxis of the Spirit in our day to operate with the same freedom?

From the theological paradigm outlined above, we should expect that the Spirit will more and more prepare the church to be the church that Christ desires to see when he returns, not the one that he left in the first century. Until we have made this theological paradigm shift we are in danger of forcing the Spirit into the constraint of historical and traditional precedence, as some in the early church attempted to do.

With the first-century church largely bound by its understanding of the traditional role of women in society and the synagogue, for example, we are not surprised to discover first-century Christianity in conflict over the role of women in the ministry of the church. Indeed, though Pentecost itself brought forth a vision and praxis of ministry that was only anticipated in the Old Testament, it never was fully realized in the first-century church.

When the Spirit came upon both men and women in the upper room on the day of Pentecost, Peter rightly concluded that the prophetic utterance of Joel had come to pass: "In the last days it will be, God declares, that I will pour out my Spirit upon all flesh, and your sons and your daughters shall prophesy, and your young men shall see visions, and your old men shall dream dreams. Even upon my slaves, both men and women, in those days I will pour out my Spirit; and they shall prophesy" (Acts 2:17–18).

In this case, eschatological preference was seen to prevail over historical precedence. Did the first-century church succeed in carrying out the eschatological agenda of the Holy Spirit? Hardly, even though Paul labored valiantly to bring it about. In the end, he had to make concessions due to expediency, fully assured that the Spirit would lead the church beyond what even he was able to see in his lifetime.

At critical points, Paul placed theological anchor points for this eschatological preference, such as the one in the third chapter of his letter to the Galatians: "As many of you as were baptized into Christ have clothed yourselves with Christ. There is no longer Jew or Greek, there is no longer slave or free, there is no longer male and female; for all of you are one in Christ Jesus" (Gal. 3:27–28).

While he permitted the circumcision of Timothy (Acts 16:3) out of expediency, he refused to have Titus circumcised (Gal. 2:3) as a sign of liberation from this historical and physical sign of membership in the covenant community. While he apparently restricted the role of women in the church at Ephesus (1 Timothy 2), he openly acknowledged the ministry of Lydia in the church at Philippi, of Phoebe, a *diakonos,* and of Junia (apparently a woman) who was "prominent among the apostles" (Rom. 16:1, 7).

Paul allowed for the eschatological preference of the Holy Spirit where it could be implemented without causing disorder and confusion in the church. Giving way to expediency where it was necessary for the ministry in special situations apparently was not considered by Paul to establish a principle and precedent for all time. To make what was merely expedient normative would have supplanted the eschatological freedom of the Spirit of Jesus to prepare the church for the last century. Regarding circumcision, Titus represented what was normative, not Timothy. With regard to the role of women in church leadership and apostolic ministry, Lydia and Junia represent what is normative, not the women in the church at Ephesus.

In figure 17 I have attempted to depict the liberation that occurred through the death and resurrection of Christ, with the praxis of the Spirit following Pentecost. Here again we see the *ex nihilo* that separates historical and natural determinism from the creative and liberating power and grace of God.

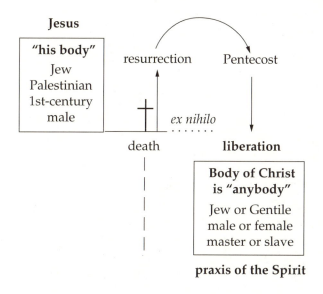

Figure 17

Note, in particular, the specific limitation represented by the physical body of Jesus as the incarnation of God. Jesus was a circumcised Jewish male, speaking his mother tongue of Hebrew (or Aramaic) and possibly Greek, in a first-century Palestinian cultural context. With the death of Jesus, all of these limiting factors were "put to death," so to speak. Though chosen by God as the temporal form in which the revelation of the Word occurred, these biological, cultural, and historical forms came to an end on the cross. In the resurrection we have the continuity of the person of Jesus without the continuation of these factors.

Whereas Jesus was a Jew, "anybody," Jew or Gentile, can now be gifted with the Spirit. In conformity to tradition and practice, the twelve disciples were male. Following the gift of the Spirit at Pentecost, "anybody," male or female, can now be anointed with the Spirit of Jesus for ministry. How do we know this? Because the praxis of the Holy Spirit in the church following Pentecost provided the context for the new theological paradigm.

It is worth noting that the action of the eleven men, in selecting a replacement for Judas following the resurrection and ascension of Jesus preceded Pentecost! Anxious to establish their own credentials and to maintain historical continuity, they probably were premature. When Jesus took leave of his followers, he instructed them to "wait there for the promise of the Father," not to develop criteria for leadership and lay down administrative guidelines!

But Some Will Ask!

But some will ask: "Does this mean that we are free to justify *everything* that claims to be done in the name of the Spirit?"

I have thought of that, too! Does eschatological preference mean that there is nothing normative in the history of divine revelation as given to us in the Bible? If that were the case, we would be close to spiritual anarchy, a situation not uncommon in some movements found within Christianity today. Let me attempt to answer the question this way.

As nearly as I can see, for every case in which eschatological preference was exercised by the Spirit in the New Testament church, there was a biblical *antecedent* for what appeared to be revolutionary and new.

For example, Paul's argument in support of treating circumcision as no longer necessary was not based on the visitation of the Spirit upon uncircumcised Gentiles alone. When Paul faced the reality of the Spirit's praxis in this context, he looked again at the Scriptures and found an antecedent for his position in the case of Abraham. Within the tradition of the Jews following Abraham and Moses, there was no precedent for allowing uncircumcised males to enjoy the full privileges reserved for the people of promise, i.e., descendants of Abraham, Isaac, and Jacob. This was the position taken by those Christian Jews who opposed Paul.

In going back to the story of Abraham, however, Paul discovered that it was *before* Abraham was circumcised that he received the promise and was declared righteous before God (Gen. 15:6; 17:10). "Faith was reckoned to Abraham as righteousness," Paul reminded his readers. "How then was it reckoned to him? Was it before or after he had been circumcised? It was not after, but before he was circumcised" (Rom. 4:9–10; cf. Galatians 3). Paul thus found the biblical antecedent for the Spirit's ministry with the Gentiles.

Role of women [handwritten margin note]

The case of the role of women in the church is similar. When the Holy Spirit set aside certain women for ministry, including that of diaconal and apostolic leadership, a biblical antecedent could be found for women who served God in the Old Testament. While these cases were exceptional and did not set a historical precedent, they nonetheless constitute a biblical antecedent. We need only to recall women who were called prophets, such as Huldah (2 Kings 22:14; 34:22); Deborah (Judg. 4:4–5); Miriam (Ex. 15:20); Noadiah (Neh. 6:14).

There was a strand of tradition in the first-century church that clung to historical precedent as the criterion for establishing the ministry of the church. Those today who seek to justify certain forms of first-century Christian life and ministry rely strongly on the passages in the New Testament that represent this tradition. For those who cling to historical precedent, Pentecost and the power of the Holy Spirit were constrained by institutional forms and doctrinal formulas.

At the same time, there was another movement in the first century that followed the leading of the Holy Spirit and looked back into historical revelation for antecedents rather than precedence. Such a movement was that of the apostle Paul.

I suggest that these represent two theological paradigms, one oriented to first-century Christianity and historical precedent, and the other oriented to eschatological precedence, biblical antecedent, and a vision for the "last-century" church.

Divorce / remarriage [handwritten margin note]

Every pastor will sooner or later be confronted by the issue of divorce and remarriage of divorced persons. On exegetical grounds alone, the issue of whether the Bible ever allows for remarriage, or on what conditions, is a subject of debate and division. Many pastors have chosen to practice mercy and grace in such situations rather than to consign persons who have failed in one marriage to live as a casualty of that failure for the rest of their lives. But how many practice this ministry with an uneasy, if not an anxious, conscience?

I believe that the two theological paradigms developed above provide some basis for making pastoral decisions in some of these cases that are theologically sound and biblically grounded. For example, if a failed marriage and subsequent divorce is considered to be a form of the *ex nihilo* where the grace of God can create a situation where "everything has become new"

(2 Cor. 5:17), one could understand that the praxis of the Holy Spirit frees the individuals from historical determinism and opens them up to eschatological fulfillment of God's promise. A remarriage can then be viewed theologically as a gracious recovery of the biblical *antecedent* that marriage itself is given by God as a possibility within the divine image (Gen. 2:24).

In this case, there is precedent for a remarriage in the divine institution of marriage itself. It would seem that the response of Jesus to the quarrelsome question put to him by the Pharisees was of this kind. "From the beginning of God's creation, 'God made them male and female.'" Jesus then quotes the passage from Genesis 2, "For this reason a man shall leave his father and mother and be joined to his wife, and the two shall become one flesh. . . . Therefore what God has joined together, let no one separate" (Mark 10:2–9).

Cutting through the casuistry that they traced back to Moses, Jesus reminded them that when they dealt with marriage "they dealt with God." And the God that we encounter when dealing with failure and sin is the one who meets us as Jesus Christ, who forgives, renews, and restores. Certainly it was God's intention that those joined together in marriage stay together and that no human principle or law can justify this separation. But as we have seen throughout the Bible, where barrenness and death occur—and tragically, they do—God's grace operates out of this *ex nihilo* to create something entirely new. Historical precedence, even as a consequence of sin, is canceled by eschatological preference.

But What About Homosexuality?

But what about the issue of homosexuality? The question always arises at this point. If the church can accept women as pastors and bless the remarriage of divorced persons through the praxis of the Spirit, can it not also accept the homosexual person and bless homosexual unions where the same Spirit is evident?

Many churches have done just that, setting aside the biblical passages that appear to forbid this sexual practice as being irrelevant in our present understanding of same-sex relationships. At the same time, it should also be noted that many churches refuse to ordain women to pastoral ministry and refuse to bless the remarriage of divorced persons on biblical grounds. For these churches, the refusal to positively affirm homosexual relationships is consistent with their understanding of biblical teaching.

The position advanced in this chapter, however, is that eschatological preference is grounded in the praxis of the Holy Spirit in such a way that God's original purpose for humanity be realized. This means that the church must recognize and affirm the work of the Spirit in the present time in anticipation of the reconciliation of the world to God as promised through Jesus Christ.

The question, But what about the issue of homosexuality? is therefore one that cannot be avoided in this discussion.

The issue of homosexuality is one that requires a book in itself, and many are available. It would take us far beyond the purpose of this book to review this literature and to discuss the exegetical issues involved. My purpose here is to test out the theological paradigm presented in this chapter by responding to the question about homosexuality and the church.

While it might seem logical to assume that the acceptance of women as pastors and blessing the remarriage of divorced persons establishes a precedent, we must remember that it is not precedent that permits the church to move with the freedom of the Spirit, but a biblical antecedent. Where the church has recognized the role of women in ministry it has a biblical antecedent for affirming this as the praxis of the Spirit. Where the church has blessed the remarriage of divorced persons in recognition of the renewing work of the grace of God it has a biblical antecedent for this ministry grounded in marriage itself as part of God's created order. Some who argue that even as the first-century church struggled over the issue of including the Gentiles and finally accepted them, so the church today must accept homosexuals. The issue is not the same, however, for in the case of the Gentiles there is a biblical antecedent in the promise to Abraham, a point that Paul clearly made in his argument to the Galatian church (Gal. 3:8).

What can we say about the issue of homosexuality in this regard? Even if one should dismiss all of the biblical texts that appear to forbid homosexuality (in both the Old and New Testaments) as not relevant for our present understanding of same-sex relationships, we are left with absolute silence from the Bible in this regard. Those who argue for the validity of homosexual relations as fully equivalent to heterosexual relations do, in fact, argue from silence with regard to a biblical view of sexuality.

I have carefully laid the foundation for eschatological preference and the praxis of the Spirit in the need for a biblical antecedent, even without a clear precedent in the biblical tradition. The Bible, however, is not silent regarding human sexuality and the image of God. "So God created humankind in his image, in the image of God he created them; male and female he created them" (Gen. 1:27).

If one reads this text as intending that the image of God be understood to include sexual differentiation as male and female, male or female, as does Karl Barth, among others, then the biblical antecedent is clearly one of heterosexual orientation and practice as God's preference. The antecedent for

homosexual relations does not appear to be found in Scripture. As a consequence, those who argue for the normalizing of homosexual relationships
and full acceptance by the church must do so on other grounds.

The main purpose of this chapter is to present a biblical and theological paradigm for ministry based on the liberating praxis of the Holy Spirit.
I have argued that this is exactly what Peter first experienced in the house
of Cornelius with regard to the Gentiles and what Paul later developed as
the foundation for the church of the first century. The church is created
and re-created through the praxis of the Spirit, liberating it from its conformity to nature and culture and its tendency to institutionalize the
Word. The church is empowered by the Spirit and each member is
equipped for ministry through the gifts of the Spirit, as we shall discover
in the chapter that follows.

The *Charisma* of the
Spirit and the Gift of Ministry

I teach at a theological seminary whose theological stance is defined in its catalogue as "Evangelical Commitment." This is further defined as a fervor that flows out of God's character, the practice of evangelism, engagement with Scripture in the context of the responsible Christian community, Godly living, and confidence in the unity of God's truth.

This theological position is held within an ecumenical context, with a multidenominational faculty, student body, and constituency. As a result, there is a broad continuum of Christian experience and ecclesiological pluralism represented at every level within the framework of an evangelical theological commitment.

Recently, I was asked by a pastor in our Doctor of Ministry program, "Why does a school with an evangelical emphasis not also have a Pentecostal theology? I understand that you have a lot of students and some faculty who have a charismatic Christian experience and many who are members of Pentecostal churches. Is Pentecost but an experience and 'evangelical' only a theology?"

This book is written for that pastor and a multitude of other pastors and Christians who are confounded and confused about the issue of the so-called charismatic experience and the increasing emphasis on the role and gifts of the Spirit.

In the preceding chapters I have attempted to show that the praxis of the Holy Spirit following Pentecost led to a new theological paradigm, where the *charisma* of the Spirit unleashed the power of the resurrected and returning Christ. In this chapter I want to expand on that theme, showing how the *charisma* of the Spirit creates the church as the body of Christ, with each member exercising gifts of ministry.

The Early Church
Was a Charismatic Community

Luke's account of the formation of the community of believers beginning on the day of Pentecost and the days following might better be called the Acts of the Holy Spirit, rather than the Acts of the Apostles! Not only were the one hundred twenty in the upper room empowered to witness by the Holy Spirit, but their message concluded by extending the promise of receiving the same Holy Spirit to all who believed (Acts 2:38). It was Peter, "filled with the Holy Spirit," who boldly witnessed to the religious leaders who were annoyed by the claim that Jesus had been raised from the dead (4:8).

The community of believers began immediately to meet for praise and worship as well as for mutual care and ministry. Some sold their possessions and turned the proceeds over to the apostles for distribution to any who were in need. Ananias, along with his wife, Sapphira, were caught up in this euphoria and sold their property as well. They conspired to hold back some of it for themselves, however, and when questioned about the matter denied their duplicity. When this was discovered, Peter charged them with "lying to the Holy Spirit," and they were both struck dead (5:1–10). Luke adds, "And great fear seized the whole church and all who heard of these things" (5:11). Indeed! Who would not be impressed?

In his book, *The Misunderstanding of the Church*, Emil Brunner says that the key to the first-century church is not historical memory, but the "fellowship of the Spirit." The extraordinary power of this charismatic manifestation is dramatically captured by Brunner's description:

> The Spirit operates with overwhelming revolutionary, transforming results. It manifests itself in such a way as to leave one wondering why and how, and in such a way as to demolish the walls of partition separating individuals from each other. . . . People draw near to the Christian community because they are irresistibly attracted by its supernatural power. . . . There is a sort of fascination which is exercised mostly without any reference to the Word, comparable rather to the attractive force of a magnet or the spread of an infectious disease. Without knowing how it happened, one is already a carrier of the infection.

Allowing for some hyperbole on Brunner's part, it is certainly true that the role of the Spirit in directing and empowering the life and witness of the early Christian community was much in evidence.

In his last sermon before being martyred, Stephen accused those who sought to exterminate the church with "opposing the Holy Spirit" (Acts 7:51). When Simon the magician was converted through Philip's testimony to Jesus, he was so impressed with Peter and John's power to communicate the Holy Spirit that he offered money saying, "Give me also this power so that anyone on whom I lay my hands may receive the Holy Spirit" (Acts 8:19). Peter's response was not nuanced with subtlety. "May your silver perish with you, because you thought you could obtain God's gift with money!" (8:20). Eugene Peterson, in his translation of the New Testament, is more blunt and probably more accurate with respect to the original Greek: "To hell with your money! And you along with it."

It is the Holy Spirit who sent out Saul and Barnabas on the first mission trip from the church at Antioch (Acts 13:2). Paul and his team sought to expand their mission into the region of Phrygia and Galatia, when they had earlier been "forbidden by the Holy Spirit to speak the word in Asia" (16:6). When they attempted to go on into Bithynia, the "Spirit of Jesus did not allow them" (16:7). After completing his third missionary trip, and prior to going to Spain via Rome, Luke says that Paul had "resolved in the Spirit" to go back to Jerusalem with the offering raised for those who were suffering from the famine (19:21).

It is Paul, of course, who developed the basic model of what we call the charismatic community as the form of the church in the first century. In each of the churches that came into being through his ministry, he left certain individuals as overseers through the gift of the Holy Spirit. This is made explicit in the charge he gave to the elders of the church at Ephesus when he made his last visit on the way back to Jerusalem. "Keep watch over yourselves and over all the flock, of which the Holy Spirit has made you overseers, to shepherd the church of God that he obtained with the blood of his own Son" (20:28).

One way of characterizing this early charismatic community is to say that the Spirit does not create offices, but rather ministries. The need for ministry results in the creation of the office. This is apparently what took place when the early church experienced contention and division over the distribution of food to the widows. The apostles solved the problem by setting aside seven men "full of the Spirit" to attend to this ministry. The apostles laid their hands on them, which implies not ordination to an office, but the communication of the Holy Spirit as empowerment to fulfill the ministry (Acts 6:1–6). Their position with the community became more "official," as it were. But, in this case, the office of ministry was grounded in the *charisma* for this ministry. This apparently became the model for establishing the charismatic (Spirit-anointed) order of leadership and ministry for the early church.

The Roman Catholic theologian, Hans Küng, rejects the Pauline authorship of Timothy and Titus as not being consistent with Paul's teaching. He suggests that traditional ecclesiology has given priority to these pastoral epistles, which tend to locate the authority and order of the church in the office and the transmission of authority through the laying on of hands, and neglects the pneumatological and charismatic order of the church. "The rediscovery of the charisms is a rediscovery of specifically Pauline ecclesiology, the importance of which for the problems of Catholicism and ecumenism cannot be overstated. . . . Hence one can speak of a charismatic structure of the Church, which includes but goes far beyond the hierarchical structure of the Church."

Küng's point should not be missed. Despite centuries of division and quarrel over the true form of the church, the hope for unity, while maintaining diversity, is through a charismatic theology of the church as the continuing praxis of the Spirit. This does not mean to play off the so-called free church principle over and against the more connectional and hierarchical forms of church order. It does mean, however, calling the church into repentance where it has subordinated the *charisma* of the Spirit to an ecclesial "chain of command."

In his perceptive essay, "Towards a Contemporary Theology of the Holy Spirit," Wesley Carr reminds us: "If the Church is to witness to this constant relevance of the future for its existence and to the breaking in of that future to the present in the act of God in Christ, then that witness must be substantiated in the structures of the Church. These structures need to be charismatic, i.e., they must reflect the Spirit both as formative force in the community and as representing the judgment of the end upon that community."

Let me share with you an anecdote to make my point. A few years ago I was asked to participate in the ordination of one of my former students. As we met in the pastor's office prior to the service, the presiding pastor explained that when it came time for the candidate to come forward and for the prayer of ordination to be given, all ordained ministers in the congregation would be invited to come up and lay their hands on the candidate along with those of us participating in the service.

At that point, I asked, "Is this not a Baptist church and do you not believe in the priesthood of all believers? Why do you think that only those already ordained have the right or the power to confer the Holy Spirit upon the candidate?"

The pastor's response was, "I have never thought of that. I just understood that this is the way it should be done." With that he said, "You are right, of course. We will invite any who feel led to participate to come up and lay hands on the candidate." When this was done, I noted that several laypersons from the congregation who had already experienced the work of the Spirit in the candidate's life came forward to lay hands on her.

Here was a church whose own theological position concerning the ministry of the church was obscured by its conformity to a practice no doubt borrowed from a more presbyterial or episcopal practice! The need to do things with ecclesial propriety is often more compelling than authentic theological reflection concerning these practices.

The church begins its repentance by submitting its most cherished position—its polity and book of order!—to an authentic charismatic theology. But this is dangerous, some tell me! Charismatics are chaotic and undisciplined! Well, the apostle Paul thought so too at times, but he urged them to grow up, not give up!

Every Christian is Born Charismatic—Some Never Grow Up!

The reformed theologian Otto Weber—no pentecostal himself!—says, "According to 1 Corinthians 7:7 and 1 Peter 4:10, all members of the Community are charismatics." This is a good point at which to begin.

According to the apostle Paul, every Christian is "charismatic" in the sense of being born into the family of God through the *charisma* of the Spirit. For Paul, the *charisma* of the Spirit is the "birth gift" of every Christian. It is by the Spirit of God that we are given the free gift (*charisma*) of eternal life: "For the wages of sin is death, but the free gift (*charisma*) of God is eternal life in Christ Jesus our Lord" (Rom. 6:23; cf. also, Rom. 5:15–17).

This "birth gift" of the Spirit is common to all in the beginning, for each Christian is born into the body of Christ by the same Spirit. "For just as the body is one and has many members, and all the members of the body, though many, are one body, so it is with Christ. For in the one Spirit we were all baptized into one body—Jews or Greeks, slaves or free—and we were all made to drink of one Spirit" (1 Cor. 12:12–13).

Many, however, do not develop this "birth gift" of the Spirit and thus do not mature as intended. The original "birth gift" of the Spirit, as it brings us to maturity, produces gifts of ministry that are not only necessary for the growth and well-being of the body of Christ, but for the extension of Christ's ministry through each member.

It is the Christ of Pentecost who ascended on high and "gave gifts to his people" (Eph. 4:8). These gifts, Paul went on to say, were to "equip the saints for the work of ministry, for building up the body of Christ, until all of us come to the unity of the faith and of the knowledge of the Son of God, to maturity, to the measure of the full stature of Christ" (4:12–13).

In chapter 13 I suggested that unless empowering precedes equipping, many people who are encouraged to begin to exercise a spiritual gift find that their enthusiasm and motivation wanes. The empowerment comes through the life of Christ that flows through us as the Holy Spirit touches the core of our own spirit. In somewhat the same way as we are touched by the spirit of another and so are moved to respond in friendship and love, so the Spirit of God touches our spirit with the very Spirit of Christ. This is what Pentecost means, not merely power but presence, not only competence to speak in other tongues but a compelling urge to communicate the good news in our own tongue.

We cannot maintain a friendship without renewing the "touch of the spirit" through mutual encounter and sharing. Pentecost is not a once and for all baptism of the Spirit, but life in fellowship and communion with the Spirit. I refer to Wesley Carr again in order to make my point: "The dynamic force within this eschatological community is the Spirit, which creates that community and sustains it and at the same time gives to each person within the community his [or her] own individual personhood. . . . Thus the Spirit becomes for the believing community more the environment in which it lives than an object of its consciousness."

The Holy Spirit is the environment, or context, of community, not merely an object of consciousness! I wish that I could write that on the wall of every church!

There are churches whose environment is stale and sterile, with hardly a breath of the Spirit's presence. One is reminded of a wax museum, where the living and the dead mingle cautiously and circumspectly, so as not to disturb each other.

Other churches are so preoccupied with the Spirit that environmental chaos and confusion reigns, with members competing with one another for "spiritual space" in which to exercise their own gifts. One is reminded of the chaos at Christmas when several youngsters are opening their presents and playing with their toys at the same time!

Spiritual maturity is not evidenced by possessing spiritual gifts, but rather by being possessed by the Spirit in such a way that we are moved toward ministry to others. One of the marks of spiritual maturity is that we are able to sustain our ministry even when it means sacrificing our own needs and pleasure. Ministry, in this sense, is not what follows a gift but what precedes the gift. The *charisma* that makes us "charismatic" is the free gift of the Spirit of Jesus Christ experienced as a community of persons bound to his body.

In the Corinthian church where "gifts" were sought and exercised for their own sake, Paul stresses ministry one to another as the context for their deployment of gifts. Using the metaphor of the human body, Paul writes: "But God has so arranged the body, giving the greater honor to the inferior member, that there may be no dissension within the body, but the members may have the same care for one another. If one member suffers, all suffer together with it; if one member is honored, all rejoice together with it" (1 Cor. 12:24–26).

Paul's magnificent chapter on love follows immediately, demonstrating what this mutual ministry means. Without love, the gifts themselves are noisy, empty, and futile. When he was a child, Paul concludes, he acted in immature and childish ways. In growing up in Christ, he no longer permits such self-indulgence (1 Corinthians 13).

In writing to the church at Ephesus, Paul placed the gifts of Christ to the church in the context of a ministry of "speaking the truth in love." This mutual ministry is practical and precise.

> So then, putting away falsehood, let all of us speak the truth to our neighbors, for we are members of one another. Be angry but do not sin; do not let the sun go down on your anger, and do not make room for the devil. Thieves must give up stealing; rather let them labor and work honestly with their own hands, so as to have something to share with the needy. Let no evil talk come out of your mouths, but only what is useful for building up, as there is need, so that your words may give grace to those who hear. And do not grieve the Holy Spirit of God, with which you were marked with a seal for the day of redemption. Put away from you all bitterness and wrath and anger and wrangling and slander, together with all malice, and be kind to one another, tenderhearted, forgiving one another, as God in Christ has forgiven you. (Eph. 4:25–32).

Recovering the *Charisma* in the Charismatic

The *charisma* of ministry is the "birth gift" of the Spirit and is the basis for empowering the Christian for the exercise of the gifts (*charismata*). Ministry is not something that takes place as a result of acquiring a spiritual gift. The gifts of the Spirit (*charismata*) may be understood as the shaping of the "birth gift" of ministry as applied in a particular context and to meet a particular need.

The literature on acquiring and using spiritual gifts expands with every new publishing year. However, I will cite Hans Küng again, who defined a spiritual gift as "the call of God, addressed to an individual, to a particular ministry in the community, which brings with it the ability to fulfill that ministry."

The *charismata*, says Küng, are everyday, rather than sensational; serviceable, rather than merely miraculous; profane, rather than sacred: that is, not restricted to holy orders, but fully "vocational," related to the entire membership of the body. They are diverse, rather than uniform: that is, there are potentially as many different *charismata* as the needs of the body and the contribution of the members. They are extensive, rather than intensive: that is, rather than being concentrated upon particular positions or people, they are found throughout the membership of the body.

In several of Paul's letters to the churches he reminds them of the importance of developing and exercising their gifts (cf. 1 Corinthians 12; Romans 12; Ephesians 4). Paul is fond of using the analogy of the human body to describe the way in which each member of the church relates to another, and all to the whole. "Now there are varieties of gifts, but the same Spirit; and there are varieties of services, but the same Lord; and there are varieties of activities, but it is the same God who activates all of them in everyone. To each is given the manifestation of the Spirit for the common good" (1 Cor. 12:4–7).

With each of the sections in which Paul lists some of the gifts, we find some duplication and some additions. The consensus among scholars today is that there is no "official" list of gifts that can be constructed by merging the various listings given by Paul. There appear to be as many gifts available to the community as there are needs, with some highlighted in each community according to the ministry focus.

My purpose in this chapter is to stress the *charisma* of the Spirit as the "gift of ministry." In developing one's own ministry, the precise *form* which that ministry will take in any given context will determine the precise *gift* to be given by the Spirit. I have attempted to show that the essential form of the church is charismatic, in the sense that the Holy Spirit is the environment in which the church lives. Each Christian is charismatic in this sense, having received the "birth gift" of the Spirit. This gift is the gift of ministry itself, which is the *charisma* that leads the charismatic toward maturity.

All ministry is Christ's ministry, given to the members of his body as their "birth gift." Some have never unwrapped it! Others have misused and abused it. The church emerges anew in every generation as the Spirit lives and empowers witnesses to Christ's reconciliation of the world to God.

The Church as the
Formation of Christ in the World

The church that emerges with each generation is the church of which I speak, of course. It is the body of Christ comprised of persons who have received the "birth gift" of the Spirit. These are the members of Christ's body who are joined in a community of love by the "one Spirit, one hope, one Lord, one faith and one baptism" of which Paul wrote (Eph. 4:4–5). To paraphrase an old saying, "The Spirit has no grandchildren!" No one is born into the body of Christ by virtue of having Christian parents. No church can transfer entitlement to the body of Christ to the next generation. The "birth gift" of Christ is his Spirit given to each individual who believes and follows him.

The existence of the body of Christ, however, takes place in real time and in the real world. Even the first believers had to have a list of "names and addresses" and a place to gather in order to function effectively. They also had to have clear policies and procedures in order to carry out their mission and preserve a semblance of cohesion and order in their community life. Discipleship includes discipline, and where it is lacking there is a tendency toward chaos and confusion, as it was in the early church and so also today.

While the various forms of institutional life of the church have differed throughout the past two thousand years, one thing is clear: No organism can exist in this world without some form of structure and organization. The body of Christ as an organism has a life in the Spirit that finds embodiment in living persons bound by a common faith. Otto Weber reminds us that "Over against the idea of the Community as an 'institution,' we must chiefly emphasize that the Community does not live from the being and will of a past Christ, but from the existence of the present Christ."

This chapter is not concerned with the forms of the church as an institution, but with the form of Christ in the world. Conformity to Christ rather than to the world, as Paul made clear, is the task of every generation in carrying out the ministry of Christ in the world (Rom. 12:1–2). How to remain conformed to Christ and also live in the real world is the question this chapter addresses.

focus of chapter

Dietrich Bonhoeffer's Thesis

One of the most significant contributions Dietrich Bonhoeffer made to the question of the nature of the church is found in his doctoral dissertation, completed at the University of Berlin when he was but twenty-one years of age. The venerable Karl Barth paid homage to this work many years later when he wrote that Bonhoeffer's dissertation "makes far more instructive and stimulating and illuminating and genuinely edifying reading today than many of the more famous works which have since been written on the problem of the Church. . . . I openly confess that I have misgivings whether I can even maintain the high level reached by Bonhoeffer, saying no less in my own words and context, and saying it no less forcefully, then did this young man so many years ago."

The thrust of Bonhoeffer's thesis, completed in 1926 as *Sanctorum Communio,* was: Christ exists as community (*gemeinde*). In Bonhoeffer's view, the church in Germany by the early part of this century had become a monument to what he called "cultural protestantism." On the one hand it was virtually irrelevant to the everyday life of the average person and, on the other hand, so embedded in the culture as a relic of religious sentimentality that Hitler eventually took it over as a way of strengthening his hold on the psyche of the nation.

Bonhoeffer's concern can be expressed in the form of three questions that represent his theological method:

> *Who* is Jesus Christ?
>   He is the very revelation of God in the form of a human person.
> *Where* is Jesus Christ today?
>   He exists in the social reality of persons gathered as the body
>   of Christ.
> *What* am I to do as a Christian?
>   Follow Christ into the world as a true disciple.

Bonhoeffer followed out the implication of these three questions in his own life. As a leader in the Confessing Church, which renounced Hitler's takeover of the state church, Bonhoeffer put into practice his thesis: Christ exists as community. Later, he saw even that movement falter and fail to take up the cause of those who were persecuted and perishing as part of Hitler's manic quest for power. He then determined that Christ existed in the world as well as in the church and that a true disciple must follow Christ into the world. This he did, and paid for it with his death in April of 1945 at the order of Hitler himself.

While the situation that confronted Bonhoeffer was quite different from our own in many ways, the three questions remain. For they are the questions put by Christ himself, not by Bonhoeffer.

The Form of Christ
in the World

In the parable of the sheep and goats (Matt. 25:31–46), Jesus placed himself in the company of the outcasts, the imprisoned, the poor, the hungry, and the naked. Failure to give food to the hungry, to care for the ones in prison, and to clothe the naked is a failure to minister to Christ himself, Jesus warned.

Bonhoeffer took this quite literally and said, "Everything would be ruined if one were to try to reserve Christ for the Church and to allow the world only some kind of law, even if it were a Christian law. Christ died for the world, and it is only in the midst of the world that Christ is Christ."

This means that the church as an institution does not "possess Christ" on its own. The Christ who is present as the formative life of the church through the Spirit is also present in the world through a kind of "incarnational solidarity" with all humanity. We not only bring Christ to the hungry along with food. In bringing food, we meet the Christ who is already there. How else can we understand the meaning of Jesus' words in the parable?

Thomas Torrance once said, "The Church cannot be in Christ without being in Him as He is proclaimed to men in their need and without being in Him as He encounters us in and behind the existence of every man in his need. Nor can the Church be recognized as His except in that meeting of Christ with Himself in the depth of human misery, where Christ clothed with His Gospel meets with Christ clothed with the desperate need and plight of men."

The "form of Christ" in the world thus becomes the paradigm for the church in the world. This form is not a principle or style to be adopted by an already existing institution, nor is it a "shape" determined by the need of the world. Rather, it is conformity to Christ who is in the world as one who shares in human solidarity as the incarnation of God in human flesh. The form of the church is thus incarnational; not another incarnation, but a continuation of the one incarnate life of God in the form of Jesus Christ.

The church is not formed by its own efforts, nor is it conformed to the world (Romans 12). Rather, the church is conformed to Christ, who "though he was in the form of God, did not regard equality with God as something to be exploited, but emptied himself, taking the form of a slave, being born in human likeness" (Phil. 2:6).

It is not only that the world needs the church in order to have Christ; the church also needs the world in order to know Christ. There is a special kind of solidarity with the world that the church must not break in order to be conformed to Christ.

Barth once said that the church may have to engage in tactical withdrawal from the world, but that it should never engage in strategic withdrawal. The overall strategy of the church is conformity to Christ's coming to the world for the sake of its reconciliation with God. This strategy must never be abandoned, else the world would be left to its own hopeless and fatal plunge into the abyss. A tactic is a particular maneuver within the overall strategy.

Jesus had a clear vision of God's strategy, which meant that he accepted the judgment that came upon the world in order to bear the sins of the world. At various times Jesus engaged in tactical withdrawal, such as the occasion when he left the ministry of teaching and healing to go away with his disciples (Mark 6:30; cf. also, John 8:59). But he never practiced strategic withdrawal.

Listen to the words of Karl Barth:

> Solidarity with the world means that those who are genuinely pious approach the children of the world as such, that those who are genuinely righteous are not ashamed to sit down with the unrighteous as friends, that those who are genuinely wise do not hesitate to seem to be fools among fools, and that those who are genuinely holy are not too good or irreproachable to go down into 'hell' in a very secular fashion. . . . Since Jesus Christ is the Savior of the world, [the church] can exist in worldly fashion, not unwillingly nor with a bad conscience, but willingly and with a good conscience.

But Isn't This Dangerous?

An inner-city church located in an economically and socially blighted area recently created a stir in the community by sponsoring a halfway house on church property for young people in trouble with the law. Despite reasonable attempts at security and supervision, the police, through an undercover agent, discovered that there had been some illegal use of drugs on the part of some of these young people at the halfway house, and made some arrests.

An emergency board meeting was called to consider what action to take in light of the incident and the account was published the next day in the local newspaper.

"How can we allow this kind of program to take place on our church property?" an elder demanded. "Pastor, you pushed this through on the basis that it was an incarnational ministry, though at the time I suspected that this was theological jargon used to cover a secular experiment in social action. Now our church has become an accomplice to illegal activity and has lost its reputation in the community."

"I have no problem with the program itself," another elder said. "But where I draw the line is with the risk that we are taking with these young people in regard to breaking the law. If we can't eliminate that risk then I vote to shut it down."

"I'm not sure where we go from here," the pastor replied. "I think we need to spend some time in prayer over this situation. Meanwhile, let me consult with the police department and see what we can do about additional security."

I have presented just enough of the details for us to use this as a case for theological reflection on what I have said thus far in this chapter.

Barth has suggested that the church must not be too holy to "go down into hell in a very secular fashion," and to do this "willingly and with a good conscience." The church did not appear to be all that willing in its rather radical effort to minister to young persons of dubious moral character, and certainly it is now suffering pangs of conscience over the consequences.

The question is: What determines the conscience of the church? Bonhoeffer would say that it is determined by the command to follow Christ, not by the church's need to preserve its reputation and moral integrity at the expense of others. When he struggled to resolve his own dilemma concerning the conspiracy to remove Hitler, even if it meant killing him, he concluded that his conscience was determined by Jesus Christ and not the law. Thus, he said, the Christian who acts responsibly must be prepared to assume guilt, if necessary.

The elder's concern for the reputation of the church, and his confession that he considered all along that the ministry project was basically secular, indicates a failure to understand that all true ministry in the world is "secular" in the sense that it seeks to recover the true humanity of the world, not to make it religious.

The Pharisees were the "worldly" ones in Jesus' day, who sought through their religion to gain preeminence and power. Jesus warned his disciples against this: "You know that the rulers of the Gentiles lord it over them, and their great ones are tyrants over them. It will not be so among you; but whoever wishes to be great among you must be your servant" (Matt. 20:25–26).

The other elder's concern for the risk involved with regard to becoming an accomplice to illegal activity forces the question as to whether or not this particular project was the right tactic, even though it fit within the strategy of reaching young people where they are in the world. It may be wise to withdraw from this ministry in order to devise a new tactic.

The pastor in this situation apparently persuaded the church to launch a ministry without considering the cost and consequences. His use of incarnational language to justify this particular mission was a wrong use of the concept. The incarnation has to do with the very strategy of the church as it exists in the world so as to make a difference to the world. The pastor used the incarnation to justify a tactic, and when that blew up in his face, he lacked the incarnational strategy to provide leadership at a critical point.

But We Are Not Bonhoeffers!

When I use case situations like this to bring home the point that the church is called to make a difference in the world, not merely to be different from the world, someone usually protests: "But we are not Bonhoeffers, and if I attempted this kind of ministry my church would blow me out of the saddle!"

Fair enough. I have used a controversial case to illustrate the difference between a strategy of encounter with the world and the tactics that one uses. It is extremely important to understand this difference.

The incarnation of God, however, was a divine strategy by which humanity—under sentence of death and with its back turned toward God—could be seized at its most tragic point and brought back within arm's length of the face of God. The strategy was to bring humanity under judgment for the sake of its liberation from the curse of death and its renewal in the image of glory and grace with which it had originally been endowed.

This strategy was no mere tactic to be abandoned when the cost became too high and the risk too great. Paul saw clearly the irrevocable commitment involved in the divine strategy when he said that Jesus, "though he was in the form of God, did not regard equality with God as something to be exploited, but emptied himself, taking the form of a slave, being born in human likeness. And being found in human form, he humbled himself and became obedient to the point of death—even death on a cross" (Phil. 2:6–8).

James Torrance puts it so eloquently that I cannot help but quote him in full:

> Christ does not heal us by standing over against us, diagnosing our sickness, prescribing medicine for us to take, and then going away, to leave us to get better by obeying his instructions—as an ordinary doctor might. No, He becomes the patient! He assumes that very humanity

which is in need of redemption, and by being anointed by the Spirit in our humanity, by a life of perfect obedience, by dying and rising again, for us, our humanity is healed *in him.* We are not just healed "through Christ" because of the work of Christ but "in and through Christ."

No theology of ministry does justice to the biblical witness to Jesus Christ without being solidly grounded in this strategy.

Once this is the fundamental theology by which the church defines its existence in the world, it is then a matter of tactics as to how best to carry through the mandate—to be in the world as Christ is in the world.

The powerlessness and irrelevance of the church is not that it lacks tactical encounter with the world, but that its strategy is one of survival rather than sacrifice, of success rather than service, of reputation rather than responsibility.

Only the evangelical church can be an incarnational church. The evangelical church is not only one that is committed to the gospel of Christ, but one that is empowered by the *charisma* of the Spirit.

The authentic *charisma* that liberates is not the spirit of power, but the Spirit of Christ. An authentic charismatic theology is one that empowers blacks in South Africa to participate in the franchise of full membership in the human race as defined socially, politically, and spiritually. It is a theology that empowers women to have full parity in every structure of society, especially the church and its ministry. It is a theology that empowers the poor, the marginalized, the weak, and the homeless to live meaningful and comfortable lives as human beings created in God's image. An authentic charismatic theology is one that disarms the church of its pride and privilege, causing it to repent and to enact repentance toward God through responsible service toward the world God loves.

Thomas Smail put it well when he said: "The charismatic Christian with his world-affirming approach and his awareness of both the demonic and the prophetic should be among those who can catch the vision. God wants to give local churches structures of relationship that have their roots in the central relationship to himself, but that express themselves horizontally and practically in such a way as to challenge the oppressive structures of society in which the church lives."

When the church is born in every generation, it is always born charismatic, because it is born of the Spirit, or it does not live at all. When the church grows up in Christ it begins to look like Christ. Whether the church knows it or not, the world knows Christ when it truly encounters him. The church is the mirror in which the world sees the face of Christ. The mirror of God is the humanity of Christ, unveiled before the world.

V

The Church's Ministry
to the World
on Behalf of Jesus

17

The Ministry of the Church
as an Apostolic Community

My students are only mildly curious and mostly disinterested in the issue of apostolic authority. "I remember a conversation I had with a Roman Catholic priest a few years ago," one pastor offered. "He was amused by my claim to have apostolic authority based only on the Scripture." "You have several hundred Protestant denominations which disagree with each other over fundamental issues of doctrine and church polity," he said. "What kind of apostolic authority does that represent? Your 'paper pope' has a thousand counterfeits."

"What did you tell him?" I asked.

"I had no good answer to that. I told him that there is only one gospel and if any church is faithful to that gospel it is apostolic, regardless of what other distinctives it claims. He just smiled, and that was the end of the conversation."

Like it or not, the question of the apostolic nature of the church is one that won't go away. In this chapter I will suggest that Christ is the chief apostle and that he continues to have a threefold apostolic ministry, which began in the first century and continues to our present day.

The first-century church is the context for the development of this threefold apostolic ministry. The present (last?) century church is the creative edge for the deployment of Christ's threefold apostolic ministry in its mission to the world.

Confusion, Crisis, and Controversy

The Corinthian church leaders were anxious and troubled. The meeting with some emissaries from James, the head of the church at Jerusalem, had just concluded. "This Paul that you look to as your pastor/founder of the church is not even an apostle," they had charged. "He was in opposition to us in Jerusalem even after the resurrection of Jesus, and we have never authorized or appointed him to an apostolic office. We are the true apostles, because we are the continuation of the apostolic ministry Jesus began with his disciples. Your church has no apostolic foundation."

The dialogue is fiction, of course, but the situation is authentic. The undermining of Paul's apostolic credentials produced a crisis in the Corinthian church. As a result, Paul apparently made a visit that he describes as painful (2 Cor. 2:2), and followed it up with a letter that he later regretted, in part at least (7:8). As it turned out, he sent Titus to Corinth in order to determine the church's response rather than make another "painful visit." When Titus brought back word of their change of heart, Paul rejoiced and expressed his gratitude in what we now have as the second letter to the church at Corinth (7:9, 13).

This was not the first time nor the last that Paul had to deal with those who followed him from place to place, seeking to destroy his work by challenging his apostolic credentials (cf. Galatians). The fact that he prevailed is indicated by the volume of his letters, which comprise the core of the New Testament theology of the church and its mission.

Fifteen hundred years later, the church again faced a crisis over apostolic authority as the Reformers broke free from the medieval church and its claim to apostolic succession through the papal office at Rome. For the medieval church apostolic authority meant having "one voice" when it came to interpreting the mind of Christ concerning what the church teaches in matters of doctrine and ethics. The authority with which this voice spoke was grounded in the transmission of apostolic authority from the first apostles to the present time through historical succession to the papal office. At the same time, the one who occupied the "chair of Peter" was later held to be infallible when speaking *ex cathedra*—from the chair of Peter and as the vicar of Christ on earth.

In the Protestant view, to be apostolic meant conformity to the teaching of the apostles as contained in the inspired and infallible Scriptures rather than to an infallible ecclesial office. Luther took his stand on Scripture alone and claimed full apostolic authority for the church, which was true to the gospel as delivered by the first-century apostles.

Karl Barth represents the contemporary Protestant consensus with regard to the apostolic nature of the church when he says:

> [T]he apostolic community means concretely the community which hears the apostolic witness of the New Testament, which implies that of the Old, and recognizes and puts this witness into effect as the source and norm of its existence. The apostolic Church is the Church which accepts and reads the Scriptures in their specific character as the direct attestation of Jesus Christ alive yesterday and today. . . . The Church is apostolic and therefore catholic when it exists on the basis of Scripture and in conformity to it.

I wonder why Barth did not say that the church is apostolic when it exists on the basis of Christ rather than Scripture? Scripture carries direct attestation to Jesus Christ, Barth has said. And he added, "Jesus Christ alive yesterday and today."

Scripture is our authority for the gospel that the first-century apostles taught, it is true. The foundation has been laid in this apostolic witness to Jesus Christ. But it is the cornerstone, not the foundation, that determines the apostolic nature and mission of the church.

Paul's view of the apostolic nature of the Christian church was clearly set forth in his letter to the church at Ephesus. "So then you are no longer strangers and aliens, but you are citizens with the saints and also members of the household of God, built upon the foundation of the apostles and prophets, with Christ Jesus himself as the cornerstone" (Eph. 2:19–20).

The author of the book of Hebrews echoes this same theme in speaking of Jesus as the apostle and high priest of our confession. "Therefore, brothers and sisters, holy partners in a heavenly calling, consider that Jesus, the apostle and high priest of our confession, was faithful to the one who appointed him, just as Moses also 'was faithful in all God's house'" (Heb. 3:1–2).

Christ, the Living Cornerstone

Jesus likened himself to the cornerstone that God had chosen. When his authority was questioned by those who were presumed to be guardians of the temple and the law, he replied: "Have you never read in the scriptures: 'The stone that the builders rejected has become the cornerstone; this was the Lord's doing, and it is amazing in our eyes'?" (Matt. 21:42; Ps. 118:22–23).

As the first apostle, Jesus is the cornerstone for the apostolic foundation. Indeed, after his resurrection and ascension Peter speaks of Christ as the "living cornerstone" and of members of the church as "living stones." "Come to him, a living stone, though rejected by mortals yet chosen and precious in God's sight, and like living stones, let yourselves be built into a spiritual house, to be a holy priesthood, to offer spiritual sacrifices acceptable to God through Jesus Christ" (1 Pet. 2:4–5).

With the resurrection of Christ, the early church was realigned to the living cornerstone, with the church comprised of "living stones." We might picture Christ as both the historical cornerstone of the original apostles as well as the contemporary "living cornerstone" of the church (see figure 18).

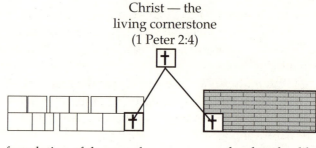

Christ — the
living cornerstone
(1 Peter 2:4)

foundation of the apostles

the church—like
living stones
(1 Peter 2:5)

ex nihilo

Figure 18

The cornerstone connects the church to its apostolic foundation, as figure 18 shows. At the same time, the risen Christ is the cornerstone of the church in every generation.

With the death of Jesus, we see the apostolic authority of the original twelve falter and fade away. Only after the resurrection of Jesus and his recommissioning of them as apostles, when he met with them behind closed doors, were they able to sustain their apostolic role (cf. John 20:19–23). There is an *ex nihilo* between the original twelve and the post-resurrection apostolic community. This destroyed the possibility of establishing apostolic authority on the period prior to the crucifixion of Jesus, a fact that Paul used in defending his own apostolic authority.

The recommissioning of the original twelve (minus Judas, of course) established the apostolic foundation of the early church. But this continuity was established solely by the "common cornerstone," which is Jesus Christ, the crucified, risen, and coming Lord.

The significance of viewing Christ as the living cornerstone is vital to our discussion of the apostolic nature of the contemporary church. The apostolic nature of the church is dependent upon the cornerstone for its identity and authority. As the living cornerstone, Christ has a threefold ministry that connects the church to its first-century apostolic foundation, to the gospel of Christ's resurrection, and, thirdly, to the risen and coming Christ present through the power of the Holy Spirit.

The Threefold Apostolic
Ministry of Christ

The *first* form of Christ's apostolic ministry is that of the historical Jesus who, as the first apostle, gathered the twelve around him and invested in them his own apostolic authority. This is what I call Christ's incarnational apostolic ministry.

The *second* is that of the resurrected Christ who gathered the eleven disciples and reconstituted them as his apostles. This is the gospel that Peter preached on the day of Pentecost and that Paul received directly from the risen Christ. This is what I call Christ's empowering apostolic ministry.

The *third* is the apostolic ministry of the Christ who will return and who is returning through the presence and power of the Holy Spirit. This is what I call Christ's transformational apostolic ministry.

This threefold apostolic ministry is, first of all, that of the historical Christ (incarnational); second, it is that of the risen and proclaimed Christ (kerygmatic); and third, it is that of the coming Christ (eschatological). These three are simultaneous and always contemporary, for it is Jesus Christ who is the living cornerstone, the same "yesterday and today and forever" (Heb. 13:8).

I picture it something like this:

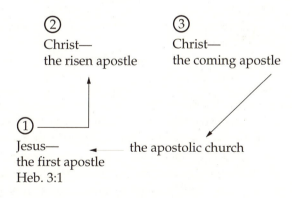

Figure 19

We can read figure 19, which depicts the threefold apostolic ministry of Christ, through the sequence of Christ's life, death, resurrection, and ascension as recounted in the biblical narrative.

At the baptism of Jesus the Spirit descended upon him and a voice came from heaven, "This is my Son, the Beloved, with whom I am well pleased" (Matt. 4:17). This was repeated on the Mount of Transfiguration: "This is my Son, the Beloved; with him I am well pleased: listen to him!" (Matt. 17:5). The apostolic authority of the historical Jesus was conferred upon him by God the Father.

In this first form of apostolic ministry, we see the *incarnational ministry* of Christ as one sent into the world by the Father taking up the cause of those who are oppressed and under the bondage of sin.

Following Jesus' resurrection from the dead, Paul writes of the "gospel concerning his Son, who was descended from David according to the flesh and was declared to be the Son of God with power according to the spirit of holiness by resurrection from the dead, Jesus Christ our Lord, through whom we have received grace and apostleship. . . . " (Rom. 1:3–4). The gospel of resurrection had apostolic authority because it was grounded in the mighty work of God in raising Jesus from the dead.

As the resurrected Lord, the apostolic ministry of Jesus is the power of God unto salvation for all who receive the Spirit of the resurrected Lord. "But in fact Christ has been raised from the dead, the first fruits of those who have died. . . . If the Spirit of him who raised Jesus from the dead dwells in you, he who raised Christ from the dead will give life to your mortal bodies also through his Spirit that dwells in you" (1 Cor. 15:20; Rom. 8:11).

In this second form of apostolic ministry, we see the *empowering ministry* of Christ as one present in power through the proclamation of his Lordship over sin and death.

As the risen and ascended Lord who is coming, Christ's apostolic authority reaches back into the present time as the creative power for the church's apostolic ministry in every generation.

> Think of us in this way, as servants of Christ and stewards of God's mysteries. Moreover, it is required of stewards that they be found trustworthy. But with me it is a very small thing that I should be judged by you or by any human court. I do not even judge myself. I am not aware of anything against myself, but I am not thereby acquitted. It is the Lord who judges me. Therefore do not pronounce judgment before the time, before the Lord comes, who will bring to light the things now hidden in darkness and will disclose the purposes of the heart. Then each one will receive commendation from God. (1 Cor. 4:1–5)

Paul viewed the coming Christ as his apostolic authority who, by virtue of his Holy Spirit, was already at work in transforming the old into the new.

Following Pentecost, Paul considers Jesus to be the apostle through whom all apostolic ministry is released in the world by the Holy Spirit.

"Now the Lord is the Spirit, and where the Spirit of the Lord is, there is freedom" (2 Cor. 3:17). The Holy Spirit is the "advance work" of the coming Christ, leading the church in its mission into the world and equipping the church through all of its members for the apostolic ministry of Christ.

In this third form of apostolic ministry, we see the *transforming ministry* of Christ as one creating the new patterns and paradigms for ministry in the church's mission to the world. "We have the mind of Christ," said Paul (1 Cor. 2:16). With full assurance of Christ's continuing apostolic ministry, Paul welcomed the uncircumcised into the church upon evidence of the Spirit's ministry and set the church free from legalistic and crippling constraints where he saw the Spirit bringing gifts of grace to each member.

Christ's threefold apostolic ministry will continue until the Kingdom reign is completed. When that is accomplished, Christ will hand over the Kingdom to the Father and his apostolic commission will be completed. As Paul anticipates the end of the age, he envisions the apostolic ministry of Christ coming to a close. In the sequence of final events, the coming of Christ will bring about the resurrection of all who belong to him. "Then comes the end, when he hands over the kingdom to God the Father, after he has destroyed every ruler and every authority and power. . . . When all things are subjected to him, then the Son himself will also be subjected to the one who put all things in subjection under him, so that God may be all in all" (1 Cor. 15:24, 28).

A Dynamic View of Christ's Continuing Apostolic Ministry

Earlier in this book I suggested that historical precedence gives way to eschatological preference. While there must be a biblical antecedent for the contemporary work of the Holy Spirit, it may be that there is no clear historical precedent. In the case of the admission of uncircumcised Gentiles through baptism into the body of Christ, for example, Paul found a clear biblical antecedent in the promise given to Abraham before he was circumcised.

This is how we are to understand the apostolic ministry of Christ. The historical precedence of the twelve disciples was set aside by the eschatological preference of the resurrected and coming Christ through the empowering and transforming act of the Holy Spirit in the life of Saul of Tarsus.

The impasse created in the discussion between my student and his Roman Catholic friend was because of their shared static views of apostolic authority. The traditional Protestant view looks back to the original message of the apostles, which is "frozen in time." When it is "thawed" in attempts to make it relevant for today's church it melts away into a thousand rivers of interpretation.

The traditional Roman Catholic view looks back to the original office of apostolic authority and locks the door with only one key handed down from generation to generation. Attempts to duplicate the key result in ecclesial scuffles at the door. Meanwhile, windows are being cut into the side walls faster than they can be patched up.

The Protestant theologians scoff at the idea of an "office" of apostolic authority while Roman Catholics scorn the spectacle of the "paper pope" in the hands of every maverick minister and television preacher.

The threefold apostolic ministry of Christ provides us with a more dynamic view of Christ's apostolic ministry. Here the focus is not so much on the historical foundation, though it includes that element. In the same sense, the apostolic message of Christ's resurrection is not the main focus, though it is included. The true emphasis is upon Christ himself as the living and coming Apostle revealed through the Holy Spirit.

Wolfhart Pannenberg has contributed much to this discussion with his emphasis on the eschatological nature of the apostolic life of the church, when he says that the first-century apostolic order of the church may not be determinative for our present century. "That which was apostolic then may be irrelevant today or may even be a hindrance to our apostolic tasks. This insight enables the church to be free to live in its own historicity as opposed to that of the apostolic age and still remain in continuity with the mission of the apostles."

I suggest that Pannenberg's thesis can only be understood in light of the threefold apostolic ministry of Christ. The same Christ who chose the twelve is the Christ who chose Saul of Tarsus rather than relying on the early Christians to establish their own criteria based on historical precedence. The same Christ who chose only males as his disciples, but who treated females as having equal dignity and worth, anointed women with the Holy Spirit, after Pentecost, for apostolic authority (e.g. the case of Junia, or Julia, Rom. 16:7).

Those appointed in the early church for leadership and ministry included apostles as well as prophets and teachers (1 Cor. 12:27–29). There is thus biblical antecedent for the ministry of apostolic leadership in the church of this century.

What might one expect from this kind of dynamic apostolic ministry as the continuing ministry of Christ through the Holy Spirit?

Certainly it would be incarnational, which is the first form of Christ's threefold ministry. This means that the church will assume forms and methods that are relevant to contemporary human social and cultural forms, critically challenging them while creatively using them to touch the lives of people.

Certainly such a dynamic apostolic ministry would be empowering, as the second form of Christ's threefold ministry. This means that the church will carry out a ministry that is a direct challenge to the powers of this age that hold people captive. The kerygma of resurrection is not only a message proclaimed but it is a power enacted, as Paul reminded the Christians at Thessalonica: "For we know, brothers and sisters beloved by God, that he has chosen you, because our message of the gospel came to you not in word only, but also in power and in the Holy Spirit and with full conviction; just as you know what kind of persons we proved to be among you for your sake" (1 Thess. 1:4–5).

Certainly such a dynamic apostolic ministry would be transforming, as the third form of Christ's threefold ministry. This means that the church will penetrate and seek to renovate social and political structures that dehumanize persons while, at the same time, will create humanizing and liberating conditions for those who are bruised and broken.

Let me be more specific.

Those who took leadership within the South African Dutch Reformed church in defining apartheid as sinful and heretical demonstrated apostolic ministry even at great cost to themselves, in some instances. The resulting transformation of the political structure that has begun is due in no small measure to the apostolic courage and commitment of a few among the many. For the first time in centuries, the Reformed church in South Africa has begun to move beyond its static confession of an apostolic foundation into the liberating and creative power of an apostolic ministry.

In the light of domestic violence and abuse that pervades the fundamental structures of marriage, family, and home, even with the church, dynamic apostolic ministry will mean the exposure and the transformation of the structures that perpetuate such evil. The incarnational apostolic ministry of Jesus is not a first-century historical monument, but it is a contemporary humanizing movement that will not tolerate abuse for the sake of preserving traditional forms of privilege and power.

When Christ's apostolic ministry is present, the institutional church itself will be called to account for polity and practice that preserve its own tradition as a barricade against change. The third form of Christ's apostolic ministry is one of transformation. Not everything that claims to be new or novel is apostolic, but there is no apostolic ministry where there is no spirit open to change as the church navigates its way in the modern world.

To be apostolic the church must *be* a mission, not merely *have* a mission. The apostolic Christ calls to the church from the side of the world. The church *sends* but Christ *summons*. That is what it is to be an apostolic church.

18

The Ministry of the Church as a Community in Mission

Those who gathered in the home of Prisca and Aquila near the outskirts of Rome were buzzing with excitement. The word had already spread through the home churches scattered throughout the city. "Phoebe has arrived from Corinth with a letter from Paul," Prisca informed the group when they were all assembled. "She is with us this evening to share news of our brothers and sisters in Cenchrae and will explain the purpose of Paul's epistle and leave it with us for further study" (cf. Rom. 16:1–2).

"Paul asked me to be sure to share with you his comments at the end of his letter," Phoebe began. "Though he has been hindered many times from coming to visit you due to his extensive commitments to preach in Asia, Macedonia, and Achaia, he is eager to visit and, as he writes, will come directly following his trip to Jerusalem to personally deliver the money collected for those who have suffered famine" (cf. 15:22–29).

"You will note that he has plans to go to Spain to preach the gospel there," Phoebe continued. "Paul confessed to me that he wanted to be sure that you would understand his reasons for spending some time with you here in Rome before going on to Spain. He would not come right out and say it, but I know that he will need some assistance in making this venture. Let me read you what he wrote:

> But now, with no further place for me in these regions, I desire, as I have for many years, to come to you when I go to Spain. For I do hope to see you on my journey and to be sent on by you, once I have enjoyed your company for a little while. (Rom. 15:23–24; cf. Acts 20:2–3; 1 Cor. 15:25–27; 16:1–5; 2 Cor. 8).

"You well know," Phoebe added, "he could go directly to Spain on his own as he has done elsewhere. He has worked to pay his own way before and is quite willing to do it again. He would prefer to be free to devote full time to this ministry, and thus would deeply appreciate some financial assistance from the church at Rome. This is what he means when he wrote, 'to be sent on by you;' and note that he repeated that phrase so it has a special meaning" (15:24, 29).

"There will be no problem with that," Rufus responded. "We all know what sacrifices Paul has made, and there would be no church here in Rome if it were not for his ministry. Just look around and see how many of us have been directly affected by his life and ministry!"

"This is what Paul was afraid of!" replied Phoebe. "He did not want his letter to be only an appeal for money. He could have written that in a page or two. You will notice when you have time to study his letter that he places his request in the context of a theological treatise on the gospel of God's mission into the world through his Son, Jesus Christ. I have read the letter many times on my journey to Rome, and I have never heard him explain the relation of the gospel to our mission in the world so profoundly and eloquently. I have the feeling that this is one letter you will want to keep and study over and over again."

"I see what you mean," Prisca said. "It always seemed to me that Rome was the center of the world and when we arrived here that the mission was over. Now I am beginning to understand that we cannot be the community of Christ without being a community of mission. In fact," she added slowly, "we here in Rome need to be reconnected with the gospel through our partnership with Paul in mission."

"That's an insightful comment," Aquila said to his wife. "You always were the first one to catch the theological and spiritual meaning of Paul's teaching. It's obvious that you should be the one to lead us in our study of Paul's letter."

The imaginary dialogue I have created, which might have taken place upon receipt of Paul's letter by the church at Rome, helps re-create the context in which we can better understand the book of Romans. Paul's letter to the church at Rome is a foundational statement on the relation of the gospel that Paul preached to the mission of the church. Paul could indeed have by-passed Rome and gone directly to Spain. Instead, he sought the partnership of the church at Rome in the mission to Spain.

In reading Paul's letter, we discover that his purpose in writing to the Christians in Rome was not primarily to gain financial aid for his mission. Tactfully, he suggests that his visit will lead to mutual enrichment. "For I am longing to see you so that I may share with you some spiritual gift to strengthen you—or rather so that we may be mutually encouraged by each other's faith, both yours and mine" (Rom. 1:11–12).

Paul then immediately launched into an exposition of the gospel, of which he is "not ashamed" (1:16). The mission to the Gentiles is bracketed with God's mission to the Jews, so that there is no difference, "both Jews and Greeks, are under the power of sin" and both the circumcised and uncircumcised given access to forgiveness and the righteousness of God through faith (3:9, 29–31). The purpose of the law as well as God's purpose through the Jews can now be revealed as fulfilled through the gospel of Christ who is the redeemer of both persons under the law and persons apart from the law.

Paul's theological reflection on the gospel of Jesus Christ was triggered by his proposed mission to Spain. If this is what led to the book of Romans, one of the most important theological writings of the New Testament, then we might well ask, "Can the church have an authentic theology without a compelling vision and contemporary involvement in God's mission to the world?" The answer is no, and this is why.

Mission Precedes and Creates the Church

For Paul, mission precedes and creates the church. The mission is always God's mission through Christ to reach the world. Earlier, in his second letter to the Corinthian church, Paul had written:

So if anyone is in Christ, there is a new creation: everything old has passed away; see, everything has become new! All this is from God, who reconciled us to himself through Christ, and has given us the ministry of reconciliation; that is, in Christ God was reconciling the world to himself, not counting their trespasses against them, and entrusting the message of reconciliation to us. So we are ambassadors for Christ, since God is making his appeal through us; we entreat you on behalf of Christ, be reconciled to God. (2 Cor. 5:17–20)

The church is the result of this mission to the world. But, at the same time, the church is the agent of this mission as it proclaims and expounds this "gospel" and penetrates into the world in partnership with God's mission to the world. The church, as the "missionary people of God," connects gospel to mission and mission to gospel.

Writing from Corinth, Paul viewed Spain through the lens of the apostolic mandate. The church at Rome emerged as the vital connection between mission and gospel. Mission is driven by the gospel and the apostolic mandate, not by the church. At the same time, the church is drawn into mission as the source of its own existence and grounded once more in the gospel as the driving force of mission.

Figure 20 depicts this twofold orientation of the church as being "in the middle" of the gospel and mission.

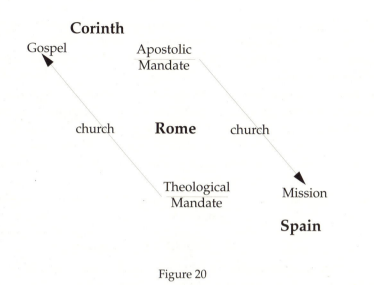

Figure 20

Paul's mission theology was anchored on the one end by the gospel, which he had received directly from Christ by revelation through personal encounter (Gal. 1:12). It was anchored on the other end by the Spirit's mission of making Christ known in regions not already evangelized by this gospel:

> For I will not venture to speak of anything except what Christ has accomplished through me to win obedience from the Gentiles, by word and deed, by the power of signs and wonders, by the power of the Spirit of God, so that from Jerusalem and as far around as Illyricum I have fully proclaimed the good news of Christ. Thus I make it my ambition to proclaim the good news, not where Christ has already been named, so that I do not build on someone else's foundation. (Rom. 15:18–20).

Paul has already preached his gospel as a fulfillment of Isaiah's messianic prophecy: "I have set you to be a light for the Gentiles, so that you may bring salvation to the ends of the earth" (Isa. 49:6; Acts 13:47). This is Christ's apostolic and messianic mission that continues the trajectory of God's mission as revealed in the Old Testament. This is God's mission through the Spirit of the Messiah (Christ) by which the church as a missionary people of God continues the purpose set forth in the calling and consecration of Israel in the Abrahamic blessing (Genesis 12). The gospel through which mission receives its mandate is truly Christ's gospel, and as such it is also God's gospel from the beginning.

In faithfulness to his apostolic mandate, Paul envisioned Spain as the next mission horizon for the gospel. His mission theology included the church as strategic and instrumental for this mission. He wrote to the church in Rome for the sake of seeking their investment in this mission. He did this so that the church could itself demonstrate its apostolic and missional character. In making this attempt, however, Paul now must fulfill the theological mandate, reflecting back on the gospel from the perspective of the projected mission to Spain.

The church exists in the center of this continuum between gospel and mission as the body and presence of Christ. The apostolic mandate is to move from the gospel through church to mission. From the perspective of mission, the theological mandate then reflects back to the gospel through the church. In this way, the church cannot be the church simply by encasing the gospel in its liturgical practice, nor can the church be the church by defining itself solely by mission, without accountability to the gospel. The apostolic mandate, as we have seen from Paul, is rooted in God's original purpose for all people as revealed through the Abrahamic covenant, of which the children of Israel became the "suffering servant."

The universality of this mission, first promised in Abraham, and then fulfilled through Jesus Christ, is established by Paul in the fourth chapter of his letter to the Roman church. Citing the fact that Abraham was declared righteous by faith prior to his circumcision, Paul concludes that it is the free gift of faith and not the law that leads to salvation from sin. Furthermore, as the promise through Abraham was to "many nations," the people of Spain are included (4:9–17).

Paul does not define the church using a theological treatise, but in the context of the gospel and mission as constitutive of its life and purpose. Jesus as the beloved Son, anointed by the Spirit, completes the messianic mission given to Israel in his own self-offering for the sins of the world. The Holy Spirit, as the contemporary presence and power of this messianic kingdom promise of redemption, creates the missionary people of God out of every nation, tribe, and culture. This is to fulfill Christ's mission of reconciling the world to God.

Jürgen Moltmann, in *The Church in the Power of the Spirit*, suggests that the messianic mission of Jesus is not entirely completed in his death and resurrection. Through the coming of the Spirit, his history becomes the church's gospel for the world. The church participates in his mission, becoming the messianic church of the coming kingdom. There is, says Moltmann, a "conversion to the future" through which the church enters into the messianic proclamation of the coming of the kingdom. Moltmann suggests that the "sending of the Spirit" can be viewed as a "sacrament of the Kingdom."

Charles Van Engen says that "the biblical theology of the Word-made-flesh, Jesus Christ, contains the concept of 'sentness.' The incarnation was a sending forth. . . . The church becomes *mission* in following the Lord as an apostolic community that is in constant, dynamic movement, proclaiming the gospel of the kingdom of light in the midst of the kingdom of darkness."

The Kingdom of God
Precedes and Empowers the Church

Another way of saying that ministry precedes and creates the church is to say that the kingdom of God precedes and empowers the church. The church is not the kingdom, says George Ladd, but is the result of the dynamic power and presence of the kingdom in the world.

The temptation for the church has always been to identify its own existence and institutional life with the kingdom of God. When that occurs, the existence of the church tends to take priority over the mission of the kingdom of God. The church tends to develop its theology by looking backward to its historical foundation. The prevailing theology of the church can easily become "historical theology," with its dogmatic theology strongly rooted in the past. The result is that the church often lacks a vibrant mission theology that moves it toward the future. I tell my students that the day they graduate from seminary all of their theology will become historical theology!

Mission theology has its orientation to the work of the Holy Spirit in the coming reign of God, which is what we mean by the phrase "kingdom of God." The theological task of relating the present work of the Holy Spirit to what has preceded in history should not be neglected. Paul accomplished that task more than any other theologian of the first century. But that task *follows* the theological task of interpreting the Spirit's work in the present in the context of the mission of God as the power of the kingdom that precedes and creates the church.

The church does not *drive* the kingdom into the world through its own institutional and pragmatic strategies. Rather, it is *drawn* into the world as it follows the mission of the Spirit. The church is constantly being re-created through the mission of the Spirit. At the same time, it has historical and ecclesial continuity and universality through its participation in the person and mission of Christ Jesus through the Spirit.

The Holy Spirit is the continued presence of Jesus, but, as such, the Spirit is also the presence of the kingdom of God in an eschatological sense. Wesley Carr says, "The dynamic force within this eschatological community is the Spirit, which creates that community and sustains it and at the same time gives to each person within the community his [or her] own individual personhood."

When I say that mission precedes the church I am speaking of God's mission that began with the gospel proclaimed to Adam and Eve immediately after the fall (Gen. 3:16), embodied in the people of Israel as the vicarious representative of God's purpose of reaching "all the families of the earth" (Genesis 12), and completed and continuing through Jesus Christ and the coming of the Holy Spirit following Pentecost to reach beyond Judea, Samaria, and to the "ends of the earth" (Acts 1:9).

Mission Precedes and Creates Theology

"Can the church have an authentic theology without a compelling vision and contemporary involvement in God's mission to the world?" According to what we have set forth above, it cannot. A theology that is authentic to the gospel of Christ must be grounded in the mission of Christ. It is in this sense that mission precedes and creates theology.

The theological mandate falls upon the church from the side of mission and is Spirit-led through the church to anchor its proclamation and programs in gospel truth. The apostolic mandate falls upon the church from the side of the gospel as God's mission, not from mission imperatives diagnosed out of contemporary needs and manufactured out of sociological and technological pragmatics and possibilities.

The church will always be tempted to make itself and its confession of faith the agenda and content of its theological reflection. If it does this, it loses its apostolic witness and authority. For the church to be apostolic it must also follow the Holy Spirit's leading through the apostolic mandate of mission. An apostolic church clearly understands the gospel as the mission of God originating in God's redemptive purpose for all humanity, fulfilled through Christ Jesus and released into the world through the Holy Spirit. The church is apostolic when it does its theological reflection from the standpoint of already being invested in mission beyond the doctrinal and parochial boundaries of the church.

Paul was very clear about the continuity between Pentecost and incarnation, not as a historical or institutional projection from the past into the future, but as the continuing mission of God. This mission of God is apostolic as represented by the sending of Israel into the world as a special people of God through whom the Messiah would come. The messianic anointing of Jesus by the Spirit continued this apostolic continuity. The messianic mission is given to the One sent by the Father as the divine Son of God incarnate. Following Pentecost, the sending Father, the sending Son, and the sending Spirit constitute the apostolic mission of God through which the church is drawn into its mission and discovers its nature.

Mission precedes and creates theology, I have said. Let me give some examples.

In the period immediately following Pentecost, the early church was empowered by the Holy Spirit to proclaim the coming of the Messiah Jesus in Jerusalem in such a way that thousands of Jews were led to acknowledge him as Lord and Savior. The formation of the church began as an enclave of circumcised Jews who devoted themselves to "the apostles' teaching and fellowship, to the breaking of bread and the prayers" (Acts 2:42). The miracles, signs, and wonders that accompanied their proclamation of Jesus as the Messiah caught the attention of the entire city, resulting in persecution by those who rejected the message in fear of losing power and prestige among the people.

The mission of the Holy Spirit, however, was not contained within this enclave. Peter was the first one to venture out under the instruction of the Spirit as received in a vision, proclaiming the gospel to the uncircumcised Cornelius who, upon believing in Christ, was baptized. Peter justified his actions to the "circumcised believers" of the church in Jerusalem by saying, "who was I that I could hinder God?" (Acts 11:17).

In this incident we see the first opening of the church to the Gentiles. At the same time, there was no theological reflection on this remarkable event. That remained for Paul to do when he also experienced the coming of the Holy Spirit upon the Gentiles. Based outside of the Jerusalem community in Antioch, Paul began to see the mission of the Spirit to the Gentiles not as an exception to the norm, but as normative for the gospel in its appeal to all persons, Jew and Gentile, male and female, slave and free (Gal. 3:28).

It was not merely Paul's practice of including Gentiles in the church but his theology that circumcision was no longer required for admission to the kingdom of God that aroused hostility and attacks upon Paul from some of the same "circumcised believers" in Jerusalem (Gal. 2:12). Paul did not deal with the issue of circumcision out of the principle of expediency, but dealt with it as a theological issue and created a new theological position as to how circumcision is related to the gospel of Christ. "For in Christ Jesus neither circumcision nor uncircumcision counts for anything; the only thing that counts is faith working through love" (Gal. 5:6).

This led Paul to relegate the issue of circumcision to a matter of relative indifference. "Was anyone at the time of his call already circumcised? Let him not seek to remove the marks of circumcision. Was anyone at the time of his call uncircumcised? Let him not seek circumcision. Circumcision is nothing, and uncircumcision is nothing; but obeying the commandments of God is everything" (1 Cor. 7:18–19).

Let me give a more contemporary example.

When I was a seminary student, the student body consisted of 292 men and 8 women. The women students were not permitted to take the degree leading to ordination, as the position of the faculty was that women could not be ordained to serve as pastors. During the next several years, many more women students began to enroll in the seminary and said to the faculty, in effect: "Our church has recognized and affirmed the anointing of the Holy Spirit upon our lives and sent us to the seminary to be trained for ordination as pastors—what do you intend to do about it?"

The faculty, as some of them later confided to me, were quite disconcerted. At first they created a special degree for the women, allowing them to take biblical languages and some of the theology courses. Some of the male students then petitioned to take this degree, as they felt it was more suitable to their needs than the standard B.D. degree! The faculty, not willing to allow this, finally conceded that they had better listen to the voice of the Spirit as affirmed by the churches who were sending the female students. As a result, the curriculum was opened up to both men and women with no discrimination.

What happened next proves my point, I think. The same faculty who earlier were quite convinced that women should be excluded from ordination and pastoral ministry, on biblical grounds, went back to look at the biblical texts and said: "What do you know! Now we see that there *is* biblical support for ordination of women!" The biblical antecedents for the role of women in God's mission were quickly found, and the texts that had been used to forbid this practice were now read in the context where Paul, for the sake of expediency, departed from what he considered normative and limited the role of women in specific situations and places.

In God's mission through the power and ministry of the Holy Spirit, allowing women to serve alongside men is not what is exceptional. The freedom of women to minister emerges out of the center of the gospel of Christ. What is exceptional is a provisional limit on their role in specific circumstances due to existing cultural and social factors not yet liberated by the gospel. This appears to be the case in both Corinth and Ephesus, while in Rome and Macedonia women are recognized leaders in the church. The gospel of Christ provides a hermeneutic by which one can read Scripture so as to discern which situations addressed by Paul were exceptions and which were normative in terms of the mission of the Spirit.

This issue, however, is still a matter of much debate within the church at large. But the faculty of this particular seminary developed a theology that supports the ordination of women and their role as leaders in the church only *after* women enrolled, in the power of the Holy Spirit and with the support of the church as the body of Christ. If these women had never come, led by the Holy Spirit, the faculty would still be clinging to their selective reading of Scripture much in the same way that the Jerusalem church resisted the ministry of Paul, who was led by the Spirit in his theology as well as in his practice.

It was as though this faculty began to see that refusal to permit women to prepare for ordained ministry only because of their gender was, to paraphrase Peter's statement, "to hinder the work of God."

Did Paul ever reach Spain? We have no record of such a mission. We know that he reached Rome finally as a prisoner. There are some who believe that he was released from prison briefly before eventually being executed at Rome. In his letter to the church at Philippi, written from his prison cell in Rome, Paul expressed no regrets and stated his full confidence that the mission of Christ would continue, whether he lived or died (Phil. 1:12–26).

We do know, however, that Phoebe reached Rome with Paul's letter. She indeed was a "benefactor of many" (Rom. 16:2). Perhaps we should have a Saint Phoebe as well as a Saint Paul in our archives of saints. Those of us who lack the calling of a Paul can certainly find our counterpart in the commission of Phoebe—to be bearers of the gospel across stormy seas and into strange lands.

19

The Ministry of the Church as a
Sacrament of Forgiveness and Healing

"Pastor, Joe is standing out in the parking lot and wants to talk with you," said the usher. It was only a few minutes before the beginning of our evening service, at which we were gathering for the communion service. I was immediately concerned because Joe, while a committed Christian, struggled with an alcohol problem. As I greeted him, my concern was validated.

"Pastor," Joe began, "I have slipped and fallen again and had too much to drink. I am in no shape to attend the service tonight and came by to let you know why I wouldn't be there." While it was evident that he had been drinking, he was not out of control.

"Joe," I responded, putting my arm around his shoulders, "this is exactly the place you should be. When we gather, it is the Lord that is the host of our table, and we all are present as needy persons. I want you to come in with me and be with us."

He did enter, and participated in our celebration of the Lord's Supper. His condition, of course, was quite evident to those around him, and the incident caused somewhat of a stir among the leaders of the church.

Some considered Joe's participation under the influence of alcohol to be a violation of the sacrament, arguing that he should have waited until he was sober before partaking of the elements. Paul's warning to the Corinthian church about "partaking in an unworthy manner" was suggested as warrant for excluding him (1 Cor. 11:27). In the end, the discussion led to an examination of the concept of the church as sacrament, and that inclusion in the body of Christ is itself participation in the sacramental life of Christ, of which the bread and wine are signs.

One has only to mention the word "sacrament" and the Episcopalians think of a mystical spirituality while the Baptists reach for the Bible and run for the pulpit. Martin Luther and Huldrych Zwingli parted ways over the different meanings each gave to the sacrament of the Lord's Supper. John Calvin and the Anabaptists fought a pitched battle over the issue of re-baptism following conversion.

Aware of these issues, I debated the wisdom of putting the word "sacrament" in the title of this chapter. I finally decided that theological controversy over the nature and number of the sacraments should not be allowed to eclipse the saving significance of Jesus' life and ministry as the primary sacrament.

Follow me as I trace out the contours of Jesus as the sacrament of God's saving and healing presence and the church as the sacrament of Jesus' presence. Following that, I want to return again to the issue of Joe and discuss the relation of forgiveness of sin to the healing of persons—spiritually, emotionally, and physically.

Jesus as the First and Primary Sacrament

The very fact that God approaches humans in their condition of brokenness and estrangement due to sin is a sacramental act. "Revelation means sacrament," Karl Barth once said. When the divine Word became flesh the real presence of divine being became touchable and graspable in the form of the humanity of Jesus Christ. The apostle John, who was part of the intimate circle of disciples around Jesus, reminds us:

> We declare to you what was from the beginning, what we have heard, what we have seen with our eyes, what we have looked at and touched with our hands, concerning the word of life— this life was revealed, and we have seen it and testify to it, and declare to you the eternal life that was with the Father and was revealed to us— we declare to you what we have seen and heard so that you also may have fellowship with us; and truly our fellowship is with the Father and with his Son Jesus Christ. (1 John 1:1–4).

The apostle Paul spoke of this revelation of God through Jesus Christ as the *mysterion* of our faith (1 Tim. 3:16). The Greek word *mysterion* was translated as *sacramentum* by Jerome in the Vulgate (Latin) Bible (e.g., Eph. 5:32). The word *mysterion* as used by Paul does not mean a mystery in the form of a hidden secret, but a revealed reality: God is present in the form of a human person, Jesus of Nazareth.

The incarnation is not of grace but of God. God is the source of grace, and where God is present grace flows out of the inexhaustible center of God's life toward humans under the sentence of death. "From his fullness we have all received, grace upon grace," wrote John. "The law indeed was given through Moses; grace and truth came through Jesus Christ" (John 1:16–17).

Where Jesus is present there is grace, because he is himself the sacrament through which grace flows. The sacrament does not precede the presence of Jesus, as though it could manipulate and dispense grace.

Rather, Jesus is the sacrament of saving and sustaining grace that flows through the "sacramental" acts of Baptism and the Lord's Supper, as especially constituted for the church, as well as through the very existence of the church itself as the sacrament of forgiveness and healing.

When the Pharisees threw the woman caught in the act of adultery at the feet of Jesus, demanding that he carry out the explicit judgment of the law given by Moses against such acts, he placed his own presence, as it were, between the law and the woman. "I do not condemn you," said Jesus to the woman, "Go your way, and from now on do not sin again" (John 8:11). The forgiveness came from Jesus as the very incarnation of God, and the encounter was a sacramental one.

Confronted with the man suffering paralysis who was lowered through the roof, Jesus conducted no inquiry into his state of repentance or faith but said, "Son, your sins are forgiven" (Mark 2:5). When the question arose as to whether anyone but God could forgive sin, Jesus healed the man as a sign that he indeed had the authority to forgive sin. In this case, the man received both forgiveness of sin and physical healing in the same encounter. The presence of Jesus was, for this man, a sacrament that brought both forgiveness and healing as an eschatological event into his life—a sign of God's power and blessing.

Let me expand on that. Forgiveness of sin has to do with removing the consequences of sin which, according to Paul, is death. "The wages of sin is death" (Rom. 6:23). Sin is not a condition, like a virus, that corrupts and weakens life. Rather, sin produces death, and sin is not removed until death has been destroyed. Forgiveness of sin is not like a medicine that removes an infection, nor is it a legal pardon that cancels a debt. While both might be included, until the death that sin causes is destroyed, sin is not forgiven.

This is why Paul can say with regard to the resurrection, "If Christ has not been raised, your faith is futile and you are still in your sins" (1 Cor. 15:17). Forgiveness is ultimately grounded in resurrection. The death that Jesus died on the cross was the consequence of sin—not his own sin, but the sin of all humanity, which he assumed in becoming human. Being born a human person, Jesus was descended from Adam, as all humans are, and thus subject to death. This "death nature" was not something from which he could be healed, short of death itself. Though without sin and filled with the Spirit of God, Jesus could atone only for the death that he assumed as the consequence of the sin of others. Jesus had nothing for which he himself needed forgiveness. At the same time, Paul argued, if Jesus had not been raised from the dead, there would be no forgiveness of our sin, because death is the fatal consequence of sin and only the resurrection of Jesus could overcome the power of death.

This "atonement" for sin began with the conception and birth of Jesus, led directly to the cross and the grave, and was completed through his resurrection. Both forgiveness for sin and healing of the body are thus grounded in this atonement as the final act in our own salvation. The healing of the body of the paralyzed man was, in effect, a sacrament, or sign, of his own resurrection and forgiveness. He still will face an earthly death, but now with the present assurance that his sins are forgiven and that he will experience the final healing that resurrection will give.

The raising of Lazarus from the grave (John 11) was itself a "sacrament," one might say, which affirmed the sacramental offering of Jesus' own life and gave him assurance of resurrection. In the priestly ministry of Jesus, he was both the sacrifice and the officiant at the altar of the cross, and, in his resurrection, he continues that priestly and sacramental ministry through the power of the gospel and the presence of the church in the world.

This is what I mean by saying that Jesus is the first and primary sacrament. His birth, life, death, and resurrection constitute the saving purpose of God toward humans as well as the actual salvation of humans through union with the resurrected Christ.

The Church as the Continuing Sacramental Presence of Jesus Christ

With the ascension of Jesus following his resurrection and the coming of the Holy Spirit at Pentecost, the church is formed as the "body of Christ" in the world and continues to be the *mysterion* of God's presence. In writing to the church in Ephesus, Paul reminds them of the "mystery" [*mysterion*] that was made known to him through revelation as the "mystery" of Christ.

In former generations this mystery [*mysterion*] was not made known to humankind, as it has now been revealed to his holy apostles and prophets by the Spirit: that is, the Gentiles have become fellow heirs, members of the same body, and sharers in the promise in Christ Jesus through the gospel . . . so that through the church the wisdom of God in its rich variety might now be made known to the rulers and authorities in the heavenly places. This was in accordance with the eternal purpose that he has carried out in Christ Jesus our Lord, in whom we have access to God in boldness and confidence through faith in him. (Eph. 3:5–12)

The church as the body of Christ now lives between the cross and the return of Christ (*parousia*). The original sacramental relation of God to humanity through Jesus Christ is now represented through the enactment of the life of the church itself. But in this representation the full presence of the *parousia* is screened, permitting the church to have a genuine history in relation to the world. This is a point that Karl Barth has stressed. In God's self-revelation in Jesus Christ to the world through the church, God also is concealed in order to be present, not merely as another "presence" alongside the existence of others, but in and through their existence. What Barth means by this is that the visible church is the real church. The human community that comprises the body of Christ is the people of God through whom Christ continues to be present, despite their failure, sinfulness, and disobedience.

It is in this sense that I suggest that the church as the body of Christ is a sacrament of forgiveness and healing. I am using the concept of sacrament in the same way that Paul used the word *mysterion*. The primary reference is to the real presence of God, first in the incarnate life of Jesus of Nazareth, and then continuing through the visible life of the people of God as constituted by the indwelling and empowering Spirit of Christ.

The Word of the gospel (*kerygma*) that the church proclaims, as Thomas Torrance has said, "is in the fullest sense the sacramental action of the Church through which the mystery of the Kingdom concerning Christ and His Church, hid from the foundation of the world, is now being revealed in history . . . in *kerygma* the same word continues to be 'made flesh' in the life of the Church."

The church's life is thus sacramental in the sense that it is the continuing life of the historical Jesus ministering to the world on behalf of God while, at the same time, the church is the eschatological presence of the coming Jesus Christ who has destroyed the power of death and gives assurance of resurrection and forgiveness through the Holy Spirit.

Forgiveness of Sins
and the Ministry of Recovery

Let me return to the issue raised by my including Joe in the communion service. Joe considered that his problem with drinking was a sin that led him to believe that he was not worthy to participate in our communion service. By including him we were practicing the sacramental life of Jesus.

When we recall the presence of Jesus amid his contemporaries, we remember that it was especially those who were considered marginal, disreputable, and truly needy that were welcomed by Jesus. Those who sought to protect Jesus from being contaminated or "violated" by association with sinners were themselves scolded by him. Paul's warning to the Corinthians was not that they were including sinners, but that they were excluding the poor and needy. They were ignoring and despising those who had too little and were keeping for themselves what they ought to have shared (1 Cor. 11:21–22).

Failure to "discern" that Joe was indeed part of the body of Christ and thus to exclude him, or even to accept his own offer to be excluded, would have constituted the offense that Paul warned against.

Joe had received the assurance of forgiveness of sins as a liturgical act on many occasions, but had not yet experienced healing and recovery from his personal addiction. When the church pronounces forgiveness of sins and spiritual peace with God without also providing the power to overcome the effect of sins in one's daily life, this may not only be a liturgical fraud but spiritual malpractice!

When confession of sin is followed immediately by the granting of absolution, without making any attempt to see that the effects of sin are removed from the person's life, the granting of absolution as assurance of the forgiveness of sins is little more than a legal transaction. If my language seems too strong in calling liturgical absolution without personal healing "malpractice," I will explain.

Suppose a man went to a medical doctor for a diagnosis concerning a pain in some part of his body and was told there was a malignant tumor that could cause death. Before leaving the office, after some massage and manipulation, the man was told by the doctor that he was now completely healed, based upon his authority as a medical professional, and needed no further treatment. When the man died of cancer only a few weeks later, would not the doctor be liable for charges of malpractice?

In somewhat the same way, if sin is a condition that affects our personal life and leads to death (the wages of sin is death), then assurance that forgiveness has been granted without removing the effect of the sin would be equivalent to spiritual malpractice. Why are we uncomfortable with this?

One might respond that sin is not a physical disease but a spiritual condition that requires forgiveness, not healing. If someone does wrong to me, it is the relationship that has been ruptured, not my spleen. I have it within my power to grant forgiveness, and if offered, the other person has the right to take it as a fact and act upon it. If the other person should continue to feel guilty, then we would say that this guilt has no objective basis and is merely "psychological guilt," which can be expiated through believing the words of forgiveness, not by repeated confession.

This is partly the truth, but not the whole truth.

The splitting of the spiritual from our personal and social life is the root of the problem. According to the Bible, sin is not only a transgression of God's law that does require God's pardon, it also has its effect on our physical, psychological, and social life. When the Christians at Corinth were so disorderly at the Lord's table—excluding others and not "discerning the body"—Paul warned them that "For this reason many of you are weak and ill, and some have died" (1 Cor. 11:30).

Those who have received the Spirit of Christ and forgiveness of sins in his name, Paul wrote, should no longer live under the "works of the flesh," as he put it. In naming these, Paul included: "fornication, impurity, licentiousness, idolatry, sorcery, enmities, strife, jealousy, anger, quarrels, dissensions, factions, envy, drunkenness, carousing, and things like these" (Gal. 5:19–21). In contrast, he listed the effects of living a life under the power of the Spirit as: "love, joy, peace, patience, kindness, generosity, faithfulness, gentleness, and self-control" (Gal. 5:22–23).

Clearly, the effects of forgiveness of sin through union with Christ go far beyond the removal of an objective guilt through divine pardon, though that is surely included. The whole truth of forgiveness includes the effects of sin as a continuing struggle in the Christian life that also must come under the sacrament of grace.

The church as the body of Christ is the sacrament of forgiveness and healing as the members share mutually in their common struggle and break the power of sin by mutual confession.

Dietrich Bonhoeffer introduced mutual confession of sins to his seminary students as a way of breaking through the self-deception of confessing only to God, as he put it. He asked why we should think it easier to confess our sins to God who is altogether holy than to a brother or sister who is a sinner like we are? He concluded that we are in essence only confessing to ourselves and granting ourselves absolution, which provides an explanation for backsliding and the lack of growth through confession.

While we may not institutionalize mutual confession as a ritual in the way that Bonhoeffer attempted, we can see the truth of his insight. The power of sin is its secret life. The church becomes an accomplice in keeping this secret by affirming only those who appear to be righteous. All too often the last place that the Christian who is struggling with the addictive power of sin can share that struggle is with brothers and sisters in the church.

Joe attempted to keep his problem with alcohol a secret from his Christian brothers and sisters, while finding support and encouragement from his open confession at the AA meetings he attended several times a week. Eventually he was able to move into recovery, but not through the sacraments of the church. The members of his AA group became his sacramental community with whom he could share honestly his need and receive from them affirmation and encouragement.

Did the church fail at precisely the point where it needed to have a ministry of forgiveness and healing? Probably. At the same time it should also be said that Joe's participation in the body of Christ enabled him to name the "higher power" that his twelve-step program included as part of his recovery. Confession of faith in Jesus Christ, with Baptism and the Lord's Supper as foundational sacraments of the church, provide a vital function in the ministry of forgiveness and healing, but the sacramental life of Christ must be extended further through mutual confession of need and the empowerment of healing grace.

Joe was not miraculously delivered from his addiction to alcohol. There was no extraordinary intervention that removed this problem from his life and family in answer to prayers of faith. Slowly and painfully, he began his recovery through participation in a twelve-step program. His wife and family were brought into the process in order for the family system to receive healing as well.

Could this process have been shortened through a miracle of divine healing? If atonement for sin includes not only forgiveness but healing, should we expect healing as well as forgiveness through faith in Christ?

We often hear testimonies of apparent miraculous deliveries from physical illness and immediate healing of the body in answer to prayer. How then should we account for the miraculous aspect of healing, particularly as it relates to physical healing?

The Sacramental Presence of the Resurrected Christ

The church is redeemed, not in Word only, but in power, and yet it waits for the redemption of the body. The sacrament functions to preserve this unity between Word and power while maintaining the eschatological tension. The word of forgiveness is proclaimed, yet the final healing of the body (resurrection) is delayed. This means, for example, that all physical healing is provisional, and a miraculous healing may be understood itself as a kind of sacrament of the resurrection.

Some have argued that physical healing is promised in the present time in the same way as forgiveness of sins. This has led some to adopt what Ken Blue has called the "faith formula" as the basis on which miraculous healing of all physical deformity and disease can be claimed. If we have the gift of salvation based on our faith, some have argued, then we should also be able to receive the gift of physical healing based on the same faith, as both have been covenanted for us in the atonement of Christ. T. J. McCrossan, for example, has suggested that every Christian can "exercise the very same appropriating faith in the bruised body of Christ for their healing as they formerly exercised in His shed blood for their salvation."

My response is to agree that forgiveness of sins and healing of the body are both part of the atonement that Christ accomplished through death and resurrection, but that both are linked to the future resurrection of the believer in Christ. It is not just that healing of the body is in the atonement; resurrection of the dead is also in the atonement, and healing of the body as well as the final act of forgiveness is grounded in this resurrection.

We have *present assurance* of forgiveness of sins through the Word of God and the witness of the Holy Spirit even as we have *present assurance* of our resurrection from the dead by the same Spirit. Assurance of forgiveness is not the same as a miraculous delivery from temptation and sin. Though we fall into sin, as John reminds us: "If we say that we have no sin, we deceive ourselves, and the truth is not in us. If we confess our sins, he who is faithful and just will forgive us our sins and cleanse us from all unrighteousness. If we say that we have not sinned, we make him a liar, and his word is not in us" (1 John 1:8–10).

In the same way, we have the promise of ultimate healing of the body through the resurrection, even though we still struggle with physical infirmity and, eventually, must die. Some do testify to the miracle of physical healing, and there is no reason to deny that such healings do occur. The fact that such miracles do not occur in response to every prayer of faith, and that such a healing does not remove the threat of eventual death, tells us that the miracles of healing may not be God's way of removing all sickness and suffering in the present time.

When these miracles of healing do occur, they are a sign, or a kind of sacrament, of the resurrection, which gives us assurance that our faith placed in the power of God to raise us from the dead and forgive all sin is valid. The "sacrament" of a miraculous physical healing is meant to encourage and empower all believers to remain steadfast in faith as well as giving a witness to unbelievers of the power of God unto salvation.

As the sacrament of forgiveness and healing, the church must not become the advocate of a God who heals occasionally and intermittently and abandons the ones who suffer pain and affliction as though God is not also their advocate.

A ministry of reconciliation is a ministry of advocacy, not merely healing. God's advocacy for human persons who suffer and live with deformity and disease is to give assurance that these torments are not the consequence of sin or lack of faith. Where God gives the gift of faith that produces the miracle of healing, this too is a form of advocacy for all who are unhealed. In receiving assurance that we are, through faith, empowered by the God who raises the dead and forgives sin, we are lifted out of futility and despair into a life of hope in God's ultimate healing.

In the practice of the ministry of advocacy and healing, there is need of a pastoral strategy by which the unhealed are not placed at a disadvantage by the testimony of the healed. There is need of a pastoral strategy by which the release of divine power and presence is exercised on behalf of the unhealed as a continuing and constant upholding of life and faith.

I have stressed in this chapter the fact that the person of Christ, as "the sacrament," underlies all sacraments. If Christ is the first and final sacrament, then the body of Christ continues the sacramental ministry of Christ in touching and transforming human life in the struggles, conflicts, and pain of everyday life. The sacrament that empowers and restores the life of ordinary persons in this struggle is the extraordinary one.

The Ministry of the Church as the Advocate for the Abused and Oppressed

If there are two sides to humanity, Jesus will be found on the wrong side. He was not a religious person, though he lived amid a religious society that prized appearance and cultivated piety as a discipline of outward form. He did not have access to the privileged sanctuaries of the priests. He recoiled from the public display of piety by the religious professional and turned toward the common people who thrust upon him their anxious care and world-weary lives.

Where lines were drawn between the sacred and the profane that tended to dehumanize and marginalize common people, he acted with uncommon decency toward those whose dignity was shredded by the disgrace that comes from misfortune, mistreatment, and moral failure. He appeared in the world, as Dietrich Bonhoeffer once said, "incognito as a beggar among beggars, as an outcast among the outcast, despairing among the despairing, dying among the dying."

The Lebanese philosopher, Kahlil Gibran, expressed the same thought in his own vivid way:

> Long ago there lived a Man who was crucified for being too loving and too lovable.
>
> And strange to relate I met him thrice yesterday.
>
> The first time He was asking a policeman not to take a prostitute to prison; the second time He was drinking wine with an outcast; and the third time He was having a fist fight with a promoter inside a church.

Jesus as Public Defender

In our system of justice, every person, no matter how destitute, is entitled to a legal defense before the court. Where the defendant has no resources, the court appoints legal counsel—an attorney who serves as public defender, an advocate for the rights of the individual before the bar of justice.

A second kind of advocacy is needed for the rights of the individual who suffers injustice at the hands of others. In cases where children have been abused and/or molested in their own homes, the court will appoint an advocate for the child, whose responsibility is to ensure that the rights of the child are protected from violation by either the parents or public institutions.

The concept of advocacy for the defenseless and powerless has roots that go further back than modern civil law. The Judeo-Christian tradition has as its central core the concept of advocacy for the orphan, the "stranger within the gates," and the poor and oppressed in the land.

The biblical account of the first act of violence as a result of the fall contains a reference to advocacy for the "blood of Abel" that Cain spilled on the ground. It is this "blood of the innocent" that first draws God into the scene.

"Then the LORD said to Cain, 'Where is your brother Abel?' He said, 'I do not know; am I my brother's keeper?' And the LORD said, 'What have you done? Listen; your brother's blood is crying out to me from the ground! And now you are cursed from the ground, which has opened its mouth to receive your brother's blood from your hand'" (Gen. 4:9–11).

There was also divine advocacy for Cain, who murdered his brother Abel. Fearing for his own life at the hands of those who would seek vengeance against him for his dreadful act, Cain cries out, "My punishment is greater than I can bear! Today you have driven me away from the soil, and I shall be hidden from your face; I shall be a fugitive and a wanderer on the earth, and anyone who meets me may kill me" (Gen. 4:13–14).

So be it, we might be tempted to say. What does he expect? Has he not forfeited all of his rights in taking the life of his brother?

"Then the LORD said to him, 'Not so! Whoever kills Cain will suffer a sevenfold vengeance.' And the LORD put a mark on Cain, so that no one who came upon him would kill him" (Gen. 4:15).

I wonder if any text of Scripture has been more misrepresented than this one! The "mark of Cain" has often been interpreted as a stigma placed on one who has done something wrong so as to make visible that person's disgrace and shame. On the contrary, the mark placed upon Cain was a sign that whoever sought vengeance against Cain would have to deal with God. God became the advocate of Cain when he had no covering for his shame and no refuge from the moral outrage directed against him by the family of Abel.

Advocacy does not excuse—nor does it condone—wrong. It is as concerned for the victim as for the perpetrator of the wrong. Advocacy asks that justice be allowed to fit punishment to the crime as restraint against human passions that collapse into the abyss of inhuman moral outrage. "Vengeance is mine, I will repay, says the Lord" (Rom. 12:19; Heb. 10:30; Deut. 32:35).

Throughout Scripture, both in the Old and New Testaments, God's advocacy for the abused and oppressed is as strongly represented as God's judgment and wrath against sin and wrongdoing. The Mosaic law itself made provision for the poor and unfortunate as well as for the widows and orphans. In harvesting the crops, some was to be left for the "gleaners," those who had no land and had to live off what could be picked up when the harvesters were through (Deut. 24:21). The alien who entered into the community of Israel was to have the same protection of law as the Israelite (Num. 15:16). "Cities of refuge" were established within the land for those who sought sanctuary from those who wanted vengeance against them for crimes committed (Numbers 35).

This is the background for the role of Jesus as advocate for those who were victims of social stigma, devastating disease, humiliating moral failure, and oppression both demonic and economic. He accepted the hospitality of Zacchaeus, a despised collaborator with Rome (Luke 19). He affirmed the value of both the woman and her ministry to him when others complained that she was unworthy to touch his feet (Luke 7:37–50). He placed himself on the side of the woman caught in adultery when the law called for her execution (John 8). On the cross, Jesus assured the criminal who confessed his guilt and asked to be remembered that he would be with him in paradise (Luke 23:42–43).

It is this Jesus of whom the apostle John wrote, remembering his words concerning the sending of the Holy Spirit. Jesus was the first advocate, and the Spirit will come to be another advocate. "And I will ask the Father, and he will give you another Advocate, to be with you forever "(John 14:16). The Holy Spirit will continue the role of advocate that Jesus began, and those who receive the Spirit as their advocate then become advocates for others (14:26; 15:26; 16:7).

The Greek word translated as advocate is *paraklete*. It literally means "called to the side," and denotes a role of comforting, exhorting, and encouraging. The ministry of serving as a *paraklete* is one that continues the ministry of Christ through the presence and power of the Holy Spirit.

James Torrance reminds us of Christ's paracletic ministry when he says: "Christ does not heal us by standing over against us. . . . He is the true Priest, bone of our bone, flesh of our flesh. As such, he bears upon his divine heart our sins and injustices and effects in his vicarious humanity our reconciliation." Through the Holy Spirit that Jesus promised and that we have received, Christ continues to stand with and for persons who are in need of divine advocacy.

The Continuing
Paracletic Ministry of Christ

Jacob Firet, in his book *Dynamics of Pastoring,* suggested three ways in which the ministry of Christ takes place.

1. Kerygmatic ministry: God has come; the kingdom of God stands opposed to the presumption and powers of this world, and offers healing and hope to all who enter;
2. Didactic ministry: God has come; this is how one should live as a member of the kingdom of God.
3. Paracletic ministry: God has come; he wants to live in my house and my situation; he will walk with me as I enter and experience the blessings of the kingdom.

The church does pretty well with the first two forms of Christ's ministry through the proclamation of the Word and through teaching the Word. What is too often neglected is the paracletic ministry of Christ through which persons experience the presence and power of Christ "alongside" them in their need and struggle for dignity, meaning, and belonging. "Paraclesis," says Firet, "is the consolation and admonition of God which reorients people toward salvation in the concreteness of their situation; for the [caregiver] this means that he knows the concreteness of the situation of those people by participation in it."

Thomas Smail reminds us that Christians who are inspired and empowered by the Holy Spirit not only have their roots in relationship to God but "express themselves horizontally and practically in such a way as to challenge the oppressive structures of society in which the church lives." Our concern, Smail continues, should be as much for the socially demonic, in the form of oppressive structures, as for the personally demonic.

Where then in our society should we look for the kind of advocacy that will make an intervention into the "socially demonic," which causes oppression and abuse? Can we expect that the institutions of marriage and family will provide such a sanctuary for healing when it is these very social structures that are often the cause of so much violence and neglect of basic human rights and dignity? Unfortunately we cannot.

Stanley Hauerwas reminds us that "Unless marriage has a purpose beyond being together it will certainly be a hell." Many who have suffered spouse abuse will testify to that. As for the family, Hauerwas comments, "Ironically, . . . the family is threatened today partly because it has no institutions that have the moral status to stand over against it to call into question its demonic tendencies. The first function of the church in relation to the family must, therefore, be to stand as an institution that claims loyalty and significance beyond that of the family."

The Church's Ministry to
Victims of Abuse and Violence

The focus of this chapter now sharpens. The church's ministry to the world as advocate for the abused and oppressed begins close to home. This does not exclude the global concerns of the church for peace, justice, and freedom from oppression wherever it occurs. We agonize and grieve over violence to innocent persons in every land as vividly portrayed before our eyes in virtually every newscast. These pictures and reports of violence horrify us but do not inform us as to what can be done on a personal basis. Even as Jesus heard the cries and felt the pain of those who were closest to him, so the church must hear, see, and respond to those who live in closest proximity and must become the advocate of those who are victims of abuse.

The Dynamics of Intimacy and Abuse

The most dangerous place for women and children today may be the home. Sociologists Richard Gelles and Murray Straus tell us, "You are more likely to be physically assaulted, beaten, and killed in your own home at the hands of a loved one than any place else, or by any one else in our society. . . . In our society, a person's earliest experiences with violence come in the home—spankings and physical punishment from parents. We learn that there is always going to be a certain amount of violence that accompanies intimacy."

The kind of abuse and violence that takes place in the home is different from all other forms of violence in that it has its highest potential for injury where there is the greatest potential for intimacy and love. Difficult as it is for us to accept, violence and love can coexist within the same relationship. Gelles and Straus stress this point when they write: "That violence and love can actually coexist in families is perhaps the most insidious aspect of intimate violence because it means that, unlike violence in the streets, we are tied to abusers by the bonds of love, attachment, and affection. . . . Perhaps the greatest challenge to understanding intimate violence and devising adequate social polity is to see violence and love as coexisting in the same relationship."

Persons who abuse and commit violence within marriage and against children in the home are ordinarily "normal" persons when measured by accepted societal standards. The solution is not, therefore, to explain incidents of abuse as perpetrated by aberrant persons who are sociopathic and pathological personalities. While some instances may well be due to deranged and distorted minds, the greater share of abuse and violence in the home is the result of a breakdown of the capacity to give the care and love that should be expected in marriage and family. The first step in uncovering such abuse and making an intervention is hearing the pain and becoming an advocate of the victim.

Whenever abusive relationships occur there is a violation of the personal being of one person by another. The risk of abuse is greater where persons are in primary relationships where intimate contact is experienced. This accounts for the high incidence of abuse between family members. Primary relationships tend to be intimate, personal, and sensitive. Secondary relationships tend to be more functional, impersonal, and task-oriented.

In marriage and family relationships there is more risk of abuse, and the abuse is more devastating, precisely because it comes from those to whom we look for support, care, and love. When those on whom we are dependent for economic, emotional, and spiritual support violate our trust by exploiting, injuring, and otherwise abusing us, often under the pretext of love itself, where does one turn for relief? When the only nurture and the only source of one's day-to-day living is from the same person who abuses us, to escape is often as terrifying as to submit. Under the threat of even greater harm, secrecy is mandated. To reveal the abuse may intensify the abuse and produce even greater violence. The power of the abuser over the victim exploits this fear and vulnerability.

By the time abuse has escalated to the point where it leads to violence and can no longer be kept a secret, people are amazed and astounded that this has been going on without their knowing about it. The first response is often denial, which exposes the victim of the abuse to further rejection and offers opportunity for the abuser to regain credibility and control. My concern in this chapter is to analyze the origins of abuse within relationships where intimacy, trust, and dependence on others for nurture and support are promised and expected. The church's advocacy for those who are abused and oppressed must begin where abuse begins.

Where Does Abuse Begin?

The typical pattern in abusive incidents is one in which the need to control is strongly present, coupled with perceptions of self-inadequacy. The victim experiences the offender as oppressive, coercive, demanding, exploitative, destructive, and crippling. These are the negative aspects of an abusive relationship. The positive counterparts are relationships which are safe, responsive, nurturing, productive, and empowering. These can be placed on a continuum of relationships ranging from loving to abusive, correlated with positive and negative self-esteem.

Figure 21 illustrates this continuum.

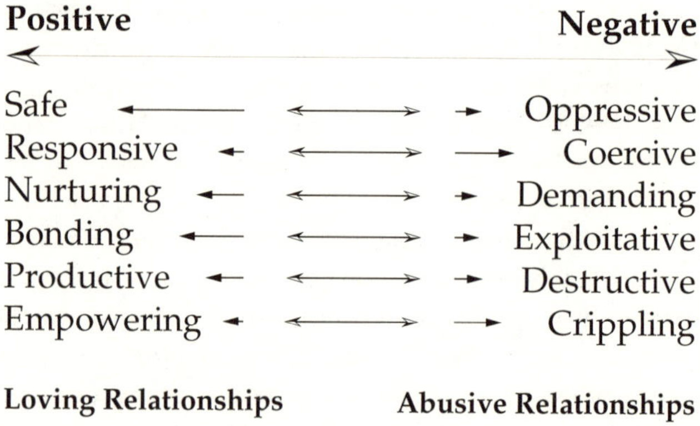

Positive			Negative
Safe	←	← →	→ Oppressive
Responsive	←	← →	→ Coercive
Nurturing	←	← →	→ Demanding
Bonding	←	← →	→ Exploitative
Productive	←	← →	→ Destructive
Empowering	←	← →	→ Crippling

Loving Relationships   **Abusive Relationships**

Figure 21

The left side of the continuum represents loving relationships, which tend to be experienced as safe, responsive, nurturing, bonding, productive, and empowering. The right side of the continuum represents abusive relationships, which tend to be oppressive, coercive, demanding, exploitative, destructive, and crippling. Note that there is a continuum on which each of the contrasting relationship pairs are placed. When a relationship no longer feels safe, it is already abusive to the degree that it is experienced as oppressive. When one no longer feels free to respond but is coerced into responding, it is abusive. When a person *feels* abused, abuse has occurred.

I have used the above diagram to enable couples to talk about how they feel in a marriage or premarital relationship. As each plots on the diagram a point for each of the six areas that most accurately describes how they feel in the relationship, hidden levels of abuse begin to appear. Often the other partner is totally unaware of these feelings. When I ask, "Why did you not express discomfort or feelings of being exploited or oppressed before?" the answer is usually, "Because I was afraid that he/she would not like me or give me what I was looking for in the relationship."

Some are shocked to discover that their partner experiences such feelings of being coerced or exploited at points in the relationship. Much of our day-to-day life in marriage and family relationships becomes "normalized" by cultural, traditional, and social conventions as to our roles. This is one clue as to why abuse and violence can quietly and sometimes explosively occur in what we consider to be normal relationships between normal people.

Advocacy begins where there are feelings of abuse, even when such feelings are concealed within what appear to be normal marriage and family relationships. Where the church fails to perceive such abuse, it fails to become the advocate of those who are victims.

The Power Dynamics
in Abusive Relationships

An abusive relationship is fundamentally based on power dynamics. Where the abuser has a power advantage by virtue of gender, role, professional status, or financial assets, controlling the type of the behavior is extremely effective. When this power differential is coupled with negative self-esteem, the offender may carry a hidden "moral rage" at feeling so inadequate that abusive behavior brings a certain satisfaction to this primitive moral instinct.

The power struggle is not between the gospel and culture, but between the gospel and the "powers" within any culture that dehumanize and enslave persons. Paul sought the renewal of the social structures and the humanization of culture, not the replacing of these structures and culture with a kind of freedom that destroys them. The continuity of order and stability through social change and cultural pluralism is thus grounded in human nature itself as that which produces and lives by culture. The challenge facing advocacy for victims is to make an intervention that restores the humanity of those who are part of the abusive system rather than merely to destroy the system. This cannot always be done, as the nature of abusive power is based on the immediate rewards to the abuser.

Gelles and Straus suggest that acts of violence occur when the costs of being violent do not outweigh the rewards. "Clearly, the immediate rewards of using violence to work off anger or frustration are quite valuable to some individuals who would rather not wait to see the longer-term benefits of more reasoned and rational discipline and conversation with their children or partners."

Strangely, the need to exercise power and control over others is not because the abuser feels strong but because he or she feels powerless and weak. The "payoff" in using abuse to control others is the feeling of gaining power over that person and compensating for one's own feeling of powerlessness. This is one aspect of the immediate "reward" of which Gelles and Straus speak.

In figure 21, each of the six areas offer a continuum on which perceptions of abuse can be determined on the part of the recipient. In each area, the degree to which one is under the control or power of another is an indicator of a propensity toward abuse, if not actual abuse.

The Anatomy of Advocacy

The ministry of the church as advocate must be one in which it perceives the effects of the abusive use of power in the same way as does the victim. This will ordinarily mean a paradigm shift for the church, as it assumes the role of advocate for the ones who are most powerless and vulnerable in its own constituency and its own community. The paradigm shift is a shift away from representing the appearance of virtue and toward becoming an advocate for victims of the seemingly virtuous and righteous.

Jesus was such an advocate, suffering rejection and persecution from the religious establishment of his own day because of this.

When Jesus healed on the Sabbath, ate with publicans and sinners, and asked a Samaritan woman to minister to his thirst, he penetrated through all racial, sexual, social, and cultural barriers to restore true humanity to others. Indeed, his own humanity could hardly have been the true humanity that it was if he had drawn back from the real humanity of others.

In drawing persons around him, Jesus re-created humanity in the form of a community of shared life and common identity. Even this narrower circle, defined by the specific calling of the twelve, was structurally open to the unclean leper, the tormented demoniac, the self-righteous Pharisee, and the women of ambiguous reputation. In contact with Jesus, humanity was liberated from the blind and capricious powers of nature and disease, as well as from the cruel and inhuman practices of the social and religious tyranny of the strong over the weak. In the real humanity of Jesus we see the humanization as well as the socialization of humanity.

Being an advocate means living as this specific person belonging to these particular people who speak the same language and participate in the same rituals of community life. This is to suffer rejection from one's own people, in many cases. Not to have the social approval of one's own people is to suffer estrangement, if not derangement. Jesus himself experienced this powerful social judgment when he was thought to have an "unclean spirit" by the standard of the self-perception of the Pharisees (Mark 3:30). Even his mothers, brothers, and sisters sought to intercept his ministry and remove him from public exposure because they concluded that "he is beside himself" (Mark 3:21). Advocacy is costly!

The effects of sin as inhumanity are not overcome through a more rigorous form of spirituality, but through a renewed structure of sociality. Advocacy seeks to restore the value of love as a social reality. Love is defined as living peaceably in a domestic setting, as clothing the naked, feeding the hungry, and loving the neighbor as oneself.

The anatomy of advocacy is grounded in the love of God expressed through Jesus Christ as both its source and goal. Jesus is the first advocate, and from him we learn the inner dynamic of advocacy.

1. He *felt* the pain of the powerless and tormented as his own pain.
2. He *heard* the cry of the desperate and needy with his own ears.
3. He *transferred* to the side of victim his own power.
4. He *exposed* the evil of abuse at the cost of his own privilege.
5. He *transformed* the dynamics of oppression by his own presence.

We cannot hear what we do not feel. The advocate hears because the advocate feels the pain of those who suffer. We cannot see what we do not hear. The victim remains invisible as long as we do not hear their cry for help or do not believe their words when they speak of it. We do not respond to what we do not see. Failure to act is due to blindness, not to lack of courage.

"I don't see the problem of which you speak," one pastor told me. "I know of no incidence of domestic violence or child abuse in my church."

Taking action against abuse means that one sees it at its earliest stages. Seeing the victim means that one can hear and believe their story. Until we feel the pain of others by placing ourselves in their situation, their words never reach our ears.

We know that the whole creation has been groaning in labor pains until now; and not only the creation, but we ourselves, who have the first fruits of the Spirit, groan inwardly while we wait for adoption, the redemption of our bodies. . . . Likewise the Spirit helps us in our weakness; for we do not know how to pray as we ought, but that very Spirit intercedes with sighs too deep for words (Rom. 8:22–23, 26).

Come, Holy Spirit.

VI

Leading God's People
in the Ministry of Christ

Leaders Who Abuse:
The Misuse of Power

Jim (not his real name) is thirty-three years old, married with two children, and is a seminary student preparing to be a pastor. Ten years earlier he and his wife joined a nondenominational community church in southern California as new Christians. Another couple, through whom they had come to know Christ as personal savior, were members of this church and introduced them to the pastor. They were immediately received into the fellowship and soon became active members of a Bible class taught by the pastor.

Pastor Bob, as he was affectionately called, was a compelling preacher and stimulating teacher. He was also a strong leader, running the church office with efficiency and leading the church board with an iron hand, though with a "velvet glove," as he liked to say.

The church operated a large preschool during the week. When the director moved away, Jim's wife was appointed by the pastor to fill the vacancy, as she had taught kindergarten for two years in public school and had administrative experience.

Jim and his wife became totally involved with the life of the church. They became part of an inner circle of couples, some of whom were board members, and all of whom were strong supporters of the pastor. After two years, Jim was elected to the board of elders along with others who had been hand-picked by the pastor as candidates.

The first stormcloud in what was to become an ominous and threatening sky appeared when Jim became concerned by some of the teachings of the pastor in the adult Bible class. The pastor insinuated in his teaching that some of the members were hindering the growth and effectiveness of the ministry of the church by criticizing his leadership. He taught that submission to the authority of the leaders of the church was a mark of spiritual humility and discipleship. When this theme began to appear in the pastor's sermons as well, Jim discussed the matter privately with two of his friends on the board.

"We have a Judas in our midst," one board member said. "The church secretary was fired by the pastor for insubordination when she refused to follow his instructions concerning some bookkeeping procedure. She has now gone to several other members accusing the pastor of unethical practices. She is attempting to undermine his authority in order to justify her own case."

Troubled by what he heard, Jim went directly to the pastor to find out for himself what had happened. He was surprised and shocked by what he heard. "Jim," the pastor told him, "you must dissociate yourself from these people who are out to destroy me. God has called me to lead this church and any one who opposes me will suffer the consequences from the Lord. I heard that your wife has some sympathy for this woman, and I expect you to get her in control if she wants to keep her job."

When Jim discussed the matter with his wife, she was outraged. She made it clear that she had no intention of closing her eyes to what she considered to be a matter of injustice and unethical behavior on the part of the pastor. "If he fires me he will have a lawsuit on his hands."

Shaken by what was taking place, Jim consulted with his friend who had first introduced them to the pastor. "I am sorry Jim, but I had no idea that the pastor would take this position. My wife and I have already made plans to leave and attend another church."

Jim was inwardly torn. The pastor was the person most responsible for the development and growth of his own relationship with God. At the same time, he was concerned that his marriage would be damaged, if not destroyed, if he chose to follow the pastor rather than support his wife.

Months passed, with secret meetings between Jim, the pastor, and others who were attempting to persuade Jim that his wife was an unspiritual person who was not only damaging the church but his own relationship with God as well. Jim felt increasing spiritual anxiety and psychological turmoil. Sensing that he might leave the church, the pastor warned him of dire spiritual consequences should he depart and threatened to contact any church he attended with information regarding his "spiritual apostasy," as the pastor put it.

"Now here I am," Jim said to me, after telling me his story. "My wife and I finally escaped by contacting the person who originally led us into this church. That was two years ago. We have received some excellent therapy with a Christian counselor and I now realize that we suffered horrendous spiritual abuse from this pastor. Through this experience I have felt called to full-time ministry. I no longer feel like a victim, but I don't want to end up victimizing others when I become a pastor. Why do some people abuse their power when they become spiritual leaders, and how can it be prevented?"

His question prompted me to write this chapter. Jim's experience was more severe than many people who have suffered at the hands of pastors and leaders who have misused their power. But the incidence of this kind of spiritual abuse at any level is more frequent than we would like to admit. We need to understand the nature of spiritual power dynamics in order to prepare men and women who will not become abusers as they assume the role of spiritual leaders.

The Devastating Effect
of Spiritual Abuse

Abuse of any type occurs when someone uses authority to exercise power over another for the purpose of controlling and exploiting another's vulnerability. Spiritual abuse happens when a leader with spiritual authority uses that authority to coerce, control, or exploit a follower, thus causing spiritual wounds.

David Johnson and Jeff Van Vonderen define *spiritual abuse* as "the mistreatment of a person who is in need of help, support or greater spiritual empowerment, with the result of weakening, undermining or decreasing that person's spiritual empowerment."

Jesus scolded the Pharisees and teachers of the law for their abuse of authority when they "sit on Moses' seat" (Matt. 23:2). Ken Blue comments:

> We often hear today that "knowledge is power." In Jesus' day, the knowledge of the law of Moses was power. The Pharisees knew Moses' teaching by heart and knew how to teach and apply it. They were the experts. From this lofty position of power they looked down on the "mob" (as they called them), which they said was cursed because "it knows nothing of the law" (John 7:49). So for those ecclesiastical abusers of the first century, the seat of Moses functioned in much the same way as leadership titles, academic degrees and church offices do for today's spiritual abusers.

Spiritual abuse on the part of a spiritual leader results whenever spiritual mentoring, teaching, or guidance is used to gain control and reinforce the authority of the leader rather than to empower and nurture the ones who are led. Power over others is but one kind of power in the relationship between pastors and parishioners, between teachers and students, between parents and children, and between therapists and clients. There is always a power differential in such relationships when one has more knowledge, skill, and authority than others.

Rollo May describes five kinds of power in his search for the sources of violence in human relationships.

exploitative power → power over
manipulative power → power over
competitive power → power against
nutritive power → power for
integrative power → power with

The first three kinds of power can easily be abusive use of power. The leader who exploits the spiritual motives and desires of a church member for the sake of producing loyalty and uncritical support commits spiritual abuse. The pastoral counselor who exploits the vulnerability of a troubled person seeking spiritual care so as to fulfill emotional and/or sexual needs commits spiritual abuse.

The leader who manipulates the agenda, coerces the decision-making process, and creates adversaries between people so as to "divide and conquer," grieves the spirit of a people and commits spiritual abuse. The pastor who uses biblical texts and ecclesial authority to gain a competitive edge in conflict situations commits spiritual abuse by "making wrongful use of the name of God" (Ex. 2:7). To be put on the losing side of an argument against God is to suffer spiritual abuse!

The consequences of spiritual abuse are particularly devastating because, as Ronald Enroth says, "Unlike physical abuse that often results in bruised bodies, spiritual and pastoral abuse leaves scars on the psyche and soul. It is inflicted by persons who are accorded respect and honor in our society by virtue of their role as religious leaders and models of spiritual authority. . . . When they abuse their authority and when they misuse ecclesiastical power to control and manipulate the flock, the results can be catastrophic."

Jim experienced some of these consequences, and they were devastating. As a relatively new Christian, he allowed his pastor to become his spiritual mentor. His spiritual conscience was tender and malleable. His perception of God was filtered through his pastor's approval and affirmation. The charge of spiritual delinquency struck at the very core of his assurance of salvation. The suggestion that his wife was an evil influence on him caused him to question the grounds of their marriage and turned intimacy with her into spiritual adultery. The questions concerning the pastor's authority and control that arose in his mind drove the dagger of doubt about his own spiritual integrity deeper and deeper. He felt like he was sinking in quicksand, and his struggles to escape only increased the pressure that threatened to suck the very life out of his soul.

Jim was a victim of spiritual abuse, and it was only by the grace of God that he and his wife escaped and found healing through the support of a friend and the counsel of a Christian therapist who understood the dynamics of spiritual abuse.

What Turns Leaders into Abusers?

The German theologian and pastor, Dietrich Bonhoeffer, is well known for his resistance to Hitler and his subsequent imprisonment and death as a modern Christian martyr. What is not so well known is his early warning concerning Hitler's assumption of the title *Führer* (Leader) as part of his rise to power in the late 1920s and early 1930s. Just two days after Hitler's appointment as Reich Chancellor on January 30th, 1933, Bonhoeffer was delivering an address over German radio on "The Concept of the Leader (*das Führerprinzip*)," when his address was cut off the air by Goebbels, Hitler's newly appointed minister of propaganda. In his talk Bonhoeffer warned, "It is essential for the image of the Leader that the group does not see the face of the one who goes before, but sees him only from behind as the figure stepping out ahead. His humanity is veiled in his Leader's form."

Bonhoeffer's uncanny insight provided to be accurate as events unfolded. The use of power by Hitler obscured not only his own humanity but led to the dehumanization and death of millions of others.

All forms of abuse, as I have said earlier, results from the misuse of power for the purpose of controlling and exploiting another's vulnerability. In using power in such a way, the leader assumes a role that conceals the human weakness of the leader and blinds the leader to the human value of those who follow.

When a leader entrusted with a role of providing spiritual direction, teaching, and pastoral care uses the authority of the role to conceal his or her own human weaknesses and needs, there is a corresponding blindness to the human value of others under their care. Spiritual leaders become abusers when they use their role to break the common human bond they have with those for whom they are responsible as "priests of God."

In arguing for the more excellent priestly role of Jesus, the author of the book of Hebrews points to the transparent humanity of Jesus and reminds his readers: "For we do not have a high priest who is unable to sympathize with our weaknesses, but we have one who in every respect has been tested as we are, yet without sin" (Heb. 4:15).

The role of the priest includes the humanity of the priest.

Every high priest chosen from among mortals is put in charge of things pertaining to God on their behalf, to offer gifts and sacrifices for sins. He is able to deal gently with the ignorant and wayward, since he himself is subject to weakness; and because of this he must offer sacrifice for his own sins as well as for those of the people. And one does not presume to take this honor, but takes it only when called by God, just as Aaron was. (Heb. 5:1–4)

In the days of his flesh, the author continues, "Jesus offered up prayers and supplications with loud cries and tears, to the one who was able to save him from death" (5:7).

The priestly role of a spiritual leader is liable to abuse when the leader seeks to conceal his or her own human weaknesses and spiritual defects by projecting them upon others. The priest then turns into an accuser and judge. Using the guise of priest to uncover weaknesses in others, the leader manipulates the guilt so as to gain power over the other rather than mediating the guilt through priestly intercession so as to empower the other.

In looking for clues as to why spiritual leaders become abusers, we should be alert to ways in which those who lead use their role to gratify their needs for power and self-importance. Those who seek the priestly ministry in order to prey on the weaknesses of others are potential abusers. Those who are set apart for leadership must have demonstrated a healthy core of self-identity and a capacity to exercise authority and use of power without exploiting the weaknesses and needs of others.

The Double Bind
of Spiritual Leadership

All leadership entails the assumption of a role, the mantle of authority, and the exercise of power. The humanity of both the leader and those who follow is a check against the misuse of that role, authority, and power. Abuse occurs when the leader conceals his or her own humanity and becomes blind to the humanity of others. In this case, humanity is a value meant to be upheld and preserved.

Spiritual leadership presents a different equation. The leader who assumes the role, authority, and power of speaking and acting on behalf of God now faces what might appear to be an impossible task. For it is not only human weakness on the part of the leader that must be concealed but humanity itself. If the perception of the leader is that spiritual values take precedence over and even replace human values, then the leader will suffer the double bind of attempting to be authentically human in order to be an effective priest while denying that humanity in order to be prophet of God.

Some spiritual leaders who are uncomfortable with their own humanity can assume the mantle of a prophet and exercise their authority and power unrestrained and untouched by the inhuman effects of their leadership. In fact, those who have not fully integrated their human feelings, needs, and drives into a healthy core self may seek out the role of spiritual leader or pastor precisely with the hope that the role will provide a solution to these unresolved issues.

We have a clue then to why some spiritual leaders become abusers. It may very well lie with the motives and needs to escape one's own humanity through donning the mantle of a spiritual leader in a prophetic role. In this case, the double bind is not really experienced at all, except as a underlying terror that one will be unmasked and uncovered as only human after all. Thus one is driven by this fear into greater and greater excesses of abuse through misuse of the authority and power that comes with the office.

The role of spiritual leader is one fraught with risk, both for the one who assumes the role as well as for those who are subject to the leader. James warned: "Not many of you should become teachers, my brothers and sisters, for you know that we who teach will be judged with greater strictness. For all of us make many mistakes. Anyone who makes no mistakes in speaking is perfect, able to keep the whole body in check with a bridle" (James 3:1–2).

The apostle Paul was well aware of the danger of spiritual leadership when he spoke of his own role as "the aroma of Christ to God among those who are being saved and those who are perishing." As he considered the implications of this, he cried out, "Who is sufficient for these things?" (2 Cor. 2:15, 16).

As if to answer his own question, Paul wrote:

But we have this treasure in clay jars, so that it may be made clear that this extraordinary power belongs to God and does not come from us. We are afflicted in every way, but not crushed; perplexed, but not driven to despair; persecuted, but not forsaken; struck down, but not destroyed; always carrying in the body the death of Jesus, so that the life of Jesus may also be made visible in our bodies. For while we live, we are always being given up to death for Jesus' sake, so that the life of Jesus may be made visible in our mortal flesh. So death is at work in us, but life in you. (2 Cor. 4:7–12)

It is not difficult for most people to see that Jim and his wife were victims of spiritual abuse on the part of a pastor who used the power and authority of the pastoral office to exploit, manipulate, and coerce his people. I have attempted to show why this pastor might have become an abuser.

First, he failed in the priestly ministry of Christ by creating, exploiting, and manipulating spiritual guilt in Jim. Driven, no doubt, by his own "bad spiritual self" split off from his "good self," the pastor projected the bad part on Jim. "We have a Judas in our midst," was no doubt first said by the pastor and repeated by his supporters. Spiritual abusers are leaders who use the priestly office of ministry to create and manipulate guilt rather than to mediate and relieve it. Such abuse disempowers people as spiritual beings and creates spiritual wounds no ordinary therapy can remove.

Second, the pastor failed in the prophetic ministry of Christ by assuming a "god-like" role in dispensing judgment without regard to his own all-too-human condition. Like the Pharisees in Jesus' day, this pastor assumed that authority to speak on behalf of God was self-authenticated by his own mantle of ordination and call. To question his authority was to question the very counsel of God. Spiritual abusers are leaders who use the prophetic office of ministry to align themselves with God against the people of God. Such abuse abandons people and condemns them to the hell of spiritual apostasy.

Karl Barth once said that the call to worship is the temptation to idolatry, but we cannot stop worshiping on that account. One might paraphrase Barth by saying that the call to spiritual leadership is the first step to becoming a spiritual abuser, but that we cannot dispense with our leaders. In the next chapter, I hope to develop a model of leadership that serves the mission and ministry of Christ, rather than subverting it. It is called servant leadership.

The Ministry
of Servant Leadership

"I don't believe in the concept of servant leadership," a pastor I will call "Bill Jones" told me. "I am not the paid servant of my congregation, but their spiritual leader." I could tell from his tone of voice that this pastor was protesting as much as he was proclaiming. When pressed, he admitted that he felt like he spent more time serving the needs of the congregation than leading it. There was an angry edge to his emotions and a glint of defiance in his eyes.

More than one pastor has ended up feeling this way. Seminary graduates often enter pastoral ministry with idealistic visions of a spiritual ministry devoted largely to preparing rich and edifying sermons, giving wise counsel to lay leaders, and offering pastoral care and comfort to needy souls. After all, the call is to "full-time ministry." Sooner or later, these young pastors begin to realize that the congregation is reading from a different version of the original vision. *Full-time* is the name of the horse hitched to the cart with a dozen wheels, one or more dropping off at the most inopportune times, and *ministry* is the code word for the driver who also doubles as the mechanic.

Few pastors actually have the kind of abusive power and control practiced by Pastor Bob, as we saw in the previous chapter. Yet if a pastor feels like a slave to the people, the need to use power as a way of gaining control will be a temptation. "Don't Get Mad, Get Even," is the invisible bumper sticker on many a clergy chariot. Psychologists call it the passive/aggressive syndrome. Pastors who get stuck in this pattern often feel abused and become quiet abusers of their congregations by blaming or scolding them for lack of spiritual discipline.

In this chapter I hope to create a biblical model of servant leadership that will both empower the leader and enable the people to become the kind of community that fulfills the will and purpose of God.

An effective servant leader must possess three things: a creative vision that inspires, a delegated power that enables, and a spiritual gift for ministry.

Servant Leadership:
Trusted to Lead through Vision

The fundamental misconception with servant leadership, as reflected by the pastor cited above, is that one ends up being the servant of the people or the organization. This leads to the "doormat" concept of leadership, where one lays down whatever dreams and plans one has and invites people to walk over them. "I am only the coach," one pastor said, "my people are the players." Or, to put it in more ecclesiastical terms, "I am only the pastor, my people are the ministers." This concept of servant leadership is really the abandonment of leadership. It leads to failure on the part of the leader and frustration among the members of the church.

Robert Greenleaf, who wrote the seminal work on servant leadership, made it clear that the leader is not subservient to the desires and goals of the organization, but is a servant of the mission of the organization. It is the vision of the specific mission or goal of the organization, says Greenleaf, that marks the effective leader. "Foresight is the 'lead' that the leader has. When he loses this lead and events start to force his hand, he is leader in name only. He is not leading; he is reacting to immediate events and he probably will not long be a leader."

The leader is the servant of the mission of the people of God. This mission must be perceived as the "vision" that informs the goals and strategy of the people. The vision does not come through predicting what will come to pass in the future by reading past performance and extending present goals, but through reading the signs of the future in the present.

In the English language, the word *future* points us to that which has not yet occurred, beyond the present. Jürgen Moltmann reminds us that there are two words for *future* in Latin. One is *futurum*, from which we have the English word *future*. The other word is *adventus*, from which we have the English word *advent*.

Futurum denotes what will be or what may be. The *futurum* arises out of the present and has its potential in the possibilities that emerge out of the present. In this sense of the word, the future cannot really be any more than extrapolation out of the past and present. The "future" is already a "future past," because nothing can be imagined that has not already left some trace in the past. There is indeed "nothing new under the sun" (Eccl. 1:9).

In contrast, the word *adventus* (advent) points to that which is "coming to the present." This kind of future does not arise as a possibility out of the past, but rather as a manifestation in the present of what the future is. The ancient Greek writer Hesiod described the eternal being of Zeus by saying, "Zeus was and Zeus is and Zeus will be." In contrast, John, in the book of Revelation, writes, "Grace to you and peace from him who is and who was and who is to come" (Rev. 1:4). God's future is not in "what comes to be," but in him "who comes."

For example, John the Baptizer did not point into the future and predict the coming of the Messiah. Rather, he pointed to Jesus standing in their midst and announced that the coming of the Messiah as the promised one (future), was now present. "Here is the lamb of God who takes away the sin of the world," exclaimed John (John 1:29). John's vision was not of an event that lay in the future, but of the future that had come into the present. This is why the church announces the "advent" of Christ in the weeks prior to the celebration of the birth of Jesus.

As John understood his role, it was to "prepare the way of the Lord," in fulfillment of the promise of Isaiah 40:1–5. The spiritual leader does not manipulate the people to advance his or her own program and plan, but "prepares" the people for the coming and presence of the Lord in their midst. Leaders who do this will be trusted to lead because their vision has integrity and their preparing of the way of the Lord is directed toward the spiritual and personal health of the people. Rather than abusing the people by coercing them into being followers, the leader who has a compelling vision of what God's purpose is for the people prepares them to receive the blessing and benefits of the Lord.

Effective leadership means reading the signs of God's promise in the context of present events and translating these signs into goals; this is "preparing the way of the Lord."

Servant Leadership: Trusted to Lead through Power

Can leaders be trusted with the authority and power necessary to "prepare the way of the Lord" as servants of the vision, without also abusing that power? If the leader is a true servant, the answer is yes. It is the misuse of power that causes abuse, not power itself. Jesus commended the faith of the centurion who sought healing for his son, when he suggested that Jesus only had to "say the word," and his son would be healed. "I also am a man set under authority," the centurion said, "and I say to one, 'Go,' and he goes, and to another 'Come,' and he comes" (Luke 7:1–10). Faith does not rest on powerlessness, but uses power to accomplish God's vision and purpose for humanity.

The servant leader is a "steward" of the resources needed to attain the vision. And the power to carry out this stewardship is a delegated power. What the author of the book of Hebrews said of the one who serves as priest is also true of the leader: "And one does not presume to take this honor, but takes it only when called by God, just as Aaron was" (Heb. 5:4).

As a good steward, the servant leader is faithful and accountable to the Lord who cherishes and loves the people. One of the most compelling metaphors in the Bible is that of the steward. Jesus used the concept to develop the theme of faithfulness and accountability in some of his parables (e.g., Luke 12:42–48). Paul wrote that a bishop "as God's steward, must be blameless; he must not be arrogant or quick-tempered or addicted to wine or violent or greedy for gain. . . . " (Titus 1:7).

Ken Blue says, "Most people understand that if someone is dedicated to building them up and solving their problems, that person can be trusted with power. True servants diffuse any fear of their leadership." David McKenna wrote of the grace to lead and the power to follow, indicating that empowering those who follow is really the graceful use of power.

Discipline and direction are the twin components of effective leadership. Power in the service of vision serves as a discipline against disorder as well as direction for the disorganized.

Moses exercised servant leadership when he responded to God's call and brought the vision of liberation from bondage and entrance into a "promised land" to his people in Egypt. The story of their forty years of wandering in the wilderness before they actually entered into the land under Joshua's leadership is a case study in servant leadership using power both to discipline and give direction. Confronted with disorder that threatened the very existence of the people, Moses exercised discipline after first becoming their advocate.

When the people turned away from God to worship the golden calf, Moses made intervention on their behalf directly to God (Ex. 32:11–14; 30–34). Having earned the right to be their leader by risking his own standing with God on their behalf, Moses confronted their disorder and brought them under discipline. "When Moses saw that the people were running wild (for Aaron had let them run wild, to the derision of their enemies), then Moses stood in the gate of the camp, and said, 'Who is on the Lord's side? Come to me!' " (32:25–26).

With the power to discipline came the power to lead through directing the people back toward the Promised Land in fulfillment of the vision. Though in the end he himself was not allowed to enter due to his own disobedience, he nonetheless led the people to the very threshold of the land before turning the leadership over to Joshua.

Power in the service of vision issues in a strategy that unites the wisdom of God with the work of God in order that the will of God may finally be accomplished. Figure 22 depicts this process.

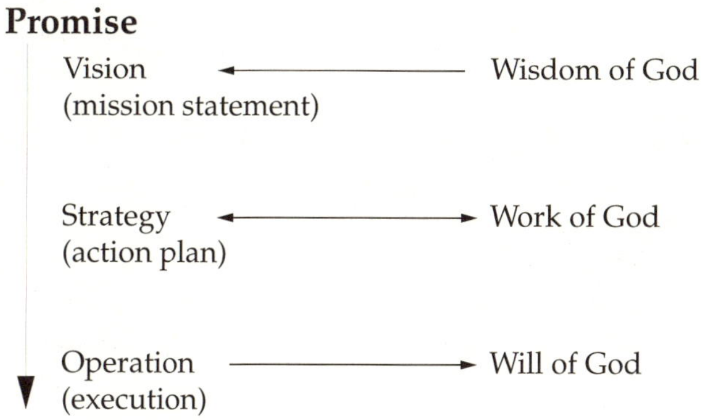

Promise

Vision ◄─────────────── Wisdom of God
(mission statement)

Strategy ◄──────────────► Work of God
(action plan)

Operation ──────────────► Will of God
(execution)

Figure 22

The *wisdom* of God provides the common sense of leadership. God's wisdom is not esoteric or mysterious. Rather, it enables the leader to censor outrageous idealism and sense the wisdom of working with God on behalf of the people. A clearly defined mission that the people of God seize as their own task leads to singleness of purpose.

The *work* of God takes place through the creative strategy of leadership. Strategic planning with steps for implementation translates wisdom into work. An action plan informed by mission does the work of God as it moves toward the will of God.

The *will* of God is discovered through the consummation of leadership. It is important to note that the will of God is not the same as the wisdom of God. The will of God is the result of leadership that discerns the vision of God and implements that vision through a strategy that includes planning and directing the process.

The power of leadership is not a claim to know the will of God more than anyone else, but in having the vision, based on promise, that leads to the will of God through doing God's work. When leaders claim to know the will of God as a private revelation, they are close to misusing power and abusing the people. Any use of power to abuse the people is contrary to the will of God, because God's desire and purpose is directed toward the ultimate good of his people.

Effective use of leadership power involves discipline that corrects disorder and direction that overcomes disorganization and confusion. Effective servant leadership means directing and coordinating the energies and resources of the people of God; this is being a "faithful steward" of God's vision.

The kind of servant leader who can be trusted with power will have these qualities:

> The servant leader will be able to articulate more clearly than anyone else the vision of the people of God as a contemporary interpretation of its mission.
>
> The servant leader will be more closely aligned with the promise that leads to the will of God than anyone else, and will factor that promise into the planning process.
>
> The servant leader will lead others who are responsible for implementing the planning process into full disclosure of the promise, vision, and goals that he or she holds to be essential to the planning process.
>
> The servant leader will exercise power by empowering others to see the vision, work the plan, and reap the benefits and blessings of doing God's will.
>
> The servant leader, more than anyone else, will be an advocate for those who stumble and fall through their own failure or who are wounded by others through the process.

Servant Leadership: Empowered to Lead through Spiritual Gifts

When the apostle Paul itemized the many spiritual gifts that enable the people of God to carry out the ministry of Christ, he strongly suggested that every member of the body of Christ should expect to receive and exercise a gift. "To each is given the manifestation of the Spirit for the common good" (1 Cor. 12:7).

At the same time, Paul recognized that those who are placed in positions of leadership have their authority and power by virtue of the spiritual gift. It is "Christ's gift," he wrote, that is the basis for the "grace gifts" (*charismata*). "The gifts he gave were that some would be apostles, some prophets, some evangelists, some pastors and teachers, to equip the saints for the work of ministry, for building up the body of Christ, until all of us come to the unity of the faith and of the knowledge of the Son of God, to maturity, to the measure of the full stature of Christ" (Eph. 4:11–13).

In the contemporary concern for the role of spiritual gifts in the equipping of the ministry of the laity, it should also be noted that those in positions of leadership are also "gifted" by the Spirit of Christ for that ministry. The thrust of much of the literature on spiritual gifts for ministry has been on equipping the laity for the ministry, and rightly so. But we need to be reminded that there are gifts of leadership as well.

When leaders misuse power and abuse their people, one might call this spiritual malpractice—the abuse of the gift of the Spirit. Spiritual leadership, as Oswald Sanders has pointed out, is characterized by the gift of the Spirit as the motivating factor in the exercise of power and authority.

The centerpiece of Paul's theology of spiritual gifts is the continuation of Christ's ministry through Christ's gifts to the people of God through the Spirit. It is the ascended Christ, wrote Paul, who "gave gifts to his people" (Eph. 4:8). With the gift comes the character of Christ. "Let the same mind be in you that was in Christ Jesus," Paul exhorted the Philippians (2:5). He then went on to enumerate the qualities of humility, non-exploitiveness, servanthood, and obedience to the mission and will of God as those that exemplify Christ.

In looking for qualities of leadership within the people of God one should look, first of all, for evidence of the spiritual giftedness of the leader. This is not manifested only by leadership skills but by a leadership spirit. Because skills and competence can be identified and quantified against proven performance of successful leaders, there is a temptation to assume that if one has the "right stuff" one has the gift.

What we often fail to see in measuring effective leaders by these criteria is that, in the secular world, effective leadership measured by performance alone may be more easily attained by the absence of the very qualities attributed to Christ. I was informed by an organizational psychologist that people with sociopathic tendencies tend to make the most effective leaders because they are not troubled by conscience! When exploiting others makes good business sense it is common sense to the one who has no spiritual sense. When we honor leaders in the church for their skill in using power we should not be surprised to discover that they are often the very ones who misuse power and become spiritual abusers.

When leaders abuse their people, spiritual abuse has already occurred as abuse of the spiritual gift of leadership. An arrogant spirit is not hard to detect, nor is a self-serving use of authority easy to conceal. We should not be interested as much in how one's superiors have evaluated a candidate for a position of leadership, but in the candid comments of those who have worked with and under this person.

The profile of Christ is clearly drawn through the recorded history of those who were his followers. He was not the servant of the people, but of God. When pressured by the crowd to assume a role that was contrary to the wisdom of God for his life, he simply disappeared from their midst

(John 6:15). Urged by his disciples not to go to Jerusalem because of the danger that faced them, Jesus rebuked them and said, "If any want to become my followers, let them deny themselves and take up their cross and follow me" (Matt. 16:24).

He was the leader, no doubt about that. Just ask Peter! But he exercised that leadership in the power of the Spirit, not for his own self-interest or glory. Following his baptism, "full of the Holy Spirit," he was immediately led by the Spirit into the wilderness to be tempted (Luke 4:1). In his first sermon in the synagogue at Nazareth he applied the words of Isaiah to himself: "The Spirit of the Lord is upon me, because he has anointed me to bring good news to the poor. He has sent me to proclaim release to the captives and recovery of sight to the blind, to let the oppressed go free, to proclaim the year of the Lord's favor" (Luke 4:18–19).

Reading the account of his ministry from baptism to crucifixion, one would surely conclude that Jesus was an effective servant leader based on this job description!

Perhaps every leader should place this text before those who follow as the criteria on which evaluation will be made and the effectiveness of one's leadership judged. To say, "the Spirit of the Lord is upon me," is to hold before the people of God the character of Christ and to subdue one's own spirit to that of the Lord.

An effective servant leader, I have said, must possess three things: a creative vision that inspires, a delegated power that enables, and a spiritual gift for ministry. Pastors are servant leaders of the people of God. They are not accountable by virtue of always having the right vision, but of submitting their vision to the wisdom of God and being willing to abandon their own in favor of God's. They are not accountable for every strategic plan, but that the plans are worked so as to lead to the will of God. They are not responsible to succeed at every point but at every point, to be accountable to the gift of the Spirit and the character of Christ in exercising that gift.

The final test of the servant leader is that the "little ones" who belong to Christ are not despised and abused, for "in heaven, their angels continually see the face of my father" (Matt. 18:10). The effective servant leader is not one who "works the angles," but who sees the angels.

God's servant leader does not stand between the people and God, but stands with the people as the faithful steward, to provide discipline and correction and to prepare the way for the coming of the Lord. Maranatha!

Churches That Abuse:
Domestic Disorder in the Family of God

There are abusive churches as well as abusive leaders. Pastor Bill Jones, to whom I referred in the previous chapter, may well have been serving an abusive church. Churches that abuse not only have a history of mistreating their leaders but also of spiritually wounding their own members. Many pastors have accepted a call to a church with spiritual zeal and sacrificial love only to end up in the lion's den without Daniel's deliverance. Steven Krantz, a pastor who speaks from first-hand experience of such a church says, "The pastor who is called to a bruised church will be picking shrapnel from the shredded hearts of a wounded people for a long time."

Like a dysfunctional family, the church often demonizes the one who diagnoses the sickness. Instead of seeking the cure, the church, twisted and tormented by its own inner pain, collapses back into the primitive instincts of survival that lurk beneath the surface of all domesticated beasts. So too they sent Jesus away after he confronted the demons in the Gerasene village because, as Luke records, "they were filled with great fear" (Luke 8:37). In the end, those who opposed the ministry of Jesus finally spoke the words openly: "Are we not right in saying that you are a Samaritan and have a demon?" (John 8:48).

A bit melodramatic, you say. But then you have not read the increasing flow of papers that come across my desk written by bruised and battered pastors who have retreated from the battle to lick their wounds. Take my word for it. There are churches that create spiritual wounds in their leaders and in their own members that may never completely heal. There are churches that are injured through pastors who have abused them. There are churches with people who have been abused but who now become abusers themselves.

I want to talk about such churches in this chapter. I do not intend to suggest that many churches are this way, but that there are churches that abuse and they can be found in any community. No church has complete immunity from this disorder.

The Dysfunctional Nature
of Churches That Abuse

The most dangerous place for a woman is in an intimate relationship, and the most dangerous place for a child is in the home. So say those who work with victims of domestic violence. This is because most abuse takes place where there is the highest level of intimacy and personal contact.

It can also be said that the most dangerous place for spiritual abuse to occur is in the church. As with domestic violence, there is a paradoxical twist. We cannot survive and grow to maturity without personal contact with others who provide the context for relationships that touch the core of our being. We cannot exist as whole persons without relationships, and yet it is in relationships that we are most vulnerable to abuse and violence.

In the same way, we cannot exist with Christ without relationship and participation in the body of Christ—the church. Yet it is in the body of Christ that we are most vulnerable to spiritual abuse. This is what makes spiritual abuse, like domestic violence, so insidious. The most obvious attack of the devil would not be as destructive as the rape of our souls by those who present themselves as our spiritual caretakers, companions, and guides. The Psalmist cries out: "It is not enemies who taunt me—I could bear that; it is not adversaries who deal insolently with me—I could hide from them. But it is you, my equal, my companion, my familiar friend, with whom I kept pleasant company; we walked in the house of God with the throng" (Ps. 55:12–14).

Churches that abuse are like dysfunctional families where the only glue that holds the members together is their common pain and their conflicted patterns of interaction. In a paradoxical way, conflict in the dysfunctional church family is the normal form of communion. Conflict energizes the passions at the same time that it exhausts the spirit. Mistaking the arousal of passion for the moving of the Spirit, the members stimulate themselves by touching the exposed nerves of their opponents.

"Conflict exists *inside* of people not *between* them," says psychologist Newton Malony. Conflict does not result from lack of discipline, but from insatiable desires and unmet needs. These needs are themselves often due to experience of previous abuse. Abusers are most often themselves victims of abuse from earlier in their lives. A church that abuses is a church with members who carry, deep within, unresolved anger, unhealed pain, and untouched feelings. Conflict becomes an addiction because it is a stimulant that creates its own need. "Beware of the habits learned in controversy," warns Francis Schaeffer.

Where one might expect that chronic conflict would lead to disintegration of the church, the exact opposite is true. A dysfunctional system is the most stable of all because it is extremely rigid. Resistance to change causes the rigidity, and the rhythm of conflict and communion maintains the balance. Social psychologists speak of this as homeostasis. Homeostasis functions as a thermostat of the social system, regulating those behaviors that are acceptable within a certain range.

Family therapist Virginia Satir suggests that members of the family help to maintain this balance overtly and covertly. The family's repetitious, circular, predictable patterns of interaction reveal this balance. "When the family homeostasis is precarious," she writes, "members exert much effort to maintain it."

This is why conflict energizes a community rather than blowing it up. This is also why a conflicted community constantly seeks new sources of energy by drawing everyone into the conflict, even when it means turning on its own most vulnerable members.

This is illustrated by the recent campus dispute at Rutgers University (Newark, N.J.), following President Francis Lawrence's comments that African American students perform poorly on standardized tests because of "genetic, hereditary backgrounds." Dinesh D'Souza commented, "It's ironic, this man has been appeasing campus activists for a long time. The revolution is eating its own children."

The metaphor is a chilling one. But unfortunately, also an accurate one. Churches that abuse end up "devouring their own children." Not only are unsuspecting pastors often the victims of spiritual abuse by their own people, but the members can turn on each other when the energy level is depleted. Contrary to Darwin's evolutionary thesis, it is the most unfit who survive in the frenzy of spiritual cannibalism.

The Devastating Consequences of Spiritual Abuse

1. *Spiritual abuse is the violation of our trust placed in God by someone who betrays that trust by using God's name to gain entrance into our secret soul, destroying our experience of the goodness of God.*

What Linda (not her real name) shared with me was a story that I had heard before, with different names and different faces. She and her husband became members of a new church that suddenly sprang up in their suburban community. They were attracted by the friendliness of the people and the vibrant, contemporary worship service. Having no family close and with no long-term friends nearby, Linda responded eagerly to the invitation to join a small group that met weekly for prayer and informal Bible study. All went well for several months.

As her friendship deepened with the members of her group, Linda began to share with the group some of her spiritual struggles. She had grown up in a traditional Protestant church, but had not made a personal profession of her faith until she met the man who was to become her husband, who was an active Christian. After they were married, her husband began to lose interest in the church they were attending and she was left to continue her spiritual journey alone.

She felt comfortable sharing some of these personal and spiritual issues with the group because one of the rules of the group was confidentiality, and she valued their spiritual concern and prayers for her. One woman in the group called Linda one day and said that she would like to meet with her alone for prayer and sharing. Linda's response was positive and they began to meet regularly in addition to the regular group meeting. The intense spiritual tone of their sharing was something that Linda had never experienced before. As she recalled the experience, she described it as being in the very presence of God. It was the most intimate and personal relationship she had ever had with another person, she told me. Her relationship with God became the focal point of her entire life.

Meanwhile, her husband became intensely jealous and threatened by this "new Linda," as he put it. Their marriage, which had gone through some shaky times, now became strained to the breaking point. Linda's prayer partner began to urge her to confront her husband with his lack of spiritual concern and suggested that he might be a "tool of Satan" to undermine her own relationship with God.

The reader can guess the rest of the story. Linda's marital problems became the prayer concerns of the small group, confidentiality was breached, and the pastor was drawn into the situation. Linda's prayer partner told the pastor that Linda's husband was an evil influence on her and on the entire group. The pastor confronted Linda's husband, his reaction was one of outrage, Linda was urged to move out of their home for the sake of her own spiritual integrity, and the end result was a divorce.

Left with a broken marriage, a sense of betrayal by her closest spiritual friend, and a feeling of abandonment by the church (divorced persons were not welcome in that church!), Linda simply quit attending. No one called her to offer support and assistance. She left that church a damaged person, with much emotional pain and deeply wounded in spirit.

"I can't even pray now," she told me. "And I cannot attend any church without feeling my stomach knot up. If those people represented who God is, I have no desire to seek him. And yet, I know that only God can heal me. What can I do?"

Linda is a woman who has suffered spiritual abuse by people who destroyed her trust in the goodness of God by gaining access into the private place in her life and violating it in the name of God. This, at the very least, is to break the commandment, "You shall not make wrongful use of the name of the LORD your God, for the LORD will not acquit anyone who misuses his name" (Ex. 20:7).

2. *Spiritual abuse is the exploitation of our sacrificial love for God as a means of advancing organizational and institutional goals, leaving our spirits undernourished and our lives over-burdened.*

When members of the church are pressed into service as unpaid workers to staff the various programs and institutional needs of the organization as a test of their love for God and their participation in the ministry of Christ, there is always the danger of spiritual abuse.

When a member of my own congregation, whom I will call Fred, came to me he was obviously in considerable distress. Part of his distress was in facing me with his complaint. The rest of his distress, as it came out, was caused by a pattern of neglect and insensitivity during recent years on my part as pastor and on the part of the church as well.

When a major building project was voted by the congregation, Fred was selected to head up the committee responsible for developing the plans and supervising the construction. As a member of the church board, he had heard me expound a concept of ministry many times. In order to enlist men and women in the organizational life of the church, I had preached and taught that love for God is both a motive and means to fulfill our Christian responsibility. For persons like Fred, this touched a strong chord of spiritual response, and the sacrifice called for seemed to be meaningful.

Now, as I listened to Fred, I saw how easily this appeal to spiritual sacrifice as a sign of love for God could be misused. "I am embarrassed to have to tell you this, Pastor," he said, "but I am sorry that I ever took that job. You will never know how many hours I worked to get the plans approved and the building completed. When we had the dedication service, I thought that I would feel some satisfaction and gratification, but it was just the opposite. Everyone seemed excited about the building, but I went home and cried. And I haven't cried since my mother died."

I waited until he was able to continue, not knowing yet what had caused him to feel this way.

"I'm probably not a very spiritual person," he finally said. "I know that we are to do everything for the glory of God and not for ourselves. But I took a lot of criticism during this process and I guess made some enemies in the church. I don't think I ever want to hold another office or take on another job in the church for the rest of my life. I'm simply tired of trying to get somewhere with God by holding up one corner of this church by myself."

I had never heard of spiritual abuse at that time in my pastoral ministry but, looking back, I can see it clearly. Fred had been exploited. We had appealed to his love for God, used him to fulfill our own vision, and lost sight of him as a child of God in the process. My priorities shifted that day. And I think that Fred experienced healing and recovery. It was a painful lesson for both of us, and he ended up being the teacher.

3. *Spiritual abuse is the addictive power of a legalistic theology that creates guilt in order to dispense grace, leaving us spiritual cripples bound to one another by the invisible cords of co-dependency.*

The following story illustrates a particularly devastating kind of spiritual abuse. The name of the church has been changed, providing an ironic twist on the details described.

Grace Church was a nondenominational church founded by a pastor whose theology was based on salvation by grace alone, whose preaching was marked by hour-long expositions of biblical texts, and whose concept of the life of faith was submission to Jesus as Lord. It is not enough that we are saved, he taught, but we must also have Jesus as our Lord.

As it turned out, submission to the lordship of Jesus was defined as rejection of anything that had to do with self, and turning everything in one's life over to God. Because grace was easy, discipleship was hard. That is the ironic twist. In order to stir the saints in his congregation up for the rigorous task of discipleship, he had to create guilt as the motivating force. "Walking with the Lord," became the badge of the spiritually mature. To practice it one had to learn the pious vocabulary, avoid the appearance of worldliness, cultivate the virtues of religiosity and, at all costs, deny one's deeper human needs and desires.

As I explored the inner life of this congregation, I wondered why people would tolerate being made to suffer such crippling guilt and shame. It then became clear that there was something addictive about this kind of spiritual abuse. People became hooked on it. Shame itself is addictive, as Lewis Smedes once said: "Most everyone walks through a valley of shame now and then. Some of us, however, take a lifelong lease on shame; it is our permanent home. We are shame-bound. . . . Some of us are so hooked onto shame that we are afraid we would be lonely without it. . . . If we lost our shame, we would not recognize ourselves."

This describes exactly the members of Grace Church. Their Christian identity had become so fixated on guilt and shame as the evidence of their spiritual quest that they would have felt, well, *guilty* for not feeling guilty! If they were comfortable wearing this mantle of spiritual shame, why describe it as spiritual abuse? Because of the casualties who quietly dropped out of sight and out of the picture at Grace Church. As with all forms of spiritual abuse, one does not move directly from being a victim into re-covery. In ministering to some who had left but remained spiritually wounded, I discovered something more about the devastating conse-quences of spiritual abuse.

4. *Spiritual abuse is the silent cancer of secret gossip and malicious rumor that causes a feeding frenzy among the sharks submerged in the troubled waters of church conflicts. We are unaware of the damage until we stand up and attempt to walk out, and find that we have no legs.*

The church resembles a family in many ways. Paul Minear reflects on the unique characteristics of the New Testament church and says, "When-ever a social whole bears the impress of a common character there the term 'family' is legitimately used." We are encouraged to call each other brother and sister, and to confess our faults to one another (James 5:16). The body of Christ has a systemic structure so that if one suffers all suffer and if one is honored, all are honored (1 Cor. 12:26). The most salient fea-tures of an abusive family are the dynamics of power and control, bound-aries, reality distortion, and secrecy.

Every family has its own secrets, and John Bradshaw reminds us that "Families are as sick as their secrets." Like a family, the church has both a public face and a domestic life. To the casual observer and marginal mem-ber, the church may appear serene and untroubled. Yet the inner life of the family of God can be vicious and pernicious for those who are sucked into the vortex of spiritual abuse.

A pastor, whom I will not name, once wrote an extended paper for me as part of a class assignment, documenting his own experience with such a church. At first the church welcomed him with open arms and positive affirmation. As he learned more about the makeup of the church board and the connections between some of the members, he discovered that the treasurer of the church was a wealthy businessman in the community, who gave large gifts to the church to make up for budget deficits and to enable the church to complete special projects. He was also considered by most members of the church to be a highly spiritual person to whom they looked for wisdom and guidance.

The plot thickens. This treasurer's daughter was also on the board of el-ders. In the course of what appeared to be rather routine church business, the pastor suggested a change in the worship service. All on the board agreed. Later, the pastor was confronted by the treasurer's daughter with the charge that he had acted arrogantly in making this change and that many in the church were disturbed by his action.

Suspecting that it was really her father that was the source of this com-plaint, the pastor went directly to him. He was treated in a condescending but gracious manner with no admission that he himself was responsible for the complaint. As weeks and months went on, it became increasingly clear that the treasurer's daughter was creating problems on the board with charges against the pastor, and that her father was the one instigating the conflict. As other members of the church were drawn into the conflict, rumors spread and unfounded charges about the pastor circulated through an informal network. The pastor felt helpless to counter this conspiracy, and attempts to deal directly with the treasurer failed to resolve the issue.

It was now revealed to the pastor that the treasurer had been responsible for driving the two previous pastors out of the church, and that virtually the entire church was controlled by him. Not only did he threaten to withhold his financial support as a means of controlling the church, he concealed his own manipulative behavior behind the facade of hyperspirituality. To resist him was to invite retaliation, though he was careful not to leave bruises that might be seen by the public. The pastor was advised by several of his friends to leave, but he felt led to bring some healing and reconciliation through the application of intervention strategies that he had learned through his continuing education. It was all to no avail.

The pastor's denominational executive was finally called in to deal with the crisis. Admitting that the church had a history of abuse toward pastors and that one man had the congregation virtually under his control, the denomination elected to remove the pastor and support him in the establishing of a new church in another part of the city, leaving the congregation to call another pastor!

In reading the letters of the apostle Paul, one discovers over and over again how many of these churches were plagued by internal strife, gossip, factions, and false teachers, and how his own leadership was maligned and undermined. It must have broken Paul's heart! His belief that the Holy Spirit was the bond between the members and that they were called to peace and unity was sorely tested by the outrageous behavior on the part of many. Yet he never gave up his conviction that even the most troubled church was truly the body of Christ, and that the members were "called to be saints" (1 Cor. 1:2).

Churches can recover from being spiritual abusers, and those who have been spiritually abused can find healing and hope in churches that embody Christ's ministry of reconciliation and recovery. In the final chapter of this book I will suggest what the characteristics of such a church would be.

The Ministry
of Care and Community

"We are born broken," wrote Eugene O'Neill. "We live by mending. The grace of God is the glue."

I was once asked to officiate at the funeral service of a young mother who, on a bright and sunny spring day, dropped off her youngest daughter at her husband's place of work and inexplicably went home to take her own life. The family was stunned and stricken with grief and remorse. "Why could we have not seen that she was suffering so much?" they asked. "Yes, she had some problems, but she seemed to be coping with them well enough."

I discovered that she was noted for her beautiful garden and her love for flowers. Lovely vases filled with fresh flowers could be found in every part of her home. At the graveside service, I commented on that, and said something like this. "Peggy herself appeared to be a beautiful vase. Yet from the inside, she saw her life as cracked and falling to pieces if she let go of it. Nor could she hand it over to someone else to hold for her, for it took both hands to keep it together, and if she took even one hand off to ask for assistance, she feared it would fall apart. What we saw was a beautiful person, like a vase, with imperfections to be sure, but with no fatal flaws. What she saw from the inside were fractures that never could be mended. Her life broke apart from the inside out. Only in this tragic end do we feel her pain as a bond with her and with God. His grace is now her healing and our comfort. "

"We are born broken, we live by mending. The grace of God is the glue."

The church may well be a place for those who "are called saints," as Paul addressed the Corinthians. But we are saints in need of mending. Writing to the church at Thessalonica, Paul said, "Night and day we pray most earnestly that we may see you face to face and restore whatever is lacking in your faith" (1 Thess. 3:10). The word "restore" is *katartizo*, and is used in Matthew 4:21, of James and John "mending" their nets. Everyone's faith needs mending at times, and the grace of God is the glue.

Paul knows that the Christians in that church need some "mending" of their faith. He is not deceived by the outward appearance, as he once was with regard to his own life. He discerns the broken edges of the spirit deep within the people; he feels their pain, sees the widening cracks in their faith, and wants to be there to administer some glue.

In this chapter I want to talk about the church's ministry of discernment, caring, and community. These are the characteristics of a church where the glue of God's grace heals the brokenness with which we were born, and where there the ministry of mending can take place for those whose spirit has been broken.

The Ministry of Discernment

A woman who was depressed came to her pastor for counseling. She had been upset for several weeks because he had not noticed her depression. He apologized and thanked her for bringing it to his attention. She replied by saying that pastors are "expected to see" things without being told. She had not thought it necessary to mention what he was expected to discern.

This pastor had stumbled on one of the unspoken rules of the church. The pastor is expected to recognize needs and discern problems without them being mentioned!

Discernment is a gift of leadership that enables one to recognize blind spots in the church's perception of reality coupled with the capacity to recognize and call forth potential in persons.

Persons who have suffered spiritual abuse have a distorted view of reality; they become confused and disoriented. One of the principal tasks of leadership, John Patton writes, is to clarify reality for people. Leaders help interpret reality, and so lower the anxiety of a group by giving answers to questions being asked. Discernment is the process that frees us from our preoccupation with our own concerns and allows us to focus deeply on the life and concerns of another person.

Discernment must be coupled with love. Discernment without love can expose another's blind spots, but one may use that blindness to control and manipulate others. Therapeutic insight is a form of power that can be used to seduce as well as heal. Love seeks the empowerment of others through discernment that enables them to grasp the reality of healing and hope, leading to growth toward their own potential.

If there is no discernment, love can be used to lead others but without noticing the damage done to those who follow. Love without discernment does not see the blind spots in another's perception of reality. When we love without discernment we pursue our own agenda and project our own identity and goals on those we love.

Theodore Roszak reminds us, "We are born into other people's intentions. We learn our names and our natures at their hands, and they cannot teach us more truth than they know or will freely tell. Can there be families whose love is not treason against our natural vocation?" And Stanley Hauerwas warns, "No one rules more tyrannously than those who claim not to rule at all because they only want to love us."

Those responsible for leading the church must have the capacity to discern where spiritual abuse has occurred or is occurring. There must be discernment of what reality is like for others. How does one gain this capacity?

The capacity for discernment begins with openness to the reality of one's own life as humanly flawed and spiritually graced.

Karl Barth spoke dramatically but insightfully when he said that Christians must not

> be ashamed to sit down with the unrighteous as friends, that those who are genuinely wise do not hesitate to seem to be fools among fools, and that those who are genuinely holy are not too good or irreproachable to go down into 'hell' in a very secular fashion . . . since Jesus Christ is the Savior of the world, [the church] can exist in worldly fashion, not unwillingly nor with a bad conscience, but willingly and with a good conscience. It consists in the recognition that its members also bear in themselves and in some way actualize all human possibilities.

I was not far into my own pastoral ministry before I began to realize that no one had come to me to confess thoughts, actions, and flaws that I did not recognize as possible failings in my own life. Barth has it right. We all "bear in ourselves and in some way actualize all human possibilities."

One of the principles of the twelve-step recovery programs is that only one who is himself or herself in recovery can be effective in helping others. The blind spot in one's own life must be recognized, admitted, and brought to light before one can discern the blind spot in another. Jesus said it first: "Why do you see the speck in your neighbor's eye, but do not notice the log in your own eye? Or how can you say to your neighbor, 'Friend, let me take out the speck in your eye,' when you yourself do not see the log in your own eye? You hypocrite, first take the log out of your own eye, and then you will see clearly to take the speck out of your neighbor's eye" (Luke 6:41–42).

Discernment also is gained through the capacity to feel the pain and hear the cry of those who are spiritually abused. In chapter 20, I wrote: We cannot hear what we do not feel. We cannot see what we do not hear. The victim remains invisible as long as we do not hear their cry for help or do not believe their words when they speak of it. We do not respond to what we do not see. Failure to act is due to blindness, not to lack of courage.

"Pastors are expected to see things without being told," replied the woman who explained her failure to tell him about her depression. In a sense, she was correct. Failure to see is really a result of being so preoccupied with our own feelings that we do not feel what it is like for others to live within the "cracked vase" of their lives. What we cannot see in others, we can discern through feelings. The woman who took her own life *appeared* to be coping well, said her friends and family. They could not see the cracks she felt.

In the diary of a girl not yet twelve, named Opal by her foster parents, the precocious thoughts of a child who experienced herself as "feeling" surprise us with their clarity and truth:

> I saw a silken cradle in a hazel branch.
> It was cream with a hazel leaf
> halfway around it.
> I put it to my ear and I did listen.
> It had a little voice.
> While I did listen, I did feel its feels.
> It has lovely ones.
> I did hurry to the house of the girl
> who has no seeing
> so she might know its feels
> and hear its heart voice.
> She does so like to feel things.
> She has seeing by feels.

Love is not only an act of volition, says theologian Emil Brunner, but it is an expression of *feeling*. "To be apprehended by the love of God, means to be smitten in the very center of one's being, to suffer it, not as a pain, but as a supreme joy, as happiness and peace. . . . "

When the Word of God becomes a living Word and not merely a dead letter, it functions in the church as a discerning Spirit, as the author of Hebrews makes clear. "Indeed, the word of God is living and active, sharper than any two-edged sword, piercing until it divides soul from spirit, joints from marrow; it is able to judge the thoughts and intentions of the heart. And before him no creature is hidden, but all are naked and laid bare to the eyes of the one to whom we must render an account" (Heb. 4:12–13).

Discernment is the sensory organ of love, registering the feelings of those who are broken and seeking the glue of God's grace. If we have not been smitten ourselves with the arrow of divine love, we will not feel, we will not hear, and we will not see what others expect us to see—the inside of their cracked vase.

The Ministry of Caring

"The inherent ideal of the personal," wrote John Macmurray, "is a community of persons in which each cares for all the others, and no one cares for himself." The apostle Paul said it first. "Let each of you look not to your own interests, but to the interests of others" (Phil. 2:4). The members of the body of Christ should have care for one another, wrote Paul, for "If one member suffers, all suffer together with it; if one member is honored, all rejoice together with it" (1 Cor. 12:26).

One cannot assume the responsibility of care for others, of course, unless one practices healthy and consistent self-care. "Let the same mind be in you that was in Christ Jesus," urged Paul (Phil. 2:5). In attempting to restore others who have fallen, Paul warns, "take care that you yourself are not tempted" (Gal. 6:1). While we are to "bear one another's burdens," we must all "carry our own load" (Gal. 6:2, 5).

The point is this. One cannot practice healthy self-care unless one is part of a community that cares for each other. The ministry of caring is not to take on another person's life as our own personal project; that leads to codependency, a dysfunction that cripples and weakens both the caregiver and the one cared for. None of us really wants to be another person's project, though we don't mind being pampered at times. We all have needs, but there is a bittersweet feeling about receiving a care package in response to an expressed need.

Early in my pastoral ministry, I shared with a fellow minister the frustrations of attempting to live on the meager salary that the church paid while attempting to keep up a standard of living that the church expected of its pastor. The confines of this friendship outside of the church freed me to indulge in a bit of self-pity and disclosure of personal pain. I felt better after the conversation and was grateful for the opportunity to share my feelings.

A few days later, I received a note from my friend with a check for $50.00, explaining that some extra money had come his way and he was glad to share some with me. In those days, $50.00 was almost a week's salary! I was stunned, chagrined, and troubled by this gift. My thank-you letter was gracious, but the feeling was bittersweet. The $50.00 was indeed a temporary help, but it was soon gone. I had not really wanted money, though the lack of money was the cause of my pain and frustration. I wanted someone to hear me, not merely to help me. I knew that I could never again have the freedom to share with him that kind of need. I didn't know how to ask for care without it also being interpreted as a request for aid.

A year later, I mentioned to the chairperson of my church that I would soon have to resign in order to get a secular job to buy the necessary clothes for the family and take care of other needs that had been deferred.

He was astonished and said, "We knew that you could not live on what we were paying you but assumed that you had other sources of income to supplement your salary!" Steps were taken immediately to raise my salary to the point where we could mange to live without falling too far behind.

I had been teaching and preaching a gospel of love and mutual care, but had not been practicing it. I had allowed my pride and concern for maintaining the appearance of having no needs to isolate me from the very community to which I looked for care. Failing to disclose to them the pain and frustration caused by an unworkable financial arrangement, I deprived them of the opportunity to share a problem that, in reality, was of mutual concern. At the same time, I could secretly blame them for not meeting my needs!

I have discovered that when someone says, "no one really cares," the complaint is not so much that a need has not been met but that one feels alone and unwanted. It is not need that isolates us, but the withholding of the pain, anxiety, and fear that lie behind our needs.

Before Peggy tragically took her own life, her emotions were on a pendulum, swinging from highs to lows, with no apparent cause other than a physiological or psychological unbalance. Over a period of several months, she had received counseling for episodes of depression that seemed to be related to PMS syndrome, as well as some medication. When these attempts to regulate her life did not help, she discontinued the therapy.

She did not lack friends and family with whom she had frequent contact. There were many who would have responded instantly to an expressed need. Peggy's extended family appeared to function at a high level of efficiency and productivity. When problems arose, they were quick to respond and offer solutions. If part of her life was broken, the solution was to fix it, so that she could function within her roles as wife, mother, and friend.

A woman who sought pastoral counseling for what she considered an intolerable marriage told me that her friends could not accept the fact that she could not find some way to fix her marriage, as her husband did not appear to be abusive or unloving. "What they don't understand," she said, "is that I could make a pretense of living in the marriage as though everything were fine, but it would literally kill me. I feel isolated, uncared for, and have thought of suicide as the only way to escape."

There is an ironic paradox in a community's response to another person's need. In attempting to provide help or to solve a problem, the person may actually be driven deeper into isolation by dealing with the symptom rather than allowing the person space to express the deeper need for caring.

There is often a "get well soon" message hidden in many of our attempts to help someone with whom we live when they have a problem or share some pain. This is especially true if we become anxious when someone we care about does not respond to our attempts to help. When caring becomes associated with curing, we do not know how to care for persons when their pain seems incurable. Sometimes caring means allowing a person space to be oneself within the bond of friendship, without expecting that person to "get well" as a condition of being accepted.

To feel that no one cares is to feel unimportant and of no value. The essence of care is valuing another person's life as much as we do our own. Paul made this clear when he applied the principle of mutual love and care to the marital relation. "As Christ cares for the church as his own body," wrote Paul, "in the same way, husbands should love their wives as they do their own bodies. He who loves his wife loves himself. For no one ever hates his own body, but he nourishes and tenderly cares for it, just as Christ does for the church, for we are members of his body" (Eph. 5:28–31).

In the previous chapter, I wrote of churches that abuse not only their own members but their pastors. Such abuse is a failure of the ministry of care and community. When pastors fail to care for the members of the church and their own families, this is abuse. When churches fail to care for their pastors and their families, this is also abuse. A recent survey of pastors revealed that 80 percent believe that pastoral ministry has affected their families negatively, that 33 percent say that being in ministry is an outright hazard to their family, and 70 percent report that they do not have someone they consider a close friend.

The ministry of care is the ministry of community. It is the ministry of Christ through the members of the body for the purpose of mutual edification, growth, and blessing.

The Ministry of Community

In the biblical concept of the church, community is a verb before it is a noun. Community is what takes place when there is mutual care, forgiveness, and a common life of the Spirit of Christ. The fruit of the Spirit, in contrast to what Paul calls the "works of the flesh," are the virtues of community life—"love, joy, peace, patience, kindness, generosity, faithfulness, gentleness, and self-control" (Gal. 5:22–23). Do not ask me whether or not I have the spiritual fruit of gentleness, ask the persons who live with me! I may think of myself as a kind person, but those who feel the effects of my words and actions are the better judges.

The mutual life of community is more like a friendship than a corpora-
tion or partnership. Unlike any other social structure, friendship exists
solely by virtue of the constant care not to hurt, offend, or devalue the
other. The ministry of community is the ministry of friendship in a context of institutional structures, roles, and other obligations. Community as
ministry can take place outside of formal structures such as an institutional and organized church. Where Christ is present in the church, it is as
community, wrote Dietrich Bonhoeffer, not as a corporate society. The
ministry of community is the ministry of Christ through the mutual care
and life of the members.

The philosopher John Macmurray reminds us that if we agree to disagree and our basic relation is only toleration or even cooperation, "we
will remain isolated individuals, and the co-operation between us, though
it may appear to satisfy our need of one another, will not really satisfy *us*.
For what we really need is to care for one another, and we are only caring
for ourselves. We have achieved society, but not community. We have become associates, but not friends."

I often remind couples who are about to marry that their marital relation depends on their relation as friends, not on their roles as husband and
wife. Often married couples say and do things to each other that would destroy a friendship. Because we value the person with whom we are friends,
we anticipate the effect of our words and actions and hold in check that
which would be hurtful and offensive. If we did not, we would soon have
no friends. If married persons valued each other as friends, care would be
taken not to violate the relation through words and actions that hurt. In the
same way, members of the body of Christ are to value each other and take
care for the effect of their words and actions upon one another.

This restraint does not mean the lack of honesty, but the practice of care.
We can speak the truth to our friends, but we must "speak the truth in
love" so that we can "promote the body's growth in building itself up in
love" (Eph. 4:15, 16). We are responsible for the intention in our words and
actions, even though, as John Macmurray tells us, we may not always be
aware of our motives. It is our intention, not merely our motives, that determines whether our words and actions are received as honest love.

This may require restraint and patience with regard to holding in check
our own words if they cause harm, and not responding in kind to the
harmful words and actions of others.

The apostle Paul urged such restraint in appealing to the members of
the body. "Bear with one another and, if anyone has a complaint against
another, forgive each other; just as the Lord has forgiven you, so you also
must forgive" (Col. 3:13). The Greek verb *anechomai* (bear with one an-

other) means literally, "keep on holding back." Patient restraint in the face of the action of others is the intended meaning. It also means "holding back" on our own need to use others to vent our anger and judgment.

David Mains describes what kind of place the church ought to be when he says, "The church is a place where people who make a lot of mistakes can come and feel loved, helped, forgiven, and given hope to go out and do better next time." Some have found this to be true. Many have not. Some who have turned to the church to find healing have instead been treated with indifference at best, and at worst, wounded further. Many within the church have left as persons with spiritual wounds and broken lives.

The church exists in a society where wounded people can be seen at every hand. Those who become casualties of abuse, failed marriages, chemical dependency, moral failure, or excessive grief are found both within the church and outside of it. As we have seen, there are many who also experience spiritual abuse rather than spiritual healing and growth as members of the church.

The ministry of community is intended by God to provide a place of recovery and healing from such experiences. Where there has been abuse, pain, and brokenness, however, recovery is not an easy—nor is it an immediate—experience.

What makes the recovery of spiritual and personal wholeness difficult is that a callus forms over the wound, masking the pain. Dennis Guernsey writes, "Much like a bruise that has been callused over, these patterns which inflict hurt and pain have never healed. The emotional calluses form to cover the hurt and keep it from dominating the person's ability to function. . . . Such is the deceptiveness of the callus. Because you no longer feel the pain, the tendency is to believe that the hurt has been healed."

"I am a survivor," one man told me, who had experienced a series of failures in his personal relationships, along with a struggle with alcoholism. As I listened I sensed that he was fighting against capitulation to despair, using all of the coping skills he could muster.

Survival is a powerful instinct of self, but it does not always lead to growth. The emotional energy needed to maintain the struggle to survive was a heavy drain on his spirit. In attempting to draw back from the broken side of his life, he was retreating from the creative power of spiritual wholeness. Behind all psychological pain and brokenness, there is a spiritual wound that can be healed only by strong doses of the grace of God.

"We live by mending. The grace of God is the glue."

"Spirituality for survivors is a topic that needs much work in the future," writes James Leehan. "Survivors do not need an emphasis on evil and sin; they have gotten more than enough of that. As victims they were constantly told how wicked and bad they were, and as survivors they are struggling to overcome that image."

There is no need to make people whose spirit is broken feel condemned, as a condition for receiving grace. In fact, this may well bruise the broken spirit and turn what could be a hopeful spiritual experience of recovery of the joy of salvation into a hopeless inward spiral of self-condemnation.

A sense of guilt is not creative and produces no positive motivation toward spiritual wholeness. We tend to forget that the cross of Christ only has significance as a place where sin is judged for those who have experienced the power of resurrection and the gift of the Spirit of God. It is true, consciousness of sin can lead to brokenness of spirit and thus to healing and wholeness.

"The Lord is near to the broken hearted," wrote David, "and saves the crushed in Spirit" (Ps. 34:18). God's touch is firm, but light. His Spirit is powerful, but not violent. "A bruised reed he will not break, and a dimly burning wick he will not quench" (Isa. 42:3).

The spiritual goal for the broken spirit is renewal and restoration through the power of God. This is the gift of God that comes freely to those who receive the Spirit. "For all who are led by the Spirit of God are children of God. . . . When we cry 'Abba! Father!' it is that very Spirit bearing witness with our spirit that we are children of God . . . " (Rom. 8:14–16).

"Pastors are expected to see things," was the woman's response to her pastor who had failed to discern that she was deeply depressed.

"No one really cared," said my friend as he explained why he had stopped attending a church where he had once held an office.

Peggy's last cry was the sound of a gun echoing in the silence of her carefully tended flowers.

"This is not fair," protested a reader of the first draft of this chapter. "You have pointed to the casualties of the church and neglected to mention the positive effects in the lives of the majority of its members. You are expecting too much of the church. It is impossible to be all things to all people."

My response was to cite Jesus: "Those who are well have no need of a physician, but those who are sick" (Luke 5:31). It was not the comfortable, the untroubled, the righteous, who revealed the healing and saving grace of God through Jesus. It was blind Bartimaeus, the despised Samaritan woman, the scorned prostitute, the desperate father of the demon-possessed boy, it was all of these that set the standard and determined the character of Jesus' ministry.

"Truly I tell you, just as you did it to one of the least of these who are members of my family, you did it to me" (Matt. 25:40). For every Peggy that walks alone into the dark night of her soul, there are hundreds who linger in the corridors of the church hoping that someone will see the stress fractures in their faith.

For every person who is clinically depressed and in need of professional therapy, there are hundreds who sit passively in the pews waiting for "pastors to see things" that are circumspectly hidden from view on Sunday morning.

For every pastor who leaves the ministry a broken and bruised person, there are hundreds who lick their own wounds and turn the other cheek that has already been struck from the blind side.

If the church is perceived as a community of discernment and caring, it will, like Jesus, find the tormented and troubled, the anxious and the curious, the desperate and the devout, coming for healing and hope.

You will want me to list the ten easy steps to becoming this kind of community. This cannot be done. There is only one rule: "Love does no wrong to a neighbor" (Rom. 13:10). Do no harm!

Discernment can only be learned by listening; it cannot be taught. Caring can only be practiced by valuing the other as much as oneself.

It was the woman who said, "pastors are expected to see," that taught the pastor. It is Peggy who teaches us that the outside appearance of another person differs from the inside view.

Jesus is our teacher and mentor in the formation of the church for ministry. And he does not enter from behind the altar, but through the door to the street.

"Preach one sermon every month," I tell my students, "to the Jesus who walks in off the street and sits alone in the back row, weary and worn, to see whether there is any good news for him today!" Then practice what you preach.

Notes

PART I. Ministry as Theological Task

Chapter 1:
Ministry as Theological Discovery

I am indebted to Karl Barth for my understanding of the seventh day preceding the first day. "We must understand that God is the measure of all reality and propriety, understand that eternity exists first and then time, and therefore the future first and then the present, as surely as the Creator exists first and then the creature. He who understands that need take no offense here" (Barth, *Church Dogmatics*, I/1. Translated by Geoffrey Bromily [Edinburgh: T. & T. Clark, 1975], 531).

In this book, I will assume that Moses was the principal author of the first five books of the Old Testament (the Pentateuch). While I am aware that the Mosaic authorship of these books is contested in much of modern scholarship, I am not so much concerned for the questions of literary authorship as I am for the theological paradigm that emerged through Moses' leadership and ministry in the exodus event. Consequently, I speak of Moses as the author of the Genesis account of creation as a theological construct more than as a critical theory of authorship. My approach is consistent with the New Testament references to Moses as source of these first five books even as Isaiah is referred to as the prophet who produced the book of Isaiah (cf. Luke 24:27; Matt. 8:17).

I drew the concept of the "silence of the Gods" from the book by Kornilis Miskotte, *When the Gods Are Silent* (London: William Collins Sons & Co., 1967). "When we start from the infinity of God and attempt to reach his particular reality, we destroy the decisive character of the encounters of God in a concrete sense and end up with the theological ambivalence which is characteristic of the silence of the gods" (p. 218).

Abraham Heschel is my source for the concept of "pathos" as the divine source of both mercy and wrath. See his book, *The Prophets,* vol. 2 (New York: Harper & Row, 1962).

> The anger of God must not be treated in isolation, but as an aspect of the divine pathos, as one of the modes of God's responsiveness to man. It shares the features that are characteristic of the pathos as a whole: it is conditioned by God's will; it is aroused by man's sins. It is an instrument rather than a force, transitive rather than spontaneous. It is a secondary emotion, never the ruling passion, disclosing only a part of God's way with man. . . . For all the terror that the wrath

of God may bring upon man, the prophet is not crushed or shaken in his under-standing and trust. What is divine is never weird. This is the greatness of the prophet: he is able to convert terror into a song. For when the Lord smites the Egyptians, he is both "smiting and healing" (Isa. 19:22) (p. 63).

Ministry Precedes and Creates Theology

One of the fundamental theological axioms of Karl Barth was that the first com-mandment is the decisive criterion for the theology task. This was set forth in his March 10, 1933 lecture in Copenhagen, "The First Commandment as an Axiom of Theology," printed in *The Way of Theology in Karl Barth,* ed. H. Martin Rumscheidt (Allison Park, Pa.: Pickwick Publications, 1986).

In my book, *Historical Transcendence and the Reality of God* (Grand Rapids: William B. Eerdmans Publishing Co., 1975), I have explored in depth the concept of God's transcendence that appears within the historical and temporal boundary of our existence, particularly as revealed in the humanity of Jesus Christ, the in-carnation of God in human form.

Every Act of Ministry Reveals Something of God

The reference to the pastor who baptized a stillborn baby can be found in the article written by Pastor John D. Stoneking, "Saying Hello and Good-bye—Would I Baptize a Stillborn Baby?" *The Circuit Rider* 9:3, 1984.

Chapter 2:
Ministry as Theological Discernment

The Inner Logic of Theological Discernment

The concept of inner logic has been taken from the thought of Thomas F. Tor-rance. Cf. *God and Rationality* (London: Oxford University Press, 1971). "[W]e let our knowledge of things and events in their own states be illuminated by the in-telligible relations directly forced on our recognition by the things and events themselves" (p. 104; cf also, pp. 94, 99, 169).

Aristotle reacted against Plato's concept that concepts existed apart from the things that we experience through our senses. Aristotle said: "Again it must be held to be impossible that the substance and that of which it is the substance should exist apart; how therefore, can the Ideas, being the substance of things, ex-ist apart?" (*Metaphysics.* The Works of Aristotle Translated into English, vol. VIII [Oxford: The Clarendon Press, 1908], 991b).

René Descartes (1596–1650) is well known for his dualism between mind and body. Using the principle of doubt, Descartes arrived at the point where every-thing known through sense experience could be doubted except the "existence of the doubter." The existence of the mind, he concluded, was the only thing that could be affirmed with certainty, thus: I think, therefore I am. See his *Meditations* (1641), in *The Philosophical Works of Descartes* (Cambridge University Press, 1912).

Martin Heidegger argues that the original Greek concept of truth (*aletheia*) as "truth disclosing itself" was distorted by Plato when truth was subordinated to an idea. With Plato *Logos* became separated from *being,* asserts Heidegger, with the result that truth becomes a "standard of correctness" (*Essays in Metaphysics* [New York: Philosophical Library Inc., 1960]). It is interesting to reflect on the fact that the Greek concept of truth prior to Plato was much closer to the Hebrew concept of truth as divine self-disclosure.

The reference to Francis Thompson is from his poem, "The Kingdom of God," in *The Treasury of Religious Verse*, compiled by Donald T. Kauffman (Old Tappen, N.J.: Fleming Revell, 1966), 18–181.

Theological Discernment: A Case Study

Rebekah's deception of her husband raises the question of whether the means justify the ends. Certainly Rebekah violated the formal principle of truthfulness when she deliberately deceived Isaac by inducing Jacob to pretend to be his brother in order to receive the blessing. What is actually involved in this case is not the securing of a desirable end though an immoral means. There are several levels of truth that impinge on this situation at the same time. God's revealed Word to her is God's truth just as much as is her relation to her husband. Her decision is not only a moral one, it is a matter of discernment as to which truth-relationship has higher priority.

Dietrich Bonhoeffer discussed just such a situation in his essay, "What is Meant by 'Telling the Truth'?" *Ethics* (New York: Macmillan, 1973), 363–72. Bonhoeffer used the example of a boy in school who is asked by his teacher in front of the whole class whether it is true that his father often comes home drunk. It is true, but the child denies it. The fact that his father is an alcoholic cannot be admitted in this context without betraying the truth of the boy's relation to the father. In another setting, he may be free to admit the fact. In this setting, to admit to the truth would be a betrayal of his father. Bonhoeffer's point is that betraying the father is not a truthful act. At the same time, in remaining true to the father, the boy is guilty of telling a lie. Rebekah's action has no moral justification. This is why one cannot argue that the means is justified by the end. Rebekah acts responsibly in accordance with God's intention, even though she needs God's forgiveness for her act.

Chapter 3:
Ministry as Theological Innovation

Are There No Absolutes Left?

Immanuel Kant is well known for his agnosticism concerning knowledge of entities beyond that which can be known through sense experience. At the same time he postulated a universal moral law that was binding on every person. See his *Critique of Pure Reason* (London: Longman Green & Co., 1909) and *Critique of Practical Reason* (London: Macmillan & Co., 1929). From Kant's categorical moral imperative is derived the concept of deontological ethics. The ethical obligation is a universal moral law by which one can predict what moral behavior should be prior to entering actual situations.

The older dualism between an objective physical world and the human as pure subject has given way to a more dynamic and holistic view of nature. Fritjof Capra argues persuasively that modern physics has overcome this mechanistic view of nature in favor of a holistic and dynamic conception of matter (*The Turning Point: Science, Society and the Rising Culture* [London: Collins, Fontana, 1963], 89). Capra's latest book extends his thinking on the relation of nature, God, and human knowledge. See Fritjof Capra and David Steindl-Rast, *Belonging to the Universe—Explorations on the Frontiers of Science and Spirituality* (San Francisco: Harper, 1991). See also Thomas F. Torrance, *The Christian Frame of Mind—Reason, Order, and Oneness in Theology and Natural Science* (Colorado Springs: Helmers & Howard Publishers, 1989).

The relation of human language to objective reality lying beyond the words themselves has been argued by Thomas F. Torrance.

> We are unable even to determine the formal-syntactic coherence of biblical statements or passages in any consistent way unless we introduce into the equation at least some *direct reference* to objective realities and intelligibilities beyond the statements themselves, for it is finally through that metasyntactic reference that syntactic systems may be coherently organized. In other words, . . . no syntactics contain its own semantics. When interpretation is prepared to give a pivotal place in the determination of a consistent and coherent connection in biblical statements to their objective semantic reference, many of the difficulties and perplexities that crop upon the linguistic level disappear. . . . Hence we must take great care to preserve the open texture of the inner rational sequence of biblical statements, in virtue of which the intrinsic intelligibility of its objective pole may shine through to us, if we are really to understand and express that inner rational sequence in a consistent way (Thomas F. Torrance, *Reality and Evangelical Theology* [Philadelphia: Westminster Press, 1982], 116–17).

The Hebrew concept of the absolute is located in the historical encounter of God and the nature of truth as personal relation. This is reflected in the rabbinical tradition as the following story illustrates.

> The God of the Jews is never encountered in the abstract (as a logical necessity or mechanical proof), but always in the specific, historical and relational. Nowhere is this more apparent than in God's disclosure of his name as Yahweh. The divine being, says Gerhard von Rad, is presented "not in the sense of absolute, but of relative and efficacious being—I will be there (for you)." That is the meaning of Yahweh. God is always known by his acts, by his involvement with his people, by name.
>
> But again, the truth can best be framed in metaphor. Time before time, when the world was young, two brothers shared a field and a mill, each night dividing the grain they had ground together during the day. One brother lived alone; the other had a wife and a large family. Now the single brother thought to himself one day, "it isn't really fair that we divide the grain evenly. I have only myself to care for, but my brother has children to feed." So each night he secretly took some of his grain to his brother's granary to see that he was never without. But the married brother said to himself one day, "It isn't really fair that we divide the grain evenly, because I have children to provide for me in my old age, but my brother has no one. What will he do when he's old?" So every night he secretly took some of *his* grain to his brother's granary. As a result, both of them always found their supply of grain mysteriously replenished each morning.
>
> Then one night they met each other halfway between their two houses, suddenly realized what had been happening, and embraced each other in love. The legend is that God witnessed their meeting and proclaimed, "This is a holy place—a

place of love—and here it is that my temple shall be built." And so it was. The First Temple is said to have been constructed on that very site. The holy place, where God is made known to his people, is the place where human beings discover each other in love. The absolute is known in the personal (Belden C. Lane, "The Rabbinical Stories: A Primer on Theological Method," *The Christian Century*, Dec. 16, 1981).

The statement, "what *is* is absolute," echoes the thesis of Dietrich Bonhoeffer, who argued that what is normative is not the concept of what is real, but the ontic reality of personal being and encounter. In his early doctoral dissertation he wrote: "This brings us once again to what was said at the beginning of our inquiry, about the normative character of basic ontic relationships. In the sphere of Christian ethics it is not what ought to be that effects what is, but what is effects what ought to be" (*Sanctorum Communio* [London: Collins, 1967], 26, 146). Later, in his writings published as *Ethics* (New York: Macmillan, 1973), he wrote: "Good is the real itself. It is not the real in the abstract, the real detached from the reality of God, but the real which possesses reality only in God" (190f).

Chapter 4:
Ministry As Theological Praxis

Praxis Is Not Practice!

The difference between *practice* and *praxis* has been made clear by James Will.

> But praxis must not be misunderstood as practice. Practice has come to mean the use of external means to attain a theoretically defined end. It suggests that finite and sinful persons may so understand the meaning of God's peace as to be able to devise economic, political, diplomatic, and even military means to attain it. The end of peace is thought to be a transcendent value that appropriate external means may effect. Praxis, on the other hand, is a dialectical process of internally related events from which a result dynamically emerges. Given the finite and ideological character of our preconceptions of peace, they cannot be treated as sufficient definitions of an eternal value to guide our practice. Rather, we need a praxis; that is, peace must be allowed to emerge from a dialogical and dialectical process that may continuously correct our ideological tendencies. Praxis is thus a process of struggle, negotiation, and dialogue toward a genuinely voluntary consensus (James Will, *A Christology of Peace* [Louisville, Ky.: Westminster/John Knox Press, 1989], 24–25).

Aristotle's concept of praxis can be found in *The Nichomachean Ethics*, bk. 6, ch. 5, trans. J.E.C. Welldon (New York: Prometheus Books, 1987), 192.

I have discussed the way in which the curriculum of most theological schools is divided between practical theology and pure theology, and offered some suggestions for changes in "Memo to Theological Educators," in *Ministry on the Fireline—A Practical Theology for an Empowered Church,* (Downers Grove: InterVarsity Press, 1993).

The Praxis of the Spirit: A Case Study

My use of the term Christopraxis began with my published article, "Christopraxis: Competence as a Criterion for Education for Ministry," *TSF Bulletin* (January/

February, 1984). The use of the term *praxis* in contemporary theology has been greatly influenced by the quasi-Marxist connotation given to it by some Latin American Liberation theologians. My own attempt in using the word is to recover the authentically biblical connotation of God's actions that reveal his purpose and truth. I appreciate the concept of praxis as used by Orlando Costas (see *The Church and Its Mission: A Shattering Critique From the Third World* [Wheaton: Tyndale House, 1974]). For further reading concerning my use of praxis see *Ministry on the Fireline—A Practical Theology for an Empowered Church.*

The Praxis of Discipleship

For an insightful treatment of love as a core theological theme, see Clark Pinnock and Robert Brow, *Unbounded Love—A Good News Theology for the Twenty-First Century* (Downers Grove, Ill.: InterVarsity Press, 1994).

Jürgen Moltmann has made a convincing argument that the theological axis is laid in the presence of the resurrected Christ experienced in the praxis of discipleship.

> Christopraxis in the narrower sense must be understood as the life of the community of Christians in the discipleship of Jesus. . . . To know Jesus does not simply mean learning the facts of christological dogma. It means learning to know him in the praxis of discipleship. Theological christology remains related to this christopraxis, and has to absorb its experiences, and open people for again new experiences along this way. Christology emerges from Christian living and leads to Christian living (Jürgen Moltmann, *The Way of Jesus Christ—Christology in Messianic Dimensions* [San Francisco: Harper & Row, 1990], 42–43).

The reference to Dietrich Bonhoeffer is from *The Cost of Discipleship* (New York: Macmillan, 1963).

PART II. God's Ministry in Covenant and Creation

Chapter 5:
The Word of God Which Creates the Response

The name *Yahweh* is self-authenticating as the name for God that explains the source of the power in the event (cf. Ex. 3; 6:2–8). *Elohim* is the generic name for God. It is Yahweh who is Elohim, not the reverse. The actions of Yahweh as the covenant-making and keeping God constitute the critical content for knowing the only and true God. The formula is always: Know that Yahweh is Elohim (cf. Ps. 100:3). This is irreversible. It is as Yahweh that Israel knows her God (Elohim). This is the challenge put by Elijah (whose name means: "my El is Yahweh): "If Yahweh is God (Elohim), follow him; but if Baal, then follow him" (1 Kings 18:21). Only Yahweh has the power be Israel's Elohim because only he *acts*—the other gods are silent, and it is Yahweh who reveals their eternal silence.

Thus, the narration of the deeds of Yahweh re-presents the acts as the revelation of God. The Word (story of the deeds) provides the context for interpreting the deeds, even as the deeds constitute the criterion for the authority and validity of the narrative.

The Power of The Word: A Case Study

The phrase *ex nihilo* is not found in the Old Testament itself, but appears in the Apocrypha (2 Macc. 7:28).

The reference to Karl Barth is from *Church Dogmatics*, III/1. Translated by J. W. Edwards et. al. (Edinburgh: T. & T. Clark, 1969), 158ff.

The Ex Nihilo *as Interpretive Model*

Barth argues that sexual differentiation as male and female, male or female is the primary differentiation of humanity as co-humanity, and thus is rooted in the divine image itself. Karl Barth, *Church Dogmatics*, III/1, 195f.

Phyllis Trible shows quite convincingly that the original designation of the first human creature in Genesis 2 was the generic term for "man"—'*adam*;

> As presented in this first episode, with the definite article *ha-* preceding the common noun '*adam*, this work of art is neither a particular person nor the typical person but rather the creature from the earth (*ha-ªdama*)—the earth creature. The very words that differentiate creature from soil indicate similarity. . . . More important, this creature is not identified sexually. Grammatical gender ('*adam* as a masculine word) is not sexual identification. . . . In other words, the earth creature is not the male; it is not the first man" (*God and the Rhetoric of Sexuality* [Philadelphia: Fortress Press, 1978], 80).
>
> Only after surgery does this creature, for the very first time, identify itself as male. Utilizing a pun on the Hebrew word for woman, '*issah*, the earth creature refers to itself by the specific term for man as male, '*ish*. . . . The unit '*ish* and '*issah* functionally parallels *ha-'adam* and *ha-ªdama* (Ibid., 98.)

Trible, therefore, concludes that the creation of human persons as "male and female" ('*ish* and '*issah*) occurs simultaneously, not sequentially. "His sexual identity depends upon her even as hers depends upon him. For both of them sexuality originates in the one flesh of humanity" (Ibid., 99).

Chapter 6:
The Grace of God Which Presupposes Barrenness

The Inner Logic of Barrenness and Grace

The "scandal of particularity," as T. F. Torrance puts it, has to do with the uniqueness of God's act for which there is no natural cause. "This is something that minds of a certain type, or that are habituated to certain modes of thought, find intolerable, for they have what Professor Alan Cook of Cambridge University has called an 'obsessive horror of the unique event'" (*The Ground and Grammar of Theology* [Charlottesville, Va.: University Press of Virginia, 1980], 102–3).

For a discussion of the Hebrew custom that allowed for a servant-girl to produce a legitimate heir, see Claus Westerman, *Genesis 12–36—A Commentary*, trans. John J. Scullion, S. J. (Minneapolis: Augsburg Press, 1985), 237ff.

John Drane says that the faith of Abraham and Sarah was grounded in God's faithfulness as demonstrated in God's actions in history, coupled with the promise of his continued actions in the future.

In the Old Testament "faith" was essentially faithfulness to the experienced acts of God in history, coupled with a confidence in his future activity in the same sphere of operation. . . . [The Old Testament] revealed that those who would have an experiential understanding of the spiritual realities of biblical religion needed not *gnosis* but *pistis,* whereby they could share in those same experiences whose validity was vouched for by historical record. (John Drane, *Paul, Libertine or Legalist?* [London: SPK, 1975], 27, 42).

Chapter 7:
The Covenant of God Which Precedes Creation

The quotation from Karl Barth reminds us that as God precedes creation, and eternity time, so does the seventh day precede the sixth day (Karl Barth, *Church Dogmatics,* I/1, 531).

The "backwards kind of thinking" is similar to what Thomas F. Torrance speaks of as axiomatic inquiry. Axioms are formulated out of experience and used to penetrate deeper into the inner logic of that which is to be known. While axioms are unprovable, they serve as keys to penetrate into the inner structure of reality in order to cause this inner reality to reveal itself to us. There is also a "backward correlation" from the new to the old (cf. Matt. 13:51). See *God and Rationality* (London: Oxford University Press, 1971), 15ff. See also Thomas F. Torrance, *Theology and Science at the Frontiers of Knowledge* (Edinburgh: Scottish Academic Press, 1985):

> The spiritual reality to which we belong has a range of content which we cannot infer from what we already know, but which we may get to know more fully only through heuristic acts of exploring entirely new ground and grappling with novel connections and ideas. . . . Hence intensely personal acts of relation, discernment and judgment belong to the epistemic act in every field of rational knowledge and fundamental science (111).

Covenant as the Inner Logic of Creation

My use of the term covenant is primarily a theological one as used in this chapter. The covenant, says Karl Barth, "is the fellowship which originally existed between God and man, which was then disturbed and jeopardized, the purpose of which is now fulfilled in Jesus Christ and the work of reconciliation" (*Church Dogmatics,* IV/1, trans. G.W. Bromiley, [Edinburgh: T & T Clark, 1956] 22). I am well aware of the various attempts of biblical scholars, such as Eichrodt, who attempted to fit all of the Old Testament theologies into the single theme of covenant. It is now known that the earlier uses of the term in the Old Testament referred to the suzerainty relationships between a victorious nation and the conquered people. In this sense, a covenant was a treaty that was initiated unilaterally by the conquering leader to regulate the social and political life of the vassal. The terms of the treaty stipulated the responsibilities of the vassal, but also protected the rights of the people. For further study of the concept of covenant in biblical theology, see G. E. Mendenhall, "Covenant," in *The Interpreter's Dictionary of the Bible* (New York: Abingdon Press, 1962), 1:714–23.

Karl Barth says that the formula "Yahweh is Elohim" places the covenant-making and keeping God at the very heart of creation (*Church Dogmatics,* III/1, 224).

Creation as external form of the covenant, says Karl Barth, and the covenant is the internal basis for creation. "The history of creation is a great cosmic prelude and example of that history of Israel which is the proper theme of the Old Testament. Creation is the outward basis of the Covenant (Genesis 1) and the covenant is the inward basis of creation (Genesis 2)" (Karl Barth, *Church Dogmatics*, IV/1, 27; cf. also *Church Dogmatics*, III/1, pp. 94ff; 288ff; esp. 231–32).

Grace as the Inner Logic of Sin

Phyllis Trible points out that the designation "Adam" does not mean a "man" or a "male" in the sense in which we understand it today. Rather, the term represents a play on words, as the term Adam is derived from the Hebrew word for earth. See *God and the Rhetoric of Sexuality*, 80.

The Human Dilemma
and the Divine Deliverance

I have discussed the theological issues pertaining to whether or not the original humans had a mortal nature as well as a spiritual one in my book, *Theology, Death and Dying* (Oxford: Blackwell Publishers, 1986), chap. 3. My own position is that the human body was taken from the dust and was thus subject to mortality from the very beginning. Only through the power of God's grace were the original human pair oriented to a destiny beyond their mortal nature.

The relational nature of the atonement is emphasized by the New Testament theologian Ralph Martin:

> For Paul, as we shall see, the new sphere of living is one of sonship within a family context and no longer that of slavery under the taskmaster's stern eye. . . . In summary, justification by faith according to the more recent insight in the biblical usage of 'righteousness' and its cognate terms, is *a relational term*. (Ralph Martin, *Reconciliation: A Study of Paul's Theology* [Atlanta: John Knox Press, 1980], 35, 36).

Chapter 8:
The Sabbath of God Which Renews and Restores

The Theology of the Sabbath

The issue regarding the seventh day sabbath and Sunday as the first day of the week serving as the Christian sabbath is not my concern in this chapter. Those who wish to pursue this question should consult, among other sources, Paul K. Jewett, *The Lord's Day: A Theological Guide to the Christian Day of Worship* (Grand Rapids: Wm. B. Eerdmans Publishing Co., 1971); Willard M. Swartley, *Slavery, Sabbath, War and Women* (Scottdale, Pa.: Herald Press, 1983); Samuele Bacciocchi, *From Sabbath to Sunday: A Historical Investigation of the Rise of Sunday Observance in Early Christianity* (Rome: The Pontifical Gregorian University Press, 1977); W. O. Carver, *Sabbath Observance: The Lord's Day in Our Day* (Nashville: Broadman Press, 1940); Roger T. Beckwith and Wilfred Stott, *This is the Day: The Biblical Doctrine of the Christian Sunday in Its Jewish and Early Church Setting* (London: Marshal Morgan & Scott, 1978); Joshua Heschel, *The Sabbath: Its Meaning for Modern Man* (New York: Farrar, Straus & Giroux, 1951); Niels-Erik A. Andreasen, *The Old Testament Sabbath:*

A Tradition-Historical Investigation (SBL, Dissertation Series, No. 7, 1972); M. L. Andreasen, *The Sabbath: Which Day and Why?* (Washington, D.C.: Review and Herald Publishing Association, 1942); Carlyle B. Haynes, *From Sabbath to Sunday* (Washington, D.C.: Review and Herald Publishing Association, 1942).

A lyric rendition of the purpose of the sabbath for the benefit of humanity can be found in the writings of Thomas Watson:

> When the falling dust of the world has clogged the wheels of our affections, that they can scarce move towards God, the Sabbath comes, and oils the wheels of our affections, and they move swiftly on. God has appointed the Sabbath for this end. On this day the thoughts rise to heaven, the tongue speaks of God, the eyes drop tears, and the soul burns in love. The heart, which all the week was frozen, on the Sabbath melts with the word. The Sabbath is a friend to religion: it files off the rust of our graces; it is a spiritual jubilee, wherein the soul is set to converse with its Maker" (*The Ten Commandments* [Guildford, Eng.: Billings and Sons, Ltd., rev. ed., 1965; orig., 1692], 94–95, as cited by Willard M. Swartley, *Slavery, Sabbath, War and Women* [Scottdale, Pa.: Herald Press, 1983], 73).

Dietrich Bonhoeffer discusses the relation of the ultimate to the penultimate in *Ethics* (New York: Macmillan, 1965), 120–87.

Ernest Becker, *The Denial of Death* (New York: Macmillan, 1973).

The Ministry and Discipline of the Sabbath

I have dealt with the inner healing and recovery of the true humanity of the self in my book, *Self-Care: A Theology of Personal Empowerment and Spiritual Healing* (Wheaton, Ill.: Victor Books, 1995).

PART III.
Jesus' Ministry to the Father on Behalf of the World

Chapter 9:
The Baptism of Jesus into Messianic Ministry

Jesus as the Son of the Father

For a recent discussion of the importance of the virgin birth and the relation of Jesus as Son of the Father see Thomas F. Torrance, *The Mediation of Christ* (Colorado Springs: Helmers & Howard Publishers, 1992), 9f; 29f. The virgin birth is best expounded in light of the resurrection, argues Torrance. The early church theologians, for example, speak of the virgin birth being related to the 'virgin tomb,' showing their linking of these events (T. F. Torrance, Lecture Notes, 1971; cf. Karl Barth, *Church Dogmatics*, I/2 (Edinburgh: T. & T. Clark, 1956), 182.

The virgin birth, says Barth, is a "noetic sign" of the "ontic" reality of the incarnation. The virgin birth is a dogma given to explain the mystery of revelation, that is, the divine origin of the one who stands among us as God. Thus, the event (virgin birth) is not the basis for our belief in the divinity of Christ, for a noetic truth cannot be the basis for an ontic reality, but the reverse. The virgin birth story is a "sign" that accompanies and points to the mystery of the incarnation.

> The dogma of the Virgin birth is thus the confession of the boundless hiddenness of the *vere Deus vere homo* and of the boundless amazement of awe and thankfulness called forth in us by this *vere Deus vere homo*. It eliminates the last surviving possibility of understanding the *vere Deus vere homo* intellectually, as an idea or an arbitrary interpretation in the sense of docetic or ebionite Christology. It leaves only the spiritual understanding of the *vere Deus vere homo*, i.e., the understanding in which God's own work is seen in God's own light" (Karl Barth, *Church Dogmatics*, I/2, 170).

Barth goes on to say that there seems to be a "fatal connection" between denial of the virgin birth and the attempt to establish a "point of contact" by which a natural theology can be erected. For a denial of this type see W. Pannenberg, *Jesus, God and Man* (Philadelphia: Westminster Press, 1974), 143ff. Barth says of Brunner's denial of the virgin birth: "Brunner's contribution to this matter in his more recent book, *Man in Revolt*, is so bad that my only possible attitude toward it is silence" (Karl Barth, *Church Dogmatics*, I/2, 184).

For a discussion of the phrase Son of God, see my article, "Son of God" *International Standard Bible Encyclopedia*, vol. IV (Grand Rapids: Wm. B. Eerdmans Publishing Co., 1984). James Dunn has shown that the designation of Jesus as a divine Son of God who became incarnate in human flesh is primarily a theme of the gospel of John, with only one primary antecedent in the gospels found in the text of Matthew 11:27 (*Christology in the Making* [Philadelphia: Westminster Press, 1980]).

Spirit Empowered Ministry

Thomas Torrance points to the twofold ministry of Jesus when he says:

> He is in Himself not only God objectifying Himself for man but man adapted and conformed to that objectification, not only the complete revelation of God to man but the appropriate correspondence on the part of man to that revelation, not only the Word of God to man but man obediently hearing and answering that Word. In short, Jesus Christ is Himself both the Word of God as spoken by God to man and that same Word as heard and received by man, Himself both the Truth of God given to man and that very Truth understood and actualized in man (*Theological Science* [London: Oxford University Press, 1969], 50).

Thomas Torrance argues that the relation between Christ and Israel brings to completion the special role of Israel in acting as a vicarious mediator between God and humankind.

> And at last in the fullness of time the Word of God became man in Jesus, born of the Virgin Mary, within the embrace of Israel's faith and worship and expectation, himself God and man, in whom the covenanted relationship between God and Israel and through Israel with all humanity was gathered up, transformed and fulfilled once for all. In the revealing of God and the understanding of man fully coincided, the whole Word of God and the perfect response of man were indivisibly united in one person, the Mediator, who was received, believed, and worshipped together with God the Father and the Holy Spirit by the apostolic

community which he creatively called forth and assimilated to his own mission from the Father. Thus as both the incarnate revelation of God and the embodied knowledge of God, Jesus Christ constitutes in himself the Way, the Truth, and the Life through whom alone access to God the Father is freely open for all the peoples of mankind (Thomas Torrance, *The Mediation of Christ* [Colorado Springs: Helmers & Howard Publishers, 1992], 9).

The reference to Irenaeus is as follows:

For God promised, that in the last times He would pour Him [the Spirit] upon His servants and handmaids, that they might prophesy; wherefore He did also descend upon the Son of God, made the Son of man, becoming accustomed in fellowship with Him to dwell in the human race, to rest with human beings, and to dwell in the workmanship of God, working the will of the Father in them, and renewing them from their old habits into the newness of Christ (Irenaeus, *Irenaeus Against Heresies*, vol. 1, Ante-Nicene Christian Library, ed. A. Roberts and J. Donaldson [Edinburgh: T. & T. Clark, 1868, III/17/1] 334).

The Spirit does not come to us as "naked Spirit," but clothed with the character and personality of Christ. See Thomas F. Torrance, *Theology in Reconstruction* (Grand Rapids: Wm. B. Eerdmans Publishing Co., 1965), 247; Michael Green, *I Believe in the Holy Spirit* (Grand Rapids: Wm. B. Eerdmans Publishing Co., 1988), 47, 105–6.

The Humanity of God

Karl Barth comments with regard to the nature of the humanity that the divine *Logos* assumed in the incarnation (John 1:14): "The Old Testament testifies pitilessly what is meant by flesh . . . to be flesh means to exist with the 'children' of Israel under the wrath and judgment of the electing and loving God. To be flesh is to be in a state of perishing before this God" (Karl Barth, *Church Dogmatics*, IV/1, 171, 174–75).

The decision of the council at Chalcedon (451 A.D.) with regard to the deity of Jesus was to repeat the formula of Nicea (325 A.D.) that, concerning his deity, Jesus was *homoousion tō patri* (of the same essence as the Father). Concerning his humanity, the council added, Jesus was *homoousion hemin*, (of the same essence as we [humans]). These two natures were bound to one hypostatic union. Karl Barth is well known for his emphasis on the humanity of God. It is most clearly stated in his essay, *The Humanity of God* (London: Collins, Fontana Library Edition, 1967). This is the basis for Barth's claim that there is within the being of the basis for humanity as such:

God's deity is thus no prison in which he can exist only in and for Himself. It is rather His freedom to be in and for Himself but also with and for us, to assert but also to sacrifice Himself, to be wholly exalted but also completely humble, not only almighty but also almighty mercy, not only Lord but also servant, not only judge but also Himself the judged, not only man's eternal king but also his brother in time. And all that without in the slightest forfeiting His deity! All that, rather, in the highest proof and proclamation of his deity! . . . In this divinely free volition and election, in this sovereign decision (the ancients said, in His decree), God is *human*. His free affirmation of man, His free concern for him, His free substitution for him—this is God's humanity" (Karl Barth, *The Humanity of God* [London: Collins, Fontana Library Edition, 1967], 46, 48).

The citation from James Torrance is found in his essay, "The Vicarious Humanity of Christ," in *The Incarnation—Ecumenical Studies in the Nicene-Constantinopolitan Creed A.D. 381*, ed. Thomas F. Torrance (Edinburgh: Handsel Press Ltd., 1981); 141.

With Anselm of Canterbury (1033–1109), a new perspective entered medieval soteriology. Anselm argued strongly against the classical ransom theory, saying that the debt owed was not to Satan but to God, for the dishonor which sin had done to him. According to Anselm, the sinner is held fast by a duty to bring satisfaction of a penal nature. There is a moral duty that penance cannot satisfy. Only the perfect humanity of Christ (who has no debt of his own) can make this payment. Anselm wrote:

> This is the debt which man and angel owe to God, and no one who pays this debt commits sin . . . and this is the sole and complete debt of honor which we owe to God. . . . He who does not render this honor which is due to God, robs God of his own and dishonors him; and this is sin. . . . For God will not do it, because he has no debt to pay; and man will not do it, because he cannot. Therefore, in order that the God-man may perform this, it is necessary that the same being should be perfect God and perfect man, in order to make this atonement" (Anselm, *Cur Deus Homo?* [LaSalle, Ill.: Open Court Publishing Co., 1958], 202; 246).

The satisfaction theory was also part of Calvin's theory of the atonement, as well as the other Reformers.

> If the non-imputation of our sins to us be the benefit of the blood which he shed, it follows that this was the price of the satisfaction to the justice of God. . . . But we ought particularly to consider the relation described by Paul, that he was "made a curse for us." For it would be unnecessary, and consequently absurd, for Christ to be loaded with a curse, except in order to discharge the debts due from others, and thereby to obtain a righteousness for them. The testimony of Isaiah likewise is clear, that "the chastisement of our peace was upon him; and with his stripes we are healed." For if Christ had not made a satisfaction for our sins, he could not be said to have appeased God by suffering punishment to which we were exposed (*Institutes*, Book II, chap. xvii, par. 4).
>
> For what was the design of that subjection to the law, but to procure a righteousness for us, by undertaking to perform that which we were not able to do. Hence that imputation of righteousness without works, of which Paul treats; because that righteousness which is found in Christ alone is accepted as ours (*Institutes*, Book II, chap. xvii, par. 5).

In criticism of Anselm, Otto Weber says:

> But the fact remains that Anselm constructs "satisfaction" abstractly, as an *a priori*. This is the result of his realism. But that does not make it right. We can only speak of God's reconciling work in Christ in a regressive sense, and all theology is discourse *a posteriori*. The event is the absolute precedent. . . . Anselm gives a peculiarly unsure answer to the question as to how "satisfaction" affects man (Otto Weber, *Foundations of Dogmatics*, vol. 2 [Grand Rapids: Wm. B. Eerdmans Publishing Co., 1983], 213).

Chapter 10:
Jesus as the Servant of the Father on Behalf of the World

Need is a Relentless and Unforgiving Slave Master

The reference to "theological anemia" is from my article, "Burnout as a Symptom of Theological Anemia," *Theology News & Notes* (Pasadena, Calif.: Fuller Theological Seminary, March 1984).

Jesus' Ministry:
Service Grounded in Sonship

Conversion to God is also a part of Jesus' ministry on behalf of the world. Karl Barth says that Jesus achieved the penitence and conversion demand of humans.

> In Him God not only demands but He gives what He demands. In Him He does that which has to take place to set aside sin and remove the conflict. He shows himself to be pure and holy and sinless by not refusing in Him to become the greatest of all sinners, achieving the penitence and conversion which is demanded of sinners, undertaking the bitter reality of being the accused and condemned and judged and executed man of sin, in order that when He Himself has been this man no other man can or need be, in order that in place of this man another man who is pleasing to God, the man of obedience, may have space and air and be able to live (Karl Barth, *Church Dogmatics*, IV/1, 280–81).

Otto Weber suggests that Jesus is the "true believer," who has taken up the human task of faith and completed it in his own faithfulness to God.

> Older Christology debated whether Jesus of Nazareth was able to believe. Whoever reads the New Testament will not participate in this dispute. Jesus is the believing man, the "witness of faith." He is the "pioneer and perfector of our faith" (Heb. 12:2). He does not provide information about what faith is; he believes. He holds fast to man because he holds fast to the Father. He is "the" man who has an infinite need of God. His final word is a prayer. The other traditional words from the cross are directed to man. He endures with men to the very end and dies the death of lost man. This is how we have come to know him in this short overview of the New Testament witness to Christ (Otto Weber, *Foundations of Dogmatics*, vol. 2 [Grand Rapids: Wm. B. Eerdmans Publishing Co., 1983], 153–54).

Our Calling to Ministry:
Participation in the Ongoing Ministry of Christ

The concept of baptism as ordination for ministry is the thesis of the article produced by the Fourth World Conference on Faith and Order (July 1963), "Christ's Ministry Through His Whole Church and its Ministers." Originally published in *Encounter*, vol. 25, no. 1 (winter 1964) 105–29, it has been republished in *Theological Foundations for Ministry*, ed. Ray S. Anderson (Grand Rapids: Wm. B. Eerdmans Publishing Co., 1979), 430–57. "[T]hrough our baptism Christ incorporates us and ordains us for participation in his ministry. . . . For Jesus baptism meant that he was consecrated as Messiah. For us baptism means that we are consecrated as members of the messianic people. . . . According to this understanding of baptism, to be baptized means immediately to be called to the life of a servant" 432).

Chapter 11:
Jesus as Sent to the World on Behalf of the Father

The reference to Thomas Torrance is from "Service in Jesus Christ," in Anderson, *Theological Foundations for Ministry*, 724.

The reference to Karl Barth is from *Church Dogmatics*, IV/3. The context of his statement about "going down into hell," is as follows:

> Solidarity with the world means that those who are genuinely pious approach the children of the world as such, that those who are genuinely righteous are not ashamed to sit down with the unrighteous as friends, that those who are genuinely wise do not hesitate to seem to be fools among fools, and that those who are genuinely holy are not too good or irreproachable to go down into "hell" in a very secular fashion . . . since Jesus Christ is the Savior of the world, [the church] can exist in worldly fashion, not unwillingly nor with a bad conscience, but willingly and with a good conscience. It consists in the recognition that its members also bear in themselves and in some way actualise all human possibilities (774).

Being Found in Human Form

I have discussed the "human ecology of death and dying," in my book, *Theology, Death and Dying* (Oxford: Blackwell Publishers, 1986).

Chapter 12:
The Resurrection and Justification of Jesus
as the Verdict of the Father

How Far is Hell from Heaven?

The question of punishment after death is not brought up in the Old Testament. The concept of "hell" is ambiguous and represents a shadow form of life. It is in the New Testament that this doctrine is clearly taught. For a discussion of this subject see my book, *Theology, Death and Dying* particularly chap. 4, "Divine Judgment and Life After Death?"

The reference to Thomas Torrance is from his essay, "Questioning In Jesus Christ," in *Theology in Reconstruction* (Grand Rapids: Wm. B. Eerdmans Publishing Co., 1965).

With regard to the extent of the atonement and the question of limited atonement versus universalism, it is well to hear again the words of Karl Barth, who said that justification and sanctification are not experienced by all (*de facto*), even though given to all (*de jure*). Only those awakened to faith by the Spirit are united to Christ's justification and sanctification.

> *De facto*, however, [sanctification] is not known by all men, just as justification has not *de facto* been grasped and acknowledged and known and confessed by all men, but only by those who are awakened to faith. It is the people of these men which has also known sanctification. Only God Himself knows the extent of this people, and its members. The invitation to belong to it is extended to all. Certainly it is not co-extensive with the human race as such (Karl Barth, *Church Dogmatics*, IV/2, 511).

Christ Our Sanctification and Justification

Faith is related to justification in such a way that Christ is the "middle term." Paul's correlation of righteousness with faith shows that faith is the possibility that now exists by virtue of Christ, the justified one (cf. Rom. 4:11, 13; 9:30; 10:16; Phil. 3:9). The fact that in the resurrection of Christ justification has occurred once and for all, and that no one need be justified on any other terms than the justification that came through Christ has been eloquently argued by Karl Barth. His statement is so profound and homiletically crafted, that it can be produced in full as a kind of "mini sermon" on justification.

> In our whole description of the term justification, we have been speaking of Him and therefore of justified man, of His history and therefore of our own, of His transition from the past to the future, from sin to right, from death to life, and therefore of ours, of His present and therefore of ours. It happened that in the humble obedience of the Son He took our place, He took to Himself our sins and death in order to make an end of them in His death, and that in so doing He did the right. He became the new and righteous man.
>
> There is not one for whose sin and death He did not die, whose sin and death He did not remove and obliterate on the cross, for whom He did not positively do the right, whose right He has not established. There is not one to whom this was not addressed as his justification in His resurrection from the dead. There is not one whose man He is not, who is not justified in Him. There is not one who is justified in any other way that in Him—because it is in Him and only in Him that an end, a bonfire, is made of man's sin and death, because it is in Him and only in Him that man's sin and death are the old thing which has passed away, because it is in Him and only in Him that the right has been done which is demanded of man, that the right has been established to which man can move forward. Again, there is not one who is not adequately and perfectly and finally justified in Him. There is not one whose sin is not forgiven sin in Him, whose death is not a death which has been put to death in Him. There is not one whose right has not been established and confirmed validly and once and for all in Him. There is not one, therefore, who has first to win and appropriate this right for himself . . . not one. That is what faith believes. And in believing that it is justifying faith, i.e., a faith which knows and grasps and realizes the justification of man as the decision and act and word of God. . . . Faith comes about where Jesus Christ prevails on man, in Jesus Christ the self-demonstration of the justified man (Karl Barth, *Church Dogmatics*, IV/1, 629–30, 631).

It is worth repeating here the statement by the New Testament theologian, Ralph Martin, in support of the fact that justification is more of a relational term than an abstract forensic concept.

> Paul's thought is as much conditioned by promises of "rectification of personal relationships" as by assurances of forensic acquittal. Indeed the latter term is best avoided if it still conjures the notion of treating sinners as though they were not sinners. . . . God's royal rule is displayed in releasing offenders from guilt out of respect for his son who stands as their sponsor. . . . For Paul, as we shall see, the new sphere of living is one of sonship within a family context and no longer that of slavery under the taskmaster's stern eye. . . . In summary, justification by faith according to the more recent insight in the biblical usage of "righteousness" and its cognate terms, is *a relational term* (Ralph Martin, *Reconciliation: A Study of Paul's Theology* [Atlanta: John Knox Press, 1980] 35, 36).

PART IV. The Spirit's Ministry through Jesus for the Sake of the Church

Chapter 13:
Pentecost as Empowerment for Ministry

A Theology of Pentecostal Empowerment

For further reading on the relation of Christ to Pentecost, see the chapter, "The Christ of Pentecost," in my book, *Ministry on the Fireline—A Practical Theology for an Empowered Church* (Downers Grove Ill.: InterVarsity Press, 1993), 21–40.

The source for my statement that it is Pentecost, and not the Great Commission that orients the church to its mission is Harry R. Boer, *Pentecost and Missions* (Grand Rapids: Wm. B. Eerdmans Publishing Co., 1961). "At the beginning of the history of the New Testament Church stands the Pentecost event. It does not stand *approximately* at the beginning, or as a first among several significant factors, but it stands *absolutely* at the beginning. . . . It does not, however, stand in *isolation* from preceding and succeeding redemptive history" (p. 98).

The phrase, "missionary people of God" is used by Charles Van Engen in his book, *God's Missionary People: Rethinking the Purpose of the Local Church* (Grand Rapids: Baker Book House, 1991).

The Context of Pentecostal Empowerment

The reference to Douglas Hall is as follows:

It is particularly the Holy Spirit who provides the dogmatic basis for the insistence that theological reflection necessarily means engagement with the historical context. The corrective to a theology which has neglected or dismissed the context by means of a rationalized and doctrinaire concentration on the second person of the Trinity is a theology which is goaded into engagement with the worldly reality by a fresh apprehension of the Holy Spirit. For the Spirit will permit us to rest neither in the church nor in doctrinal formulations that know everything ahead of time. The Spirit will drive us, as it drove Jesus, to the wilderness of worldly temptation and the garden of worldly suffering (Douglas John Hall, *Thinking the Faith—Christian Theology in a North American Context* [Minneapolis: Augsburg Press, 1989], 105).

Use What You Have,
Attempt More Than You Can Do

The reference to Robert Banks is *Redeeming the Routines: Bringing Theology to Life* (Wheaton, Ill.: Bridge Point, 1993).

Chapter 14:
The Praxis of the Spirit as Liberation for Ministry

For a discussion of the theological situation in South Africa see my article, "Toward a Post-Apartheid Theology," *Reformed Journal,* May 1988. Reprinted as "Toward a Post-Apartheid Theology in South Africa," *Journal of Theology for South Africa,*" June 1988. See also Adrio König, "Covenant and Image: Theological Anthropology,

Human Interrelatedness and Apartheid," in *Incarnational Ministry: The Presence of Christ in Church, Society, and Family*, ed. Christian D. Kettler and Todd H. Speidell (Colorado Springs: Helmers & Howard Publishers, 1990), 162–75.

For a discussion of liberation theology in the context of South Africa, see John DeGruchy, "No Other Gospel: Is Liberation Theology a Reduction of the Gospel?" in *Incarnational Ministry: The Presence of Christ in Church, Society, and Family*, 176–90.

I mean by praxis something of what Aristotle meant when he distinguished between *poiesis* as an act of making something where the *telos* lay outside of the act of making, and *praxis* as an act which includes the *telos* within the action itself. The *telos* of something is its final purpose, meaning or character. Praxis is an action which includes the *telos*, or final meaning and character of truth. It is an action in which the truth is discovered through action, not merely applied, or "practiced." In praxis, one is not only guided in one's actions by the intention of realizing the *telos*, or purpose, but one discovers and grasps this *telos* through the action itself. See *The Nichomachean Ethics*, trans. J.E.C. Welldon (New York: Prometheus Books, 1987), 192, bk. 6/chap. 5.

The use of the term *praxis* in contemporary theology has been greatly influenced by the quasi-Marxist connotation given to it by some Latin American Liberation theologians. My own attempt in using the word is to recover the authentically biblical connotation of God's actions that reveal his purpose and truth. I appreciate the concept of praxis as used by Orlando Costas; see *The Church and Its Mission: A Shattering Critique From the Third World* (Wheaton, Ill.: Tyndale House, 1974). I have discussed this further in my essay, "Christopraxis: Competence as a Criterion for Theological Education," *Theological Students Fellowship (TSF) Bulletin*, (January/February 1984).

Which Century is Normative for our Theology?

Wesley Carr has clearly set forth the eschatological reality of the Holy Spirit for the life and context of the church's ministry.

> Christians hope to be one with Christ in the final resurrection and their experience in the Christian community is a partial and anticipatory experience of that end. Their place in this eschatologically oriented community has been brought about by the achievement of Christ (hence the significance of the images of the body and of suffering), and it is realised constantly by the agency of the Spirit which is present as a guarantee or first-fruits of the end—*arrhabon* and *aparche*. . . . The dynamic force within this eschatological community is the Spirit, which creates that community and sustains it and at the same time gives to each person within the community his [or her] own individual personhood. . . . Thus the Spirit becomes for the believing community more the environment in which it lives than an object of its consciousness. In particular, the importance of the Spirit as an eschatological phenomenon reminds us that its relation is both to the risen Christ and to the community which is oriented towards God (Wesley Carr, "Towards a Contemporary Theology of the Holy Spirit," *Scottish Journal of Theology*, vol. 28, no. 7, [1975], 506, 507–8).

But What About Homosexuality?

For a discussion of the issue of homosexuality as it relates to the church, see Pim Pronk, *Against Nature? Types of Moral Argumentation Regarding Homosexuality* (Grand Rapids: Wm. B. Eerdmans Publishing Co., 1993). Pim argues that biological nature cannot be used to distinguish between hetero- and homosexuality and that only moral considerations apply. He suggests a Christian and moral basis for homosexual relations; James B. Nelson, in *The Intimate Connection: Male Sexuality, Masculine Spirituality* (Philadelphia: Westminster Press, 1988), argues for full acceptance of a homosexual lifestyle with the Christian community; Andrew Comiskey, in *Pursuing Sexual Wholeness,* (Santa Monica, Calif.: Desert Streams Ministries, 1988), offers strategies for ministry to recovering homosexuals; Jeffrey S. Siker, ed., *Homosexuality in the Church—Both Sides of the Debate* (Westminster/ John Knox Press, 1994); John Francis Harvey, in *The Homosexual Person: New Thinking in Pastoral Care* (San Francisco: Ignatius Press, 1987), provides helpful guidance for pastoral care to homosexual persons, from a Roman Catholic perspective; Peter Edward Coleman, in *Gay Christians: A Moral Dilemma* (London: SCM Press, 1989), surveys the various positions, attempts balance between rejection and compassion.

Karl Barth argues that the only essential differentiation among persons at the personal and social level is in human sexuality (See *Church Dogmatics,* III/1, 186f; 195f; III/2, 289). He also holds that human sexuality is a manifestation of the image of God as co-relation (co-humanity) and that the mark of the human is this same co-relation grounded in sexual differentiation as male and female, male or female (*Church Dogmatics,* III/1, 195ff). Emil Brunner, however, separates sexuality from the image of God and suggests that the erotic sexual impulse is an "unbridled biological instinct" that can be consecrated only through marriage, or the ethical demand of abstinence (*Love and Marriage* [London: Collins, Fontana, 1970], 183, 195).

For a discussion of the church as empowered by the Spirit, see Jürgen Moltmann, *The Church in the Power of the Spirit: A Contribution to Messianic Eschatology* (San Francisco: Harper & Row, 1975).

Chapter 15:
The *Charisma* of the Spirit and the Gift of Ministry

The Early Church was a Charismatic Community

The reference to Emil Brunner is from *The Misunderstanding of the Church* (London: Lutterworth Press, 1952), 24, 49, 52. Karl Barth comments on Brunner's rather extravagant description of this charismatic first-century community by asking, "To put it bluntly, did this great miracle really happen? Even according to what we find in the witness of the New Testament not to speak of the first centuries, . . . does not this picture belong to the sphere of that which never was on land or sea, to the world of ideas and ideals? . . . Basically, is not the attempt to discuss the problem of the Church in terms of this criterion a romantic undertaking which makes no serious attempt at theological deliberation? What is the authority for this criterion?" (*Church Dogmatics,* IV/2, 686–87).

In the third volume of his *Dogmatics,* Brunner developed more fully his concept of the charismatic order of the church. "The Spirit produces and exists in *koinonia,* but perishes in an institution," wrote Brunner. The absence of formal authority, legal structures, and canonical law characterizes the life of Spirit. Then he went on to ask:

Does this charismatic order actually work? Was there not perpetual strife, or at the least uncertainty and the awkward question—what was to happen now? But this strange, this even wonderful charismatic ordering by the invisible Lord alone, did work. Precisely that is the miracle of the Ekklesia, which certainly Paul and the other Christians themselves regarded with ever renewed astonishment as a miracle. Even the worldwide scope of the Ekklesia was not able—and that is a second miracle—to call the charismatic leadership and order in question (*Dogmatics, vol. 3: The Christian Doctrine of the Church, Faith and the Consummation* [London: Lutterworth Press, 1962], 45).

However, Brunner added, by the end of the first century, Paul's vital charismatic order of the *ecclesia* had given way to the more hierarchical and organizationally structured form as found at Jerusalem. The Acts 15 council resulted in an uneasy truce, but no real theological basis for agreement. As a result, he says,

The Pauline Ecclesia was not deeply enough rooted to survive, and finally gave way to an order in which: salvation became linked with sacrament; the Ecclesia became a dispensing entity rather than a ministering fellowship; the act of administration of the eucharist became separated from the act of reception, with authority vested in the former; a distinction emerged between the holy place and the profane people, with a priestly caste mediating grace; fellowship became institutionalized and legalized; and the Word surrendered centrality to the sacrament, the fraternity to the hierarchy, the charismatic to the juristic, and the diakoniai to the dogmatic (*Dogmatics*, III, 60–66).

The reference to Eugene Peterson is from *The Message: The New Testament in Contemporary English* (Colorado Springs: NavPress, 1993), 255.

The reference to Hans Küng is from *The Church* (London: Sheed & Ward, 1967), 180–81, 188; reprinted in *Theological Foundations for Ministry*, ed. Ray S. Anderson (Grand Rapids: Wm. B. Eerdmans Publishing Co., 1979), 478.

The reference to Wesley Carr is from "Towards a Contemporary Theology of the Holy Spirit," *Scottish Journal of Theology*, vol. 28, no. 7, (1975), 507, 508, 513.

Every Christian is Born Charismatic—Some Never Grow Up!

The reference to Otto Weber is from *Foundations of Dogmatics*, vol. II (Grand Rapids: Wm. B. Eerdmans Publishing Co., 1983), 576. Michael Green has an excellent discussion of the charismatic nature of the church and each Christian in *I Believe in the Holy Spirit* (Grand Rapids: Wm. B. Eerdmans Publishing Co., 1988), chap. 11, 12.

The reference to Wesley Carr is from "Towards a Contemporary Theology of the Holy Spirit," 507, 508.

Recovering the Charisma in the Charismatic

For some helpful sources on spiritual gifts, see Bruce Bugbee, *Networking* (Pasadena, Calif.: Fuller Institute for Evangelism and Church Growth, 1994); Donald A. Carson, *Showing the Spirit: A Theological Exposition of I Corinthians*

12–14 (Grand Rapids: Baker Book House, 1987); Don and Kattie Fortune, *Discover Your God-Given Gifts* (Grand Rapids: Baker Book House, 1987); Larry Gilbert, *How to Have Meaning and Fulfillment through Understanding the Spiritual Gifts within You* (Lynchburg, Va.: Church Growth Institute, 1990); Siegfried Schatzmann, *A Pauline Theology of Charismata* (Peabody, Mass.: Hendrickson Publishers, 1987); Rick Yohn, *Discover Your Spiritual Gift and Use It* (Wheaton, Ill.: Tyndale House Publishers, Inc., 1974); C. Peter Wagner, *Your Spiritual Gifts Can Help Your Church Grow* (Ventura, Calif.: Regal Books, 1979). The reference to Hans Küng is from *The Church* (London: Sheed & Ward, 1967), 188f. See also, Hans Küng, "The Continuing Charismatic Structure," in Anderson, *Theological Foundations for Ministry*, 479ff.

Chapter 16:
The Church as the Formation of Christ in the World

Dietrich Bonhoeffer's Thesis

Karl Barth's reference to Bonhoeffer is from *Church Dogmatics,* IV/2, 641.

The reference to Dietrich Bonhoeffer concerning "Christ existing as Community," is from *Sanctorum Communio* (London: Collins, 1967), 160. For an excellent treatment of Bonhoeffer's life and teaching, see Renate Wind, *A Spoke in the Wheel—The Life of Dietrich Bonhoeffer* (Grand Rapids: Wm. B. Eerdmans Publishing Co., 1992).

The reference to Otto Weber is from *Foundations of Dogmatics,* vol. II, 514. Weber goes on to say:

> If the Community could not be confident that the present Christ were in and with it, it would not be the Community. The Community does not primarily look back upon an institutor and institutive will in the past, but looks upon the present Christ with and in it. This then means, with regard also to the contemporary Community, that it understands itself to be the Community of the age of salvation, that is, it is destined to understand itself in this way. . . . The "present Christ" is understood, under these circumstances, as a given already invested, so to speak, in the Community. He is not primarily the Expected One in faith in his presence; rather he is "there" just as anything in the world might be "there." This passive "being there" on the part of Jesus Christ is then actualized in the functions of "office," in the activity of preaching, and particularly in the "sacraments," which come to the foreground in this situation. This actualization takes place on the basis of the possibility already established by virtue of the fact that Jesus Christ is "there" already (Ibid).

The Form of Christ in the World

The reference to Dietrich Bonhoeffer is from *Ethics* (New York: Macmillan, 1955), 205–6. The church and the world do occupy two spheres, says Bonhoeffer, but both occupy the same reality through Jesus Christ:

> In Christ we are offered the possibility of partaking in the reality of God and in the reality of the world, but not in the one without the other. The reality of God

discloses itself only by setting me entirely in the reality of the world, and when I encounter the reality of the world it is always already sustained, accepted and reconciled in the reality of God. This is the inner meaning of the revelation of God in the man Jesus Christ. . . . One is denying the revelation of God in Jesus Christ if one tries to be "Christian" without seeing and recognizing the world in Christ (195f).

Otto Weber says much the same when he writes:

Seen Christologically, every rejection of the world by the Community would have to place in question "docetically" the incarnation of Jesus Christ. It would have to have been the case that God did not become "true man" in Jesus Christ if the Community were intended not to be "truly" in the world. But above all, the victory of the Resurrected One over the "cosmos" (John 13:33) would have to be disregarded if the Community were supposedly to understand the "world" solely as a confusing, alien reality, to be held at a distance and excluded (*Foundations of Dogmatics*, vol. II, 525–26).

The reference to Thomas Torrance is from "Service in Jesus Christ," in Anderson, *Theological Foundations for Ministry*, 724.

The reference to Karl Barth in regard to tactical withdrawal is from *Church Dogmatics*, IV/3, 780.

Barth's statement on the solidarity of the church with the world is from *Church Dogmatics*, IV/3, 773–74.

But Isn't This Dangerous?

The reference to Dietrich Bonhoeffer and the acceptance of guilt is from *Ethics*, 240ff.

But We Are Not Bonhoeffers!

The reference to James Torrance is from "The Vicarious Humanity of Christ," 141. Todd Speidell reinforces this when he adds:

Christ presents himself in the depths of human need—the hungry, the thirsty, the naked, the sick, the imprisoned (Mt. 25:31ff). The stranger among us, the homeless and psychologically debilitated, may be the place of Christ's presence among us. The Gospel of Matthew does not exhort us simply to be like Christ—ministering to the needy "as Jesus would" (which implies that he is not actively present but merely serves as a model for our social action)—but attests that Christ discloses himself through the stranger. We must be where Christ is, and act where he acts ("Incarnational Social Ethics," in *Incarnational Ministry: The Presence of Christ in Church, Society, and Family*, 146).

The statement, "only the evangelical church can be incarnational," was first written in my doctoral thesis, published as *Historical Transcendence and the Reality of God—A Christological Critique* (Grand Rapids: Wm. B. Eerdmans Publishing Co., 1979), 270.

The reference to Thomas Smail is from *The Forgotten Father* (Grand Rapids: Wm. B. Eerdmans Publishing Co., 1980), 179.

PART V.
The Church's Ministry to the World on Behalf of Jesus

Chapter 17:
The Ministry of the Church as an Apostolic Community

Confusion, Crisis, and Controversy

The reference to Karl Barth is from *Church Dogmatics*, IV/1, 722. For other sources see K. H. Rengstorf, *"apostolos,"* in *Theological Dictionary of New Testament Theology*, 1.407; E. F. Harrison, *The Apostolic Church* (Grand Rapids: Wm. B. Eerdmans Publishing Co., 1985); A. Ehrhardt, *The Apostolic Succession in the First Two Centuries of the Church* (London: Lutterworth Press, 1953); L. Goppelt, *Apostolic and Post-Apostolic Times* (Grand Rapids: Baker Book House, 1977); Ray S. Anderson, "An Apostolic Mandate," in *Ministry on the Fireline—A Practical Theology for an Empowered Church*, 119–33.

A Dynamic View of Christ's Continuing Apostolic Ministry

As an example of a typical Protestant theologian's rejection of the Roman Catholic claim to the "office" of apostolic authority, Otto Weber may be cited:

Now, there is no "office" in the Community (Church) which as such could protect the unity of the Community from place to place. In earliest Christendom the "Apostles" assumed this function. We can deduce from 1 Corinthians 14:34 that the Apostle appears as the spokesman of the "other" Communities. But as little as the apostolate is clearly defined (cf. Rom. 16:7), to that extent it belongs to a defined period of initiation. The later Community is then found to be in the "apostolic succession" (*successio apostolica*) when it is in the "evangelical succession" (*successio evangelica*). It does not itself possess an apostolic "office." None of the attempts to demonstrate the presence of an "apostolic succession" for any "episcopate" can alter this fact. They are dogmatic or historical reconstructions which can resist the massive claims of the "New Apostolic Movement" only with the greatest difficulty because the latter does not claim to have historic succession but rather the succession in charisma (Weber, *Foundations of Dogmatics*, vol. II, 556).

The reference to Pannenberg is from *The Church* (Philadelphia: Westminster Press, 1983), 44–60. The quotation in full reads:

In this age of historical consciousness, therefore, the church needs a new concept of apostolicity that will allow it to recognize without reservation the difference between the age of the apostles and its own day, without thereby losing its connection with the mission of the apostles. Attention to the eschatological motif in the early Christian apostolate can help us do this. The only criterion of apostolic teaching in this sense is whether and to what degree it is able to set forth the final truth and comprehensive universality of the person and work of Christ in the transforming and saving significance of his resurrection and its power that gives light to the world. To demand that the teaching of the church be apostolic cannot mean that everything that is known from the age of the apostles should be normative for the present day, nor can it mean that only that which is derived from the age of the apostles can be regarded as valid today. It follows that the true *vita apostolica* is to be sought in the life of the church's leaders and in the life of individual Christians who let themselves be permeated by the final all-encompassing, liberating, and transforming truth of Jesus. The *vita apostolica* does not mean copying the way of life of the apostolic age or what we think that way of life was, and it certainly cannot be lived by borrowing this or that form of life from the regulations of the apostles. That which was apostolic then may be irrelevant today or may even be a hinderance to our apostolic tasks. This insight enables the church to be free to live in its own historicity as opposed to that of the apostolic age and still remain in continuity with the mission of the apostles (William Pannenberg, *The Church*, 56–57).

Chapter 18:
The Ministry of the Church as a Community in Mission

The assumption that Phoebe was the bearer of Paul's letter to the church at Rome is held by many biblical scholars. It has recently been suggested by John Stott, *Romans: God's Good News for the World* (Downers Grove, Ill.: InterVarsity Press, 1994), 392. As to Paul's purpose in writing the letter, Stott views the mission to Spain as among the primary reasons for writing, as Rome was a strategic threshold to the western frontier of the Roman empire (33f).

Mission Precedes and Creates the Church

The reference to the church as the "missionary people of God" comes from Charles Van Engen, *God's Missionary People: Rethinking the Purpose of the Local Church* (Grand Rapids: Baker Book House, 1991).

The reference to Jürgen Moltmann is from *The Church in the Power of the Spirit* (San Francisco: Harper & Row, 1977), 83, 80; 199.

> In so far as Jesus as the Messiah is the mystery of the rule of God, the signs of the messianic era are also part of his mystery. In so far as the crucified and risen Jesus manifests the salvation of the world determined on by God, proclamation and faith and the outpouring of the Holy Spirit on the Gentiles are also part of this salvation. . . . It also follows that a christological-ecclesiological rendering of the term—Christ and the church as the primal and fundamental sacrament of salvation—certainly touches on a further sphere covered by the New Testament but does not go far enough, especially if the church of Christ is only understood in its sacraments and not at the same time in the context of the eschatology of world history (Ibid., 204–5).

The reference to Van Engen is from *God's Missionary People*, 78.

The Kingdom of God Precedes and Empowers the Church

The reference to George Ladd is from *A Theology of the New Testament*, rev. ed., ed. Donald Hagner, (Grand Rapids: Wm. B. Eerdmans Publishing Co., 1993).

> [T]he Kingdom creates the church. The dynamic rule of God present in the mission of Jesus, challenged men to response, bringing them into a new fellowship. The presence of the Kingdom meant the fulfillment of the Old Testament messianic hope promised to Israel; but when the nation as a whole rejected the offer, those who accepted it were constituted the new people of God, the sons of the

Kingdom, the true Israel, the incipient church. The church is but the result of the coming of God's Kingdom into the world by the mission of Jesus Christ (111).

The reference to Wesley Carr is from "Towards a Contemporary Theology of the Holy Spirit," in *Scottish Journal of Theology*, vol. 28, no. 7 (1975) 507.

Mission Precedes and Creates Theology

I have discussed at greater length the mission theology of Paul in my book, *Ministry on the Fireline—A Practical Theology for an Empowered Church*. See chapter 6 in particular.

In chapter 5 of my book, *Ministry on the Fireline*, I have discussed the issues pertaining to the ordination of women more fully.

Chapter 19:
The Ministry of the Church as a Sacrament of Forgiveness and Healing

The concept of the church as a "fundamental or primordial" sacrament (*Ursakrament*) has been advanced by Karl Rahner, *The Church and the Sacraments* (New York: Herder & Herder, 1963).

Jesus as the First and Primary Sacrament

The references to Karl Barth are from *Church Dogmatics*, II/1, 52, 55.

Otto Weber suggests that the church is the visible manifestation of Christ in somewhat the same way that God was visible in Christ.

If the "Church" is the "body" of Christ, the "people" of God, the "temple" of God, then it might seem natural to speak of it with "transcendent" formulae and to imagine it as an invisible, supraworldly structure, as an "ideal" Church. But the most superficial look at the New Testament, particularly at Paul, will show that there is no trace there of an "ideal" Church. The "Community" which is the "body" of Christ can be found in Corinth or Rome in concrete tangibility, in all of the concrete processes of life. "Body" does not mean something "mystical," but concreteness, form, reality (O. Weber, *Foundations of Dogmatics*, II, 531).

The reason [the church] is present is to pronounce God's coming and already present dominion in Jesus Christ to all the world. Thus, by analogy, it is visible in a way comparable to the way God in Jesus Christ made himself available to the eyes and ears, the judgment and the condemnation of man. Faith in Jesus Christ does not set aside the ambiguous earthly person of Jesus of Nazareth, in order to return solely to the deity who disclosed himself to us in it. . . . In Jesus Christ we recognize God himself as the "incarnate God" (*Deus incarnatus*) and in the Community we recognize the body of Christ (Ibid., 541).

The reference to Thomas Torrance is from *Conflict and Agreement in the Church*, vol. II (London: Lutterworth Press, 1960), 158–59.

Forgiveness of Sins and the Ministry of Recovery

The reference to Bonhoeffer is from *Life Together* (London: SCM Press, 1970). The full text of his remarks on confession are as follows:

In confession a man breaks through to certainty. Why is it that it is often easier for us to confess our sins to God than to a brother? God is holy and sinless, He is a just judge of evil and the enemy of all disobedience, but a brother is sinful as we are. He knows from his own experience the dark night of secret sin. Why should we not find it easier to go to a brother than to the holy God? But if we do, we must ask ourselves whether we have not often been deceiving ourselves with our confession of sin to God, whether we have not rather been confessing our sins to ourselves and also granting ourselves absolution. And is not the reason perhaps for our countless relapses and the feebleness of our Christian obedience to be found precisely in the fact that we are living on self-forgiveness and not on real forgiveness? Self-forgiveness can never lead to a breach with sin; this can be accomplished only by the judging and pardoning Word of God itself. . . . Our brother breaks the circle of self-deception. A man who confesses his sins in the presence of a brother knows that he is no longer alone with himself; he experiences the presence of God in the reality of the other person. . . . Mutual, brotherly confession is given to us by God in order that we may be sure of divine forgiveness (*Life Together*, 1115–16).

The Sacramental Presence of the Resurrected Christ

The reference to Ken Blue is from *Authority to Heal* (Downers Grove, Ill.: Inter-Varsity Press, 1987). John P. Baker, in his book, *Salvation and Wholeness* (London: Fountain Trust, 1973), would be one who uses the "faith formula" in the way that Ken Blue warns against.

The reference to McCrossan is from *Bodily Healing and the Atonement,* ed. Roy Hicks and Kenneth E. Hagin (Seattle, WA: Faith Library Publications, 1930). The full text of McCrossan's comment is as follows:

Did Christ die to save all sinners? Yes, you reply, Then every sinner in this world has a blood-bought right to be saved? Yes. But are all sinners saved? No, only a very small percentage. . . . Why are not all sinners saved, since they have a blood-bought right to be saved? Because they refuse to meet God's conditions as set forth in John 1:12, 13; John 3:16, 18, 36; John 5:24; and Rom. 10:9, 10. It is just the same with bodily healing. *Every saint has a blood-bought right to be healed, but thousands do not know that they must exercise the very same appropriating faith in the bruised body of Christ for their healing as they formerly exercised in His shed blood for their salvation* (*Bodily Healing and the Atonement,* 64).

For a critique of the view that physical healing is promised to believers during this present age in the same way as forgiveness of sins, see Ken Blue, *Authority to Heal;* Gordon D. Fee, *The Disease of the Health and Wealth Gospels,* (Costa Mesa, Calif.: The Word for Today, 1979); D. R. McConnel, *A Different Gospel: A Historical and Biblical Analysis of the Modern Faith Movement* (Peabody, Mass.: Hendrickson Publishers, 1988); Kenneth L. Bakken and Kathleen H. Hoffeller, *The Journey Towards Wholeness: A Christ-Centered Approach to Health and Healing* (New York: Crossroad, 1988); Colin Brown, *That You May Believe* (Grand Rapids: Wm. B. Eerdmans Publishing Co., 1985). Brown makes this point:

We need to recognize that there are distinctions between what God has covenanted to do and what he has not covenanted to do, between what God may do and what he has promised to do. God is the healer (Ex. 15:26) and the one who is behind all healing. But in the Old Testament health and healing were not automatically guaranteed by membership in the covenant. . . . The new covenant does not promise healing for all now. It promises forgiveness of sins (Matt. 26:28). There is no specific, unqualified promise of health and healing in the New Testament to those who have faith. But there are promises of forgiveness and grace to those who repent and believe (e.g., Matt. 11:28; John 1:12; 3:16–18; Acts 2:38–39; 16:31; 17:30). The church is given authority to pronounce the forgiveness of sins in the name of Christ and the authority of the Spirit (John 2:23; cf. Matt. 18:15–20). But it has no parallel authority to heal. If God heals, it is an uncovenanted mercy. But when he forgives, it is a covenanted mercy (*That You May Believe,* 202f.).

Chapter 20:
The Ministry of the Church as the Advocate
for the Abused and Oppressed

The reference to Dietrich Bonhoeffer is from *Christ the Center* (San Francisco: Harper & Row, 1978), 11.

The reference to Kahlil Gibran is from *Sand and Foam* (New York: Alfred A. Knopf, 1926), 40.

Jesus as Public Defender

The reference to James B. Torrance is from "The Vicarious Humanity of Jesus Christ," 130.

Todd Speidell reinforces this when he adds:

Christ presents himself in the depths of human need—the hungry, the thirsty, the naked, the sick, the imprisoned (Matt. 25:31ff). The stranger among us, the homeless and psychologically debilitated, may be the place of Christ's presence among us. The Gospel of Matthew does not exhort us simply to be like Christ—ministering to the needy "as Jesus would" (which implies that he is not actively present but merely serves as a model for our social action)—but attests that Christ discloses himself through the stranger. We must be where Christ is, and act where he acts ("Incarnational Social Ethics," in *Incarnational Ministry—The Presence of Christ in Church, Society, and Family* (Colorado Springs: Helmers & Howard Publishers, 1990), 146).

The Continuing Paracletic Ministry of Christ

The references to Jacob Firet are from *Dynamics in Pastoring* (Grand Rapids: Wm. B. Eerdmans Publishing Co., 1986), 99ff; 133.

The reference to Thomas Smail is from *The Forgotten Father* (Grand Rapids: Wm. B. Eerdmans Publishing Co., 1980), 179.

The references to Stanley Hauerwas are from *A Community of Character: Toward a Constructive Christian Social Ethic* (Notre Dame, Ind.: Notre Dame University Press, 1981), 172, 168.

The Church's Ministry to Victims of Abuse and Violence

I have dealt with the issue of abuse more fully in my book, *Self Care: A Theology of Personal Empowerment and Spiritual Healing* (Wheaton, Ill.: Victor Books, 1995), chap. 7.

The references to Richard Gelles and Murray Straus are from *Intimate Violence: The Causes and Consequences of Abuse in the American Family* (New York: Simon & Schuster, 1988), 18, 20–21, 51.

The full text of the statement by Gelles and Straus to the effect that violence yields rewards is as follows:

> Clearly, the immediate rewards of using violence to work off anger or frustration are quite valuable to some individuals who would rather not wait to see the longer-term benefits of more reasoned and rational discipline and conversation with their children or partners. . . . Power, control, and self-esteem are other rewards of family violence. . . . Being in control, being master (or apparent master) of a situation, increases one's sense of self-worth. For men or parents whose sense of self-esteem may have been damaged or devalued by experiences outside of the home . . . control at home is even more important (*Intimate Violence*, 32f.).

PART VI.
Leading God's People in the Ministry of Christ

Chapter 21:
Leaders Who Abuse: The Misuse of Power

The Devastating Effect of Spiritual Abuse

The reference to David Johnson and Jeff Van Vonderen is from *The Subtle Power of Spiritual Abuse* (Minneapolis: Bethany House, 1991), 19–20.

The reference to Ken Blue is from *Healing Spiritual Abuse* (Downers Grove, Ill.: InterVarsity Press, 1993), 27.

The reference to Rollo May is from *Power and Innocence—A Search for the Sources of Violence* (New York: Norton, 1972).

The reference to Ronald Enroth is from *Churches That Abuse* (Grand Rapids: Zondervan, 1992), 29. See also Ronald Enroth, *Recovering from Churches that Abuse* (Grand Rapids: Zondervan, 1994).

What Turns Leaders into Abusers?

The reference to Dietrich Bonhoeffer is from *No Rusty Swords* (New York: Harper & Row, 1965). The full text is as follows:

> Where there is community there is leadership . . . the group is the womb of the Leader. It gives him everything, even his authority. . . . It sees him, not in his reality but in his vocation. It is essential for the image of the Leader that the group does not see the face of the one who goes before, but sees him only from behind as the figure stepping out ahead. His humanity is veiled in his Leader's form. . . . The Leader is what no other person can be, an individual, a personality. The relationship between those led and their leader is that the former transfer their own rights to him. It is this one form of collectivism which turns into intensified individualism. For that reason, the true concept of community, which rests on responsibility, on the recognition that individuals belong responsibly one to another finds no fulfillment here (*No Rusty Swords*, 186–200).

Chapter 22:
The Ministry of Servant Leadership

Servant Leadership: Trusted to Lead through Vision

The reference to Robert Greenleaf is from *Servant Leadership* (New York: Paulist Press, 1977), 18. See also his book *The Servant as Religious Leader* (Peterborough, N.H.: Windy Row Press, 1982).

On the vision of leadership see Ray S. Anderson, *Minding God's Business* (Wm. B. Eerdmans Publishing Co., 1986) 66–68.

The reference to Jürgen Moltmann is from "Theological Perspectives on the Future," colloquium paper, Lutheran Brotherhood, Houston, Tex., 29 Jan. 1979. See also, Ray S. Anderson, *Minding God's Business*, 49f.

The reference to Ken Blue is from *Healing Spiritual Abuse*, 148.

Servant Leadership: Trusted to Lead through Power

The reference to David L. McKenna is from *Power to Follow, Grace to Lead* (Waco, Tex.: Word Publishing, 1989).

Servant Leadership: Empowered to Lead through Spiritual Gifts

The reference to Oswald J. Sanders is from *Spiritual Leadership* (Chicago: Moody Press, rev. ed., 1989). See also Michael T. Dibbert, *Spiritual Leadership, Responsible Management*, Ministry Resources Library (Grand Rapids: Zondervan, 1989); Michael Youssef, *The Leadership Style of Jesus* (Downers Grove, Ill.: Victor Books, 1982).

Chapter 23:
Churches That Abuse: Domestic Disorder in the Family of God

The reference to Steven Krantz is from *Pastoral Strategies for Ministering Christ in a Bruised Church Environment* (Pasadena, Calif.: Doctor of Ministry Dissertation, 1995), 66.

The Dysfunctional Nature of Churches That Abuse

The reference to Newton Malony is from H. Newton Malony, *When Getting Along Seems Impossible: Straightforward Help to Reduce Conflict at Home, at Church and at Work* (Old Tappan, N.J.: Fleming H. Revell Co., 1990), 18. See also Charles Cosgrove and Dennis Hatfield, *Church Conflict* (Nashville: Abingdon Press, 1994); H. F. Halverstadt, *Managing Church Conflict* (Louisville, Ky.: Westminster/John Knox Press, 1991); Paul Kittlaus and Speed Leas, *Church Fights: Managing Conflict in the Local Church* (Richmond, Va.: John Knox Press, 1973); David W. Augsburger, *Conflict Mediation Across Cultures: Pathways and Patterns* (Louisville, Ky.: Westminster/John Knox Press, 1992); Kenneth Gangel and Samuel L. Canine, *Communication and Conflict Management in Church and Christian Organizations* (Nashville: Broadman Press, 1993).

The reference to Francis Schaeffer is from *The Great Evangelical Disaster* (Westchester, Ill.: Crossway Books, 1984), 85.

The reference to Virginia Satir is from *Conjoint Family Therapy* (Palo Alto, Calif.: Science and Behavior Books, 1967), 1.

The source for the reference to Dinesh D'Souza is Helaine Olen, "Rutgers Remains Embroiled Over Power of a Few Words," *The Los Angeles Times*, Monday, 20 Feb. 1995, A5.

The Devastating Consequences of Spiritual Abuse

The reference to Lewis Smedes is from *Shame and Grace—Healing the Shame We Don't Deserve* (San Francisco: Harper/San Francisco, 1993), 41.

The reference to Paul Minear is from *Images of the Church in the New Testament* (Philadelphia: Westminster Press, 1960), 167.

The reference to John Bradshaw is from *Bradshaw on Shame: Healing the Shame That Binds You* (Deerfield Beach: Health Communications, forthcoming), 32.

Chapter 24:
The Ministry of Care and Community

The reference to Eugene O'Neill is from "The Great God Brown," in *The Plays of Eugene O'Neill*, vol. 1 (New York: Modern Library, 1982), 318.

A Ministry of Discernment

Some of my thoughts on discernment have been drawn from Steven Krantz, *Pastoral Strategies for Ministering Christ in a Bruised Church Environment*, 66.

The reference to John Patton is from *Pastoral Care in Context* (Louisville, Ky.: Westminster/John Knox Press, 1993), 75.

The reference to Theodore Roszak is from *Person/Planet* (Garden City, N.Y.: Doubleday, Anchor Press, 1979), 139.

The reference to Stanley Hauerwas is from *A Community of Character—Toward a Constructive Christian Social Ethic*, 172.

The reference to Karl Barth is from *Church Dogmatics*, IV/3, 773–74. The full text is as follows:

> Solidarity with the world means full commitment to it, unreserved participation in its situation, in the promise given it by creation, in its responsibility for the arrogance, sloth, and falsehood which reign within it, in its suffering under the resultant distress, but primarily and supremely in the free grace of God demonstrated and addressed to it in Jesus Christ, and therefore in its hope. . . . Solidarity with the world means that those who are genuinely pious approach the children of the world as such, that those who are genuinely righteous are not ashamed to sit down with the unrighteous as friends, that those who are genuinely wise do not hesitate to seem to be fools among fools, and that those who are genuinely holy are not too good or irreproachable to go down into 'hell' in a very secular fashion . . . since Jesus Christ is the Savior of the world, [the church] can exist in worldly fashion, not unwillingly nor with a bad conscience, but willingly and with a good conscience. It consists in the recognition that its members also bear in themselves and in some way actualise all human possibilities.

The reference to Opal is from Opal Whitley, *Opal—The Journal of an Under-standing Heart,* adapted by Jane Boulton (Palo Alto, Calif.: Tioga Publishing Company, 1984), 46.

The reference to Emil Brunner is from *Man in Revolt* (reprint, London: Lutterworth Press, 1939; Philadelphia: Westminster Press, 1979), 227.

A Ministry of Caring

The reference to John Macmurray is from *Persons in Relation* (London: Faber & Faber, 1961), 159.

In reference to "self care," see Anderson, *Self Care—A Theology of Personal Empowerment and Spiritual Healing.*

The source for the survey of pastors conducted by the Fuller Seminary Institute of Church Growth (1991) is H. B. London and Neil Wiseman, *Pastors at Risk* (Wheaton, Ill.: Victor Books, 1993), 22. See also Archibald Hart, *Coping with Depression in the Ministry and Other Helping Professions* (Dallas: Word Books, 1984), 12–14.

The Ministry of Community

The reference to Dietrich Bonhoeffer is from *Sanctorum Communio* (London: Collins, 1967), 62.

The reference to John Macmurray is from *Persons in Relation* (London: Faber & Faber, 1961), 150. The full text of the citation is as follows:

> I need you to be myself. This need is for a fully positive personal relation in which, because we trust one another, we can think and feel and act together. Only in such a relation can we really be ourselves. If we quarrel, each of us withdraws from the other into himself, and the trust is replaced by fear. We can no longer be ourselves in relation to one another. We are in conflict, and each of us loses his freedom and must act under constraint. There are two ways in which this situation can be met without actually breaking the relationship—which, we are assuming, is a necessary one. There may be a reconciliation which restores the original confidence; the negative motivation may be overcome and the positive relation re-established. Or we may agree to co-operate on conditions which impose a restraint upon each of us, and which prevent the outbreak of active hostility. The negative motivation, the fear of the other, will remain, but will be suppressed. This will make possible co-operation for such ends as each of us has an interest in achieving. But we will remain isolated individuals, and the co-operation between us, though it may appear to satisfy our need of one another, will not really satisfy *us.* For what we really need is to care for one another, and we are only caring for ourselves. We have achieved society, but not community. We have become associates, but not friends.

The second reference to John Macmurray is from *Persons in Relation.* The full text of the citation is as follows:

> All our activities, whether practical or theoretical, have their motives as well as their intentions, and are sustained by an emotional attitude. . . . The intention of one particular agent is therefore inherently related to the intention of the Other,

and not merely accidental. Consequently, the morality of an action is inherent in action itself. . . . No action can have contradictory intentions. We cannot aim in different directions at the same time. It can, however, have contradictory motives, one of which is suppressed, and therefore "unconscious." . . . In our relations with other persons this ambiguity of motivation is felt as a tension and a constraint between us, and therefore in each of us. The intention of one particular agent is therefore inherently related to the intention of the Other, and not merely accidental. Consequently, the morality of an action is inherent in action itself (*Persons in Relation,* 33, 117, 102).

The reference to David Mains is from *Healing the Dysfunctional Church Family* (Wheaton, Ill.: Victor Books, 1992), 113.

The reference to Dennis Guernsey is from *The Family Covenant—Love and Forgiveness in the Christian Home* (Elgin, Ill.: David C. Cook, 1984), 105.

The reference to James Leehan is from *Pastoral Care for Survivors of Family Abuse* (Louisville, Ky.: Westminster/John Knox Press, 1989), 99, 100.

Bibliography

Anderson, Ray S. "Burnout as a Symptom of Theological Anemia," *Theology News & Notes*. Pasadena, Calif.: Fuller Theological Seminary, March, 1984.

————. "Christopraxis: Competence as a Criterion for Education for Ministry," *TSF Bulletin* (January/February, 1984).

————. *Historical Transcendence and the Reality of God.* Grand Rapids: Wm. B. Eerdmans Publishing Co., 1975.

————. *Minding God's Business.* Grand Rapids: Wm. B. Eerdmans Publishing Co., 1986.

————. *Ministry on the Fireline—A Practical Theology for an Empowered Church.* Downers Grove, Ill.: InterVarsity Press, 1993.

————. *Self-Care: A Theology of Personal Empowerment and Spiritual Healing.* Wheaton, Ill.: Victor Books, 1995.

————. "Son of God," *International Standard Bible Encyclopedia*, vol. 4. Grand Rapids: William B. Eerdmans Publishing Co., 1984.

————. *Theology, Death and Dying.* Oxford: Blackwell Publishers, 1986.

————. "Toward a Post-Apartheid Theology," *Reformed Journal.* (May 1988).

Anderson, Ray S., ed. *Theological Foundations for Ministry.* Grand Rapids: Wm. B. Eerdmans Publishing Co., 1979.

Andreasen, Niels-Erik A. *The Old Testament Sabbath: A Tradition-Historical Investigation.* SBL Dissertation Series, no. 7, 1972.

Anselm. *Cur Deus Homo?* LaSalle, Ill.: Open Court Publishing Company, 1958.

Aristotle. *Metaphysics.* The Works of Aristotle Translated into English, vol. VIII. Oxford: The Clarendon Press, 1908.

————. *The Nichomachean Ethics*, trans. J.E.C. Welldon. New York: Prometheus Books, 1987.

Augsburger, David W. *Conflict Mediation Across Cultures: Pathways and Patterns.* Louisville, Ky.: Westminster/John Knox, 1995.

Bacciocchi, Samuele. *From Sabbath to Sunday: A Historical Investigation of the Rise of Sunday Observance in Early Christianity.* Rome: The Pontifical Gregorian University Press, 1977.

Baker, John P. *Salvation and Wholeness.* London: Fountain Trust, 1973.

Bakken, Kenneth L., and Kathleen H. Hoffeller. *The Journey Towards Wholeness: A Christ-Centered Approach to Health and Healing.* New York: Crossroad, 1988.

Banks, Robert. *Redeeming the Routines: Bringing Theology to Life.* Wheaton, Ill.: Bridge Point, 1993.

Barth, Karl. *Church Dogmatics,* I/1. Edinburgh: T. & T. Clark. Trans. Geoffrey Bromily, 2d ed., 1975.

———. *Church Dogmatics,* I/2. Edinburgh: T. & T. Clark, 1956.

———. *Church Dogmatics,* III/1. Edinburgh: T. & T. Clark. Trans. J. W. Edwards et. al., 1969.

———. *Church Dogmatics,* IV/1. Edinburgh: T. & T. Clark. Trans. G. W. Bromiley, 1956.

———. *Church Dogmatics,* IV/2. Edinburgh: T. & T. Clark. Trans. G. W. Bromiley, 1958.

———. *Church Dogmatics,* IV/3. Edinburgh: T. & T. Clark. Trans. G. W. Bromiley, 1961.

———. *The Humanity of God.* London: Collins, Fontana Library Edition, 1967.

———. *The Way of Theology in Karl Barth,* ed. H. Martin Rumscheidt. Allison Park, Pa.: Pickwick Publications, 1986.

Becker, Ernest. *The Denial of Death.* New York: Macmillan, 1973.

Beckwith, Roger T., and Wilfred Stott, *This is the Day: The Biblical Doctrine of the Christian Sunday in Its Jewish and Early Church Setting.* London: Marshal Morgan & Scott, 1978.

Blue, Ken. *Authority to Heal.* Downers Grove, Ill.: InterVarsity Press, 1987.

———. *Healing Spiritual Abuse.* Downers Grove, Ill.: InterVarsity Press, 1993.

Boer, Harry R. *Pentecost and Missions.* Grand Rapids: Wm. B. Eerdmans Publishing Co., 1961.

Bonhoeffer, Dietrich. *Christ the Center.* San Francisco: Harper & Row, 1978.

———. *Life Together.* London: SCM Press, 1970.

———. *No Rusty Swords.* New York: Harper & Row, 1965.

———. *Sanctorum Communio.* London: Collins, 1967.

———. *The Cost of Discipleship.* New York: Macmillan, 1963.

———. "What is Meant by 'Telling the Truth'?" *Ethics.* New York: Macmillan, 1973.

Bradshaw, John. *Bradshaw on Shame: Healing the Shame That Binds You.* Deerfield Beach, Fla.: Health Communications, forthcoming.

Brown, Colin. *That You May Believe.* Grand Rapids: Wm. B. Eerdmans Publishing Co., 1985.

Brunner, Emil. *Dogmatics, vol. 3: The Christian Doctrine of the Church, Faith and the Consummation.* London: Lutterworth Press, 1962.

————. *Love and Marriage*. London: Collins, Fontana, 1970.

————. *Man in Revolt*. London: Lutterworth Press, 1939; reprint, Philadelphia: Westminster Press, 1979.

————. *The Misunderstanding of the Church*. London: Lutterworth Press, 1952.

Bugbee, Bruce. *Networking*. Pasadena, Calif.: Fuller Institute for Evangelism and Church Growth, 1994.

Calvin, John. *Institutes of the Christian Religion*. Edinburgh: T. & T. Clark. Trans. Henry Beveridge from the 1559 ed., *Christianae Religionis Institutio*.

Capra, Fritjof. *The Turning Point: Science, Society and the Rising Culture*. London: Collins, Fontana, 1963.

Capra, Fritjof, and David Steindl-Rast. *Belonging to the Universe—Explorations on the Frontiers of Science and Spirituality*. San Francisco: HarperSanFrancisco, 1991.

Carr, Wesley. "Towards a Contemporary Theology of the Holy Spirit." *Scottish Journal of Theology*, vol. 28, no. 7, (1975).

Carson, Donald A. *Showing the Spirit: A Theological Exposition of 1 Corinthians 12–14*. Grand Rapids: Baker Book House, 1987.

Carver, W. O. *Sabbath Observance: The Lord's Day in Our Day*. Nashville: Broadman Press, 1940.

Coleman, Peter Edward. *Gay Christians: A Moral Dilemma*. London: SCM Press, 1989.

Comiskey, Andrew. *Pursuing Sexual Wholeness*. Santa Monica, Calif.: Desert Streams Ministries, 1988.

Cosgrove, Charles, and Dennis Hatfield. *Church Conflict*. Nashville: Abingdon Press, 1994.

Costos, Orlando. *The Church and Its Mission: A Shattering Critique From the Third World*. Wheaton, Ill.: Tyndale House, 1974.

DeGruchy, John, "No Other Gospel: Is Liberation Theology a Reduction of the Gospel?" *Incarnational Ministry: The Presence of Christ in Church, Society, and Family*, ed. Christian D. Ketter and Todd H. Speidell. Colorado Springs: Helmers & Howard Publishers, 1990, 176–90.

Descartes, René. "Meditations" (1641). In *The Philosophical Works of Descartes*. Cambridge, England: Cambridge University Press, 1912.

Dibbert, Michael T. *Spiritual Leadership, Responsible Management*. Ministry Resources Library. Grand Rapids: Zondervan, 1989.

Drane, John. *Paul: Libertine or Legalist?* London: SPK, 1975.

D'Souza, Dinesh. In Helaine Olen, "Rutgers Remains Embroiled Over Power of a Few Words," *The Los Angeles Times*. Monday, 20 Feb. 1995, A5.

Dunn, James. *Christology in the Making*. Valley Forge, Pa.: Trinity Press International, 1980.

Ehrhardt, A. *The Apostolic Succession in the First Two Centuries of the Church.* London: Lutterworth Press, 1953.

Enroth, Ronald. *Churches That Abuse.* Grand Rapids: Zondervan, 1992.

———. *Recovering from Churches That Abuse.* Grand Rapids: Zondervan, 1994.

Fee, Gordon D. *The Disease of the Health and Wealth Gospels.* Costa Mesa, Calif.: The Word for Today, 1979.

Firet, Jacob. *Dynamics in Pastoring.* Grand Rapids: Wm. B. Eerdmans Publishing Co., 1986.

Fortune, Don and Kattie. *Discover Your God-Given Gifts.* Grand Rapids: Baker Book House, 1987.

Gangel, Kenneth and Samuel L. Canine. *Communication and Conflict Management in Church and Christian Organizations.* Nashville: Broadman Press, 1993.

Gelles, Richard and Murray Straus. *Intimate Violence: The Causes and Consequences of Abuse in the American Family.* New York: Simon & Schuster, 1988.

Gibran, Kahlil. *Sand and Foam.* New York: Alfred A. Knopf, 1926.

Gilbert, Larry. *How to Have Meaning and Fulfillment through Understanding the Spiritual Gifts within You.* Lynchburg, Va.: Church Growth Institute, 1990.

Green, Michael. *I Believe in the Holy Spirit.* Grand Rapids: Wm. B. Eerdmans Publishing Co., 1988.

Greenleaf, Robert. *Servant Leadership.* New York: Paulist Press, 1977.

———. *The Servant as Religious Leader.* Petersborough, N.H.: Windy Row Press, 1982.

Guernsey, Dennis. *The Family Covenant—Love and Forgiveness in the Christian Home.* Elgin, Ill.: David C. Cook, 1984.

Hall, Douglas John. *Thinking the Faith—Christian Theology in a North American Context.* Minneapolis: Augsburg Press, 1989.

Halverstadt, H. F. *Managing Church Conflict.* Louisville, Ky.: Westminster/John Knox Press, 1991.

Harrison, E. F. *The Apostolic Church.* Grand Rapids: Wm. B. Eerdmans Publishing Co., 1985.

Hart, Archibald. *Coping with Depression in the Ministry and Other Helping Professions.* Dallas: Word Books, 1984.

Harvey, John Francis. *The Homosexual Person: New Thinking in Pastoral Care.* San Francisco: Ignatius Press, 1987.

Hauerwas, Stanley. *A Community of Character: Toward a Constructive Christian Social Ethic.* Notre Dame, Ind.: Notre Dame University Press, 1981.

Haynes, Carlyle B. *From Sabbath to Sunday.* Washington, D.C.: Review and Herald Publishing Association, 1942.

Heschel, Abraham. *The Prophets,* vol. II. New York: Harper & Row, 1962.

Heschel, Joshua. *The Sabbath: Its Meaning for Modern Man.* New York: Farrar, Straus & Giroux, 1951.

Heidegger, Martin. *Essays in Metaphysics.* New York: Philosophical Library Inc., 1960.

Hicks, Roy and Kenneth E. Hagin, eds. *Bodily Healing and the Atonement.* Seattle, WA: Faith Library Publications, n.d.

Irenaeus, *Against Heresies,* vol. III/17/1. Ante-Nicene Christian Library, ed. A. Roberts and J. Donaldson. Edinburgh: T. & T. Clark, 1868.

Jewett, Paul K. *The Lord's Day: A Theological Guide to the Christian Day of Worship.* Grand Rapids: Wm. B. Eerdmans Publishing Co., 1971.

Johnson, David, and Jeff Van Vonderen. *The Subtle Power of Spiritual Abuse.* Minneapolis: Bethany House, 1991.

Kant, Immanuel. *Critique of Practical Reason.* London: Longman Green & Co., 1909.

———. *Critique of Pure Reason.* London: Macmillan & Company, 1929.

Kittlaus, Paul, and Speed Leas, *Church Fights: Managing Conflict in the Local Church.* Richmond, Va.: John Knox Press, 1973.

König, Adrio. "Covenant and Image: Theological Anthropology, Human Interrelatedness and Apartheid." In *Incarnational Ministry: The Presence of Christ in Church, Society, and Family,* ed. Christian D. Ketter and Todd H. Speidell. Colorado Springs: Helmers & Howard Publishers, 1990, 162–75.

Krantz, Steven. *Pastoral Strategies for Ministering Christ in a Bruised Church Environment.* Doctor of Ministry diss., Pasadena, Calif., 1995.

Küng, Hans. *The Church.* London: Sheed & Ward, 1967.

———. "The Continuing Charismatic Structure." In *Theological Foundations for Ministry,* ed. Ray S. Anderson. Grand Rapids: Wm. B. Eerdmans Publishing Co., 1979, 458–89.

Ladd, George E. *A Theology of the New Testament.* Rev. edition, ed. Donald Hagner. Grand Rapids: Wm. B. Eerdmans Publishing Co., 1993.

Lane, Belden C. "The Rabbinical Stories: A Primer on Theological Method." *The Christian Century,* 16 Dec. 1981.

Leehan, James. *Pastoral Care for Survivors of Family Abuse.* Louisville, Ky.: Westminster/John Knox Press, 1989.

London, H. B., and Neil Wiseman, *Pastors at Risk.* Wheaton, Ill.: Victor Books, 1993.

Malony, H. Newton. *When Getting Along Seems Impossible: Straightforward Help to Reduce Conflict at Home, at Church, and at Work.* Old Tappan, N.J.: Fleming H. Revell Co., 1990.

McConnel, D. R. *A Different Gospel: A Historical and Biblical Analysis of the Modern Faith Movement.* Peabody, Mass.: Hendrickson Publishers, 1988.

McKenna, David L. *Power to Follow, Grace to Lead.* Waco, Tex.: Word Publishing, 1989.

Macmurray, John. *Persons in Relation.* London: Faber & Faber, 1961.

Mains, David. *Healing the Dysfunctional Church Family*. Wheaton, Ill.: Victor Books, 1992.

Martin, Ralph. *Reconciliation: A Study of Paul's Theology*. Atlanta: John Knox Press, 1980.

May, Rollo. *Power and Innocence—A Search for the Sources of Violence*. New York: Norton, 1972.

Mendenhall, G. E. "Covenant." In *The Interpreter's Dictionary of the Bible*. New York: Abingdon Press, 1962.

Minear, Paul. *Images of the Church in the New Testament*. Philadelphia: Westminster Press, 1960.

Miskotte, Kornilis. *When the Gods Are Silent*. London: Collins, 1967.

Moltmann, Jürgen. *The Church in the Power of the Spirit: A Contribution to Messianic Eschatology*. San Francisco: Harper & Row, 1975.

———. "Theological Perspectives on the Future." Houston, Tex.: Lutheran Brotherhood, 29 Jan. 1979.

———. *The Way of Jesus Christ—Christology in Messianic Dimensions*. San Francisco: Harper & Row, 1990.

Nelson, James B. *The Intimate Connection: Male Sexuality, Masculine Spirituality*. Philadelphia: Westminster Press, 1988.

Olen, Helaine. "Rutgers Remains Embroiled Over Power of a Few Words," *The Los Angeles Times*. Monday, 20, Feb. 1995, A5.

O'Neill, Eugene. "The Great God Brown." In *The Plays of Eugene O'Neill*, vol. 1. New York: Modern Library, 1982.

Pannenberg, Wolfhart. *The Church*. Philadelphia: Westminster Press, 1983.

———. *Jesus—God and Man*. Philadelphia: Westminster Press, 1977.

Patton, John. *Pastoral Care in Context*. Louisville, Ky.: Westminster Press, 1993.

Peterson, Eugene. *The Message: The New Testament in Contemporary English*. Colorado Springs: NavPress, 1993.

Pinnock, Clark and Robert Brow. *Unbounded Love—A Good News Theology for the Twenty-First Century*. Downers Grove, Ill.: InterVarsity Press, 1994.

Pronk, Pim *Against Nature? Types of Moral Argumentation Regarding Homosexuality*. Grand Rapids: Wm. B. Eerdmans Publishng Co., 1993.

Rahner, Karl. *The Church and the Sacraments*. New York: Herder & Herder, 1963.

Roszak, Theodore. *Person/Planet*. Garden City, N.Y.: Doubleday, Anchor Press, 1979.

Sanders, Oswald J. *Spiritual Leadership*, rev. ed. Chicago: Moody Press, 1989.

Satir, Virginia. *Conjoint Family Therapy*. Palo Alto, Calif.: Science & Behavior Books, 1967.

Schaeffer, Francis, *The Great Evangelical Disaster*. Westchester, Ill.: Crossway Books, 1984.

Schatzmann, Siegfried. *A Pauline Theology of Charismata.* Peabody, Mass.: Hendrickson Publishers, 1987.

Siker, Jeffrey S., ed.. *Homosexuality in the Church—Both Sides of the Debate.* Westminster/John Knox Press, 1994.

Smail, Thomas. *The Forgotten Father.* Grand Rapids: Wm. B. Eerdmans Publishing Co., 1980.

Smedes, Lewis. *Shame and Grace—Healing the Shame We Don't Deserve.* San Francisco: Harper/San Francisco, 1993.

Speidell. Todd. "Incarnational Social Ethics." In *Incarnational Ministry—The Presence of Christ in Church, Society, and Family.* Colorado Springs: Helmers & Howard Publishers, 1990, 140–52.

Stoneking, John D. "Saying Hello and Goodbye—Would I Baptize a Stillborn Baby?" *The Circuit Rider,* March 1984.

Stott, John. *Romans: God's Good News for the World.* Downers Grove, Ill.: InterVarsity Press, 1994.

Swartley, Willard M. *Slavery, Sabbath, War and Women.* Scottdale, Pa.: Herald Press, 1983.

Thompson, Francis. "The Kingdom of God." In *The Treasury of Religious Verse,* compiled by Donald T. Kauffman. Old Tappen, N.J.: Fleming Revell, 1966.

Torrance, James. "The Vicarious Humanity of Christ." In *The Incarnation-Ecumenical Studies in the Nicene-Constantinopolitan Creed A. D. 381,* ed. Thomas F. Torrance. Edinburgh: Handsel Press Ltd., 1981.

Torrance. Thomas F. *Conflict and Agreement in the Church,* vol. II. London: Lutterworth Press, 1960.

———. *God and Rationality.* London: Oxford University Press, 1971.

———. *The Christian Frame of Mind—Reason, Order, and Oneness in Theology and Natural Science.* Colorado Springs: Helmers & Howard Publishers, 1989.

———. *The Ground and Grammar of Theology.* Charlottesville, Va.: University Press of Virginia, 1980.

———. *The Mediation of Christ.* Colorado Springs: Helmers & Howard Publishers, 1992.

———. *Reality and Evangelical Theology.* Philadelphia: Westminster Press, 1982.

———. *Theological Science.* London: Oxford University Press, 1969.

———. *Theology in Reconstruction.* Grand Rapids: Wm. B. Eerdmans Publishing Co., 1965.

———. *Theology and Science at the Frontiers of Knowledge.* Edinburgh: Scottish Academic Press, 1985.

———. "Service in Jesus Christ." In *Theological Foundations for Ministry,* ed. Ray S. Anderson. Grand Rapids: Wm. B. Eerdmans Publishing Co., 1979, 714–33.

Trible, Phyllis. *God and the Rhetoric of Sexuality.* Philadelphia: Fortress Press, 1978.

Van Engen, Charles. *God's Missionary People: Rethinking the Purpose of the Local Church.* Grand Rapids: Baker Book House, 1991.

Wagner, C. Peter. *Your Spiritual Gifts Can Help Your Church Grow.* Ventura, Calif.: Regal Books, 1979.

Watson, Thomas. *The Ten Commandments.* 1692; reprint, Guildford, Eng.: Billings & Sons, Ltd., 1965.

Weber, Otto. *Foundations of Dogmatics.* Two vols. Grand Rapids: Wm. B. Eerdmans Publishing Co., 1983.

Westermann, Claus. *Genesis 12–36—A Commentary,* trans. John J. Scullion, S. J. Minneapolis: Augsburg Press, 1985.

Whitley, Opal. *Opal—The Journal of an Understanding Heart,* adapted by Jane Boulton. Palo Alto, Calif.: Tioga Publishing Co., 1984.

Will, James. *A Christology of Peace.* Louisville, Ky.: Westminster/John Knox Press, 1989.

Wind, Renate. *A Spoke in the Wheel—The Life of Dietrich Bonhoeffer.* Grand Rapids: Wm. B. Eerdmans Publishing Co., 1992.

Yohn, Rick. *Discover Your Spiritual Gift and Use It.* Wheaton, Ill.: Tyndale House, 1974.

Youssef, Michael. *The Leadership Style of Jesus.* Downers Grove, Ill.: Victor Books, 1982.

Index of Names and Subjects

sexual differentiation, 39–40
shame, 210
Siker, Jeffrey S., 243
sin, 54–55, 57–58, 76, 168
   confession of, 172, 249–50
   forgiveness of, 168–71
slavery, 39–40, 57
Smail, Thomas, 143, 179, 246, 251
Smedes, Lewis, 210, 254
Speidell, Todd H., 242, 246, 251
spiritual abuse, 191–93, 207–12
spiritual discernment, 214–15
spiritual gifts, 134–35, 202–3
spiritual leadership, 194–95
spiritual malpractice, 171
spiritual maturity, 134
Steindl-Rast, David, 228
Stephen, 130
Stoneking, John D., 226
Stott, John, 248
Stott, Wilfred, 233
Straus, Murray, 180, 183, 252
Swartley, Willard M., 233–34

theological antecedent, 21–22, 31
theological discernment, 10, 14–15
theological mandate, 158–59
theological reflection, 119–20
theology, 6–7
Thompson, Francis, 12, 227
Timothy, 122
Titus, 122
Torrance, James, 75, 142, 178, 237, 245, 251

Torrance, Thomas, 45, 72, 75, 87, 102, 139, 226, 228, 231–32, 234–37, 239, 246, 249
Trible, Phyllis, 231, 233
Trinity, 87
truth, 10–12, 16, 26, 30
   as absolute, 20, 23
   of Scripture, 15

Van Engen, Charles, 161, 241, 248
Van Vonderen, Jeff, 191, 252
violence, 180–81, 206
virgin birth, 56, 72, 234–35
vision, 198
von Rad, Gerhard, 228

Wagner, C. Peter, 245
Watson, Thomas, 234
Weber, Otto, 133, 237–38, 244–47, 249
Westerman, Claus, 231
Whitley, Opal, 216, 255
Will, James, 229
Wind, Renate, 245
wisdom, 201
Wiseman, Neil, 255
women, in ministry, 125, 164–65
Word of God, 16, 36–37, 41, 216
world, needs of, 79–80

Yohn, Rick, 245
Youssef, Michael, 253

Zacchaeus, 178
Zwingli, Huldrych, 166

The church is called to make a difference in the world, not merely to be different from the world." - p. 142

"The powerlessness and irrelevance of the church is not that it lacks tactical encounter with the world, but that its strategy is one of survival rather than sacrifice, of success rather than service, of reputation rather than responsibility." - p. 143

"The mirror of ⊖ is the humanity of Xp, unveiled before the world" - p. 143

The burden of Hope - p. 48

sinful nature vs. human nature - p. 59

Theology of the Sabbath - Chapter 8 (p. 60)

"When need is the master, the servant becomes a slave" p. 80

"The so-called burnout phenomenon among pastors is not so much due to over-investment in one's work as it is symptom of theological anemia." p. 82

"There are many churches that are seeking an Issue and end up with an Edsell" - p. 85

Manifesto for Xian Ministry - page 90

"The test for truth in a Christian is what the world sees in us of Jesus Christ, not what other Christians see in us as a Christian." - p. 91

"Everything doesn't have to be perfect to please God, and pleasing God is easier than pleasing others." p. 93

"Because [Jesus] understood and accepted his own humanity, he never condemned another for being human." p. 93

"[Jesus] had no uniforms for his disciples and no masks for his friends" - p. 94

Women in Ministry - ch. 14

"The Spirit that comes to the Church comes out of the future, not the past" - p. 120

Eschatological preference still linked to biblical antecedent → counter to spiritual anarchy - p. 124

Divorce and remarriage - p. 125

Homosexuality - p. 127

"Spiritual maturity is not evidenced by possessing spiritual gifts, but rather by being possessed by the spirit in such a way that we are moved toward ministry to others" p. 134

Def'n. of spiritual gift. - p. 135

"It is not only that the world needs the church in order to know Christ; the church also needs the world in order to know Christ." - p. 140

Tactical vs. Strategic withdrawal from the world - p. 140